The Sleepy Lagoon Murder Case

LANDMARK LAW CASES

AMERICAN SOCIETY

Peter Charles Hoffer

N. E. H. Hull

Series Editors

For a complete list of titles in the series go to www.kansaspress.ku.edu

MARK A. WEITZ

The Sleepy Lagoon Murder Case

Race Discrimination and

Mexican-American Rights

UNIVERSITY PRESS OF KANSAS

© 2010 by University Press of Kansas
All rights reserved

Published by the University Press of Kansas (Lawrence, Kansas 66045), which was
organized by the Kansas Board of Regents and is operated and funded by Emporia
State University, Fort Hays State University, Kansas State University, Pittsburg State
University, the University of Kansas, and Wichita State University

Library of Congress Cataloging-in-Publication Data

Weitz, Mark A., 1957–
The Sleepy Lagoon murder case : race discrimination and
Mexican-American rights / Mark A. Weitz.
p. cm. — (Landmark law cases & American society)
Includes bibliographical references and index.
ISBN 978-0-7006-1746-3 (cloth : alk. paper)
ISBN 978-0-7006-1747-0 (pbk. : alk. paper)
1. Sleepy Lagoon Trial, Los Angeles, Calif., 1942–1943. 2. Mexican Americans—
Civil rights—California—Los Angeles. I. Title.
KF224.S49W45 2010
345.794'9402523 — dc22
2010018065

British Library Cataloguing-in-Publication Data is available.

Printed in the United States of America

10 9 8 7 6 5 4 3 2 1

The paper used in this publication is recycled and contains 30 percent postconsumer
waste. It is acid free and meets the minimum requirements of the American National
Standard for Permanence of Paper for Printed Library Materials Z39.48-1992.

CONTENTS

How often have we seen on television or in the movies the story of official injustice? It features a parade of the usual suspects harried and railroaded by a politically ambitious prosecutor and an insensitive judge through the criminal justice system. The defendants are people of color, radicals, and newcomers, their names jumbled together and their faces almost indistinguishable in the heat of the moment. From the Salem witchcraft trials to the convictions of the Scottsboro Boys, from the executions of dozens of New York City slaves suspected of arson in 1741 to the deportations of anarchists in the great Red Scare of 1919, guilt was measured not by evidence but by prejudice and indifference.

In 1942, the death of a Mexican American youth led to the mass trial of suspected gang members in Los Angeles. Bias against the defendants flowed from the newspapers into the courtroom. Only five of the twenty-two young men were acquitted, for all had been convicted in the public mind long before their mass trials. The jury's verdicts were almost a foregone conclusion. In the midst of these events, the zoot suit riots erupted in the city, with sailors and local toughs wantonly attacking young Mexican American men in the streets and other public places.

But the story does not end here. An appeal to the California court of appeals led to the overturning of all verdicts, and an opinion whose criticism of the conduct of the trial stands as one of the most remarkable ever written. The men and women who set aside their own lives, like Carey McWilliams and Alice McGrath, along with a host of entertainment and artistic leaders, to announce their support for the defendants and raise funds for the appeal was extraordinary for its time and remains a landmark in American criminal justice.

Mark A. Weitz follows the story every step of its way, through the streets of the Mexican American community into the city, to the days of the trial itself and the mounting of the appeal. He has analyzed the evidence exculpating the defendants and indicting the officials who rushed to judgment. He reveals the full extent of the support for the defendants, and he demonstrates how it played into civil rights history. A tale that begins in tragedy ends in triumph.

The Sleepy Lagoon murder, the trials, and the appeal are important even though no new law was made and no great constitutional principle vindicated. Like all landmark cases, this one opened a window into the uneasy world of Mexican American–Anglo relations. Today we celebrate our diversity. It was not so long ago, as Weitz convincingly demonstrates here, that diversity bred suspicion and injustice.

The Sleepy Lagoon Murder Case

Introduction

Turn on a radio almost anywhere in America in 1942, and chances are the romantic lyrics of Harry James's "Sleepy Lagoon" would soon fill the air. The song painted a picture of an isolated tropical island and two lovers caught in a moment that would haunt them forever. In southeast Los Angeles, a local swimming hole — actually a reservoir near a place called Williams Ranch — quickly adopted James's title. This local Sleepy Lagoon served as a gathering place for young people from the surrounding neighborhoods. For many, the reservoir became an oasis, a source of relaxation and relief from the hot California summers. But on a hot summer night in early August 1942, Sleepy Lagoon provided the backdrop for a murder that electrified the city and the state for six months, preceded some of the most infamous riots in California history, and laid bare the glaring inadequacies of a legal system that, while modern, still clung to old prejudices in the first few months of World War II. The fear of outsiders fueled by America's war with Japan mixed with the racially heterogeneous environment that Los Angeles had become since the turn of the twentieth century. When the state of California put twenty-four young men on trial for the murder of Jose Diaz, all of these factors combined to produce one of the most conspicuous examples of justice gone awry in American history.

However, injustice alone is not the stuff of landmark cases. If that were the only criterion, the term *landmark* would be almost meaningless. As hard as the American legal system may strive to be righteous, injustice occurs almost every day. Throughout America, disparities exist in wealth, notoriety, and ethnicity. These differences yield jury pools from one place to another that can prejudice both defendants and prosecutors. However, *People v. Zammora*, as the case was styled, goes far beyond just the injustice of the proceeding. It illuminates several broader and developing aspects of American jurisprudence that still had far to go in 1942.

First, the case was tried amid the backdrop of war. The West Coast of the United States had lived in a state of high alert since the bombing of Pearl Harbor. Fear of attack from the Japanese fed a growing fear of subversion by Japanese Americans. As 1942 progressed, the United States government and military took affirmative steps to restrict Japanese American civil rights to the point of seizing their property and incarcerating these people in detention camps for the duration of the war. As the Sleepy Lagoon case unfolded, the prosecution and local media began to draw comparisons between the Mexican American defendants and America's new enemy, the empire of Japan. The same fear and racial prejudice that made many Americans comfortable with the treatment of the Japanese would allow Los Angelenos the same level of comfort with respect to the treatment of the young Mexican American defendants. The case was therefore not only relevant then as to how the war affected the operation of the judicial system, but, as America moved into the cold war and eventually on to our present-day war on terror, it provides a mirror to examine and compare how we acted then with how we respond now when threatened by people we deem outsiders.

Second, Mexican immigration dominates today's headlines: not only does the subject divide people over the issue of national immigration policy, but it also threatens to split communities grappling with immigrants on a local level that long ago breached the integrity of America's southern border. An estimated 12,000,000 people are in the United States illegally. A large segment of this population has not only become integrated into American society, but also have children born in this country who are full-fledged American citizens. As government at all levels debates how to handle the dilemma, local communities are beginning to either step to the forefront and enforce national immigration laws, or are refusing to do so. The problem is sure to find its way into the courts, and the strong feelings engendered by the immigration battle will come into play.

The Sleepy Lagoon case came in the wake of almost a century of Mexican immigration that began in the nineteenth century and picked up with greater intensity in 1910 with the Mexican revolution, finally abating in the early days of the Great Depression. While friction developed between Mexicans and Anglos before statehood had become a reality in 1850, as Mexican immigration continued into the twentieth century, California, and Los Angeles in particular, became home to the largest number of these immigrants. The struggle for basic rights that began shortly after the Treaty of Guadalupe Hidalgo in 1848 became more pronounced in the twentieth century. As Mexican Americans began to spread across the city, they moved into areas not previously open to them and laid claim to rights such as equal protection, school desegregation, and labor organization. In the face of a concerted effort to share in the American dream, the "native" Anglo population reacted in a manner that was driven, or at least articulated, by the local media. When Henry Leyvas and his twenty-one codefendants went to trial in October 1942, it was not perceived as the trial of twenty-two youths, but of twenty-two Mexican American youths. Although almost all of these young men were Americans, they had to fight the perception that, regardless of where they were born, they were outsiders — people who were not like "us." They had a different culture and were the product of a different past, both of which allegedly predisposed them to antisocial conduct.

The immigration aspect of the case was not unique to California or Los Angeles. The wave of immigration that hit America after the Civil War and ran into the 1920s brought a general fear of immigrants, and that fear had already begun playing out in the American judicial system, long before Jose Diaz was found dead on the morning of 2 August 1942. *U.S. v. Schenck*, *U.S. v. Abrams*, and *U.S. v. Debs*, although couched in terms of protected free speech versus subversive action, saw the creation and subsequent implementation of Oliver Wendell Holmes's famous "clear and present danger test." All these cases contained a strong element of xenophobia. Lying just below the surface of the First Amendment issues that these cases stand for today is the fact that with the exception of *Debs*, they involved defendants of European origin at a time when America was at war and nativism was on the rise. In 1921, two Italian immigrants stepped into the national spotlight. Nicola Sacco and Bartolomeo Vanzetti, tried for a murder committed in the Braintree suburb of Boston, endured a six-year ordeal that they ultimately lost: they were convicted of murder on flimsy evidence and, by today's standards, inadequate procedural safeguards. The case represents a step in the evolution of America's judicial system and its struggle to deal fairly with those whom society deems different. The Sleepy Lagoon case fits neatly into this story; it demonstrates how far America had come in almost twenty years. Sacco and Vanzetti found no relief in the appellate system, with even Oliver Wendell Holmes turning a deaf ear. The defendants in *People v. Zammora* would fare somewhat better because the California court of appeals looked beyond race and saw something clearly wrong with how these men were tried.

In addition to the national hot-button issues of war and immigration, Sleepy Lagoon provides a pretelevision example of how media coverage and the carnival atmosphere it creates can affect a defendant's rights to a fair trial. The Los Angeles press not only covered the trial itself, but for months before the murder even took place, it had preached a gospel of fear regarding the Mexican American community and its youth population in particular. The trial thus took place amid a media circus of fear and prejudice in an atmosphere that had been cultivated before the case ever arose. The Sleepy Lagoon case provides an opportunity to see how the judicial system grappled with a sensational trial in an era long before O. J. Simpson and Court TV. The trial serves as a warning to Americans today of the effect of ignoring procedural safeguards designed to protect the criminally accused.

Finally, *People v. Zammora* merits landmark status because it provides a link in the evolution of a defendant's right to counsel and to a fair and impartial trial. The Sixth Amendment had established the right to an attorney in federal proceedings early in the life of the republic. By the mid-1930s, neither federal nor state courts could deny effective representation in a capital case. In 1932, nine young black men stood trial in northern Alabama for the rape of two white women. Like the defendants in *Zammora*, the Scottsboro Boys were members of a racial minority accused of a capital crime in a hostile environment. Unable to afford counsel, the trial court allowed the defendants to go virtually unrepresented. On appeal, the United States Supreme Court began the process of defining what it meant to be represented by counsel. *Zammora* examines many of the same issues and racial dynamics that characterized the Scottsboro cases. However, although the Scottsboro trials allowed the Supreme Court to affirm the right to an attorney in a capital case even if one could not afford to pay for counsel, it did not speak to what it meant to be represented by counsel. When the Sleepy Lagoon defendants went to trial in 1942, they all had lawyers, but the case demonstrated just why the right to have a lawyer—and a lawyer able to advocate and protect his client's rights in a meaningful way—was so important.

Young lawyers come out of law school knowing they must defeat their adversary, whether another civil lawyer or a government prosecutor. But most are somewhat hesitant to cross swords with the judge. Part of becoming a lawyer is coming to grips with the realization that an advocate cannot allow the judge to undermine his case any more than he can allow opposing counsel to do so. In some ways, challenging the court is counterintuitive, because the judge is the authority figure in the judicial system. However, there are instances when failing to do so dooms one's case. The *Zammora* trial was such a case, although not because the defense bar willingly allowed the judge to run roughshod over their clients. The problem in 1942 lay in the absence of any codified rules of judicial conduct. The profession had a sense of what was right and wrong, but beyond vague canons that instructed lawyers and judges to act in a professional manner, there was little one could do if a parochial sense of justice dominated over fundamental fairness.

What this study seeks to demonstrate is how an environment of hostility and fear fostered a breakdown in the legal protections afforded to defendants, and how the level of protection in place in the 1940s, although far from what we know today, should have been adequate to cope with the fear and racial animosity that existed. Sleepy Lagoon provides insight into what it is like to be tried in the court of public opinion under circumstances where the opinion has been shaped before the trial ever begins. What is fascinating about the story from a purely legal perspective is how existing procedural safeguards and fundamental fairness were either bypassed or completely run over in an effort to convict these men on the basis of evidence that simply did not point to guilt. Thus, to some degree, this case is about legal subtleties as much as blatant public hostility. Comments made about defendants or their counsel, decisions regarding where people would sit, and the difference in demeanor between how the prosecution was treated by the court and the treatment afforded defense counsel all mattered.

The *Zammora* case remains the largest mass trial for murder in California history in terms of the number of defendants tried together. Beyond its place in the evolution of legal rights and the challenges placed on the judiciary to function normally in times of crisis and to overcome general prejudice, the case demonstrates the degree to which people from different races and walks of life can coalesce around an injustice, and by sheer weight of will and effort alter the outcome. When the jury returned its verdict of guilty for seventeen of the twenty-two defendants, twelve of these boys stood to spend a significant portion of their lives in jail, and some faced life sentences. The fact that less than two years later all of them walked out of jail as free men was a testament to the efforts of the Sleepy Lagoon Defense Committee. During the trial, LaRue McCormick, better known at the time as a labor activist, helped organize an ad hoc committee to publicize the trial. Shortly after the jury convicted seventeen of the defendants, the committee reorganized. Carey McWilliams, a Los Angeles attorney, prolific author, and social activist, became its national chairman, and Alice Greenfield, a civil rights activist, served as secretary. Its twofold mission was to publicize the injustice of the trial and raise money for the appeal. It did both, and the story of the SLDC is crucial to understanding the appeal efforts of the Sleepy Lagoon defendants.

This, then, is the story of a landmark American criminal case that began in one small community of one of America's largest cities, yet grew to become a part of our national legal culture. The events leading up to the trial and the trial itself serve as a reminder of an America that lies not so far in the past. Although much of what occurred was unique to that time and place, many of the social, political, and cultural issues that dominated America then remain with us today. Beyond its historical importance Sleepy Lagoon therefore provides valuable insight into how the American legal system functions under stress.

Throughout the book, the defendants and the young women who accompanied them to the Sleepy Lagoon that night are referred to as *boys* and *girls*. In part it is because many of them were boys and girls: most of the participants that night were minors. The references also reflect how the local media portrayed these young people, and, in many cases, they referred to each other as boys and girls. The terms are not meant to be offensive but reflect a different time and place, as

6   { *Introduction* }

well as an innocence of youth that this event would end forever for many of those who experienced it firsthand. Not only would the young men accused and convicted of murder find their lives forever changed, but many of the young women that were at the Sleepy Lagoon that night and became key witnesses at trial saw their lives adversely affected. In the end, the events that occurred at Sleepy Lagoon haunted almost everyone touched by the murder of Jose Diaz.

CHAPTER I

The World of *Zammora*

Courtrooms have been likened to cauldrons or furnaces in which all of the allegations are exposed to the heat of intense judicial scrutiny that burns away everything but the truth. If cases were tried in a vacuum, completely separated from the world in which they arose, that might be true. However, in America, trials take place in the midst of an array of events and circumstances that influence lawyers, judges, and juries. Like so many other sensational trials, the Sleepy Lagoon murder case cannot be understood outside the environment in which it was tried. Although World War II and a sense of escalating crime among minorities certainly provided important aspects of the social and cultural context, Los Angeles of the 1940s had been decades in the making. Racial tension and the struggle for physical and social space developed over time, driven largely by unprecedented immigration. Even when immigration dropped off during the Great Depression, the financial hardships fostered anti-Mexican attitudes. The combination of almost a century of rapid growth, the economic disaster of the 1930s, and the advent of World War II created a world that in some ways was unique to its time.

For the first sixty years of its existence, under Spanish and then Mexican rule, Los Angeles had been both small and racially diverse. Before 1848, the original inhabitants, although all under the umbrella of Spanish rule, consisted of a mix of mestizo, mulatto, Negro, indio, and other ethnic groups. The Treaty of Guadalupe Hidalgo that followed the Mexican-American War changed Los Angeles forever. Within ten years from the Bear Flag rebellion and the conquest of California by the United States, Los Angeles' population had tripled, and the new inhabitants included a significant Anglo contingent. Gold rushers came first, followed by more permanent settlers. The cultural collision that followed was both intense and predictable. Racial violence began almost immediately as Mexican Americans struggled to maintain their cultural, political, and economic status in the face of an Anglo population that was both large and committed to consolidating power. For the first decade of statehood, violence ran rampant, and much of it took the form of vigilante justice aimed at the Spanish-speaking population. The degree of violence directed at Mexican Americans is evident in the Spanish-language newspapers that sprang up in Los Angeles in the 1850s. The pages of these newspapers — tools for preserving some sense of racial solidarity — spoke out against lynchings, racial violence, land usurpation, and job discrimination. Manifest destiny had made it to the Pacific, and Los Angeles would never be the same.

For the remainder of the nineteenth century, Mexican Americans struggled against the prevailing current of Anglo control. Overt violence and vigilante justice gave way to more legal forms of abuse. Beginning in 1860, Los Angeles Hispanics lived under a set of local regulations called the sumptuary laws — subtle restrictions on civil behavior, sometimes referred to as "Sunday" laws, put on the books by the white and largely Protestant population. These laws created so-called victimless crimes and outlawed certain public behavior that thereby limited many Mexican religious activities and celebrations. Mexican Americans saw them as an attempt to suppress their culture. Efforts to remove the laws in 1882 failed when, despite Mexican American support for the Democratic Party, once in office the successful candidates reneged on their promise to repeal the laws. The ordinances remained on the books for most of the century.

Struggling to maintain their culture, Mexican Americans also tolerated diminished living conditions. The editors of *La Cronica* complained in 1877 of the lack of adequate roads and the shortage of public services afforded the Mexican American neighborhoods. One only had to go into the *barrio latino* to see the evidence of public neglect, causing one editor to remind the Los Angeles city council, "We have not yet returned into the land of the dead." Underlying all of this was a notion that the Mexican American community was somehow inferior and dirty. When a smallpox epidemic broke out in 1877, Anglo physicians told the city council that it was the unsanitary habits of the city's Mexicans that caused the outbreak. In reality, there had been only twenty-one reported cases, and, although most were among Spanish-speaking citizens, the Mexican American community had zealously followed all the public health regulations mandated by the city council.

Traditionally, ethnic communities in America used a variety of means to preserve their cultures. One of the most prevalent tools for doing so was the ethnic language newspaper. However, beyond just preserving culture, these papers also became vehicles for voicing opposition. There had been no Spanish-language newspapers in Los Angeles before 1848. By 1856, the city had two, and that number continued to grow. After 1850, at least fifteen community groups sprang up along ethnic lines, mostly political in nature, and they covered the full spectrum from conservative to militaristic. These organizations tried to foster solidarity among the Spanish-speaking population, a unity that became increasingly more important as the Mexican population in Los Angeles found itself more isolated. Whether born in the United States or Mexico, Spanish-speaking citizens found themselves at the bottom of what became a multitiered social structure, with Anglos at the top and a variety of other ethnic groups below. Most Mexicans found themselves living in the central business district of downtown, a location that facilitated finding work. Referred to as the *barrio*, "neighborhood," by its residents, most Anglo Los Angelenos called it Sonora Town, and, by the end of the 1880s, the barrioization process had split the Los Angeles Anglo and Mexican populations into two distinct ethnic communities.

Although the segregation of Mexican Americans and immigrants had clear negative ramifications, some historians point out that it also served as a means of social solidarity. Immigrants found comfort and a degree of safety in the barrio, and, for most residents, whether American or immigrant, the neighborhood alleviated some of the stress of the economic displacement and racism that was a part of everyday life in Los Angeles. However, as the twentieth century dawned, Los Angeles began to grow not only in population, but also as an economic and industrial center. From 1890 to 1910, the population went from just over 50,000 to almost 320,000. By 1910, Los Angeles had the highest concentration of Mexicans anywhere in the United States outside of San Antonio and El Paso, Texas. However, into the mix of Anglos and Mexicans came other immigrant and ethnic groups. Japanese, Chinese, and African American communities sprang up, and immigration from Southern and Eastern Europe brought Italians, Russians, and Armenians. Los Angeles had become an ethnically diverse city with people competing for jobs and living space. Yet in the face of all of this diversity, over three-quarters of the population of Los Angeles in 1910 were native-born Anglos, and they comprised a substantial portion of the middle class and elite.

Those at the bottom rung of society had limited housing options. Jacob Riis described Los Angeles' living conditions as "every bit as bad as the worst tenements in Manhattan," and, among inhabitants of all of the ethnic enclaves, Mexicans suffered the most. Not only was their housing situation crowded, but, in 1906, Los Angeles created a housing commission with the mandate to make Los Angeles "a city without a slum." The commission had the power to condemn and tear down buildings, and they used that power. The Mexican population found itself displaced by 1913, the result of a Mexican removal project aimed at destroying slums and relocating their inhabitants. However, most of the displaced had few new housing options, and the Mexican population began to move to other areas of the city.

The gravity of the housing situation cannot be understated. Historian Eduardo Pagan argues that to a great extent, Sleepy Lagoon and the zoot suit riots that followed grew out of a struggle over space. Space in Los Angeles became contested ground in the twentieth century, and that contest saw the Anglo population begin to move other ethnicities away from the more desirable areas. Mexicans and Mexican Americans found themselves caught up in the struggle. The industrial expansion that swept Los Angeles fed into the sense of racism that seemed to accompany the growth. Racially restrictive covenants created housing segregation. Mexican Americans found themselves competing for space not only with Anglos, but with Japanese, Chinese, and African American residents who also found themselves relegated to the status of minority outcasts.

Los Angeles Mexican Americans became caught up in what Harry Chandler, publisher of the *Los Angeles Times*, referred to as the "white spot of America." The white spot concept existed within a larger movement that historian Martin Sklar refers to as the "corporate restructuring of American capitalism." As the Los Angeles minority population grew, its growth dovetailed with a new view of capitalism that downplayed the individual, independent producer-owner. This new form of capitalism viewed American society as a collection of groups and corporations, each with its own interests and agenda. This conceptual shift had ramifications for Mexican Americans. Although as individuals most minorities lacked the ability to make their way up the social ladder, this new theory of capitalism allowed the Mexican American population and other minorities to begin to organize along ethnic and racial lines to advance social, political, and economic priorities. However, what this new restructuring did was place power in the hands of the few, and, although it presented the appearance that groups could broker for power, in reality, the new system fostered inequity. Neither Jim Crow in the South nor housing segregation in Los Angeles proved inconsistent with this new form of corporate liberalism.

What this all meant was that while the Anglo inhabitants of America's white spot needed the minority labor that Mexican Americans offered, it struggled with how to use the labor and still preserve the most desirable space. In areas of labor, this did not present a problem. Lower-level industrial and agricultural jobs kept minorities segregated in terms of the workforce. Not only were they segregated from whites, but the way industries were organized, employers kept minority groups segregated from one another. However, maintaining the purity of the white spot became more difficult in areas of social interaction. The control over housing that drove minorities away from the white spot created the risk that the various ethnic groups would interact with each other, and by identifying common interests, they would develop into a larger, more formidable force. In addition to the possibility of some kind of political solidarity, the negative aspects of crowding — disease, unsanitary conditions, and the other characteristics of slums or barrios — could not be contained.

The housing commissions and zoning ordinances that sprang up in the early twentieth century strove to clean up the areas of social blight with the hope that the areas could also be made more attractive for white inhabitation. Ultimately, the goal was to "whiten" Los Angeles and give the city its own unique urban version of the City Beautiful movement that swept America during the Progressive era. The most desirable area to live in the 1920s was the homogenous west side of Los Angeles. A megalopolis that today is known for its suburbs, incorporated Los Angeles of the early twentieth century was home to three-quarters of the city's population, and part of the goal was to move the immigrant populations away from the more desirable parts of Los Angeles, and in the process dilute those homogenous neighborhoods to the point of eliminating ethnic enclaves.

The housing "plan" and the reality that flowed from it proved to be two different things. The zoning ordinances and housing commission did not eliminate ethnic neighborhoods or "whiten" traditionally ethnic areas. Zoning clearly facilitated industrial expansion, but ethnic neighborhoods thrived, and Mexican Americans, thought by many Los Angeleno Anglos to have been on their way out as a cohesive ethnic group, made a resounding recovery. Between 1920 and 1930, the Mexican American population in Los Angeles tripled. Anglos referred to this increase as the "Mexican problem," and a state government report in the late 1920s projected that Mexicans would become the most prevalent group in California among foreign-born peoples. As the foreign-born Mexican population settled and built families, this natural increase fostered a growth in the Mexican American population.

The late 1920s saw efforts to restrict Mexican immigration into California, and these efforts brought an increase in efforts by the Los Angeles police department to sweep areas of heavy Mexican and Mexican American populations. Local authorities arrested hundreds at a time for vagrancy. Those unable to pay a fine were impressed into work for the city until they worked off the fines. Meanwhile, their families had no idea what had happened to them. Anglo Los Angeles had developed a fear of its Mexican and Mexican American population, and this fear of the Mexican problem grew from the realization that Mexican immigration into California and Los Angeles in the 1920s was on the rise.

In the midst of this ongoing struggle came the Great Depression. As financial collapse swept the nation and unemployment rose to unprecedented levels, Anglo efforts to deal with Mexican immigrants rose to new levels. When the Great Depression began, the employment situation for Mexican residents of Southern California was tenable. Before 1929, most people worked at least part of the year, but that ended with the stock market crash and the depression that followed. More importantly, racism had come not only to define whether one got work, but also the ability to move up in society. Most Mexican immigrants and Mexican Americans found employment opportunities at the low end of the wage scale. Trained and experienced brick and tile layers and potters found themselves languishing in production jobs. Efforts to organize by minority workers revealed strength in numbers, but consistent with the new corporate liberalism, such efforts yielded no results. Mexicans competed for the highly sought-after but low-paying service jobs in Los Angeles, where wages were low and upward mobility nonexistent. Even the city's garment industry, where 75 percent of the workers were Mexican or Mexican American, kept wages low and stifled efforts at unionization, thus blocking workers' ability to change conditions. But despite the poor pay, the scarcity of jobs made bad work better than no work at all.

Unemployed Mexican immigrants and Mexican Americans had few options. Mexican immigrants could return to Mexico, and some did so. For the first time in decades, Mexican immigration to the United States actually declined, a trend that indicates the lack of opportunity that drives immigration as well as a sense of what was happening to immigrants and Mexican Americans in the United States. Like most people, out-of-work Mexican immigrants and Mexican Americans sought public assistance when the job market evaporated. This increasing reliance on government help placed enormous burdens on state and local welfare systems across America. City and state officials in the Southwest and California responded by repatriating Mexican immigrants. Unfortunately, many Mexican American citizens found themselves caught up in this process. Some people left because of inducements as railroads and local city officials offered cut-rate fares for immigrants willing to return. Some immigrants saw the opportunity to get home as a blessing, given the conditions in Los Angeles and most of Southern California. However, much of the repatriation was forced, and Mexican Americans found themselves being forcibly removed from what had become their home. The 1930 U.S. census identified 1.42 million people of Mexican ancestry living in the United States. Of that number 805,535 were U.S. born, an increase of 100,000 from a decade before. Given the fact that illegal immigrants are less likely to take part in the census process, the percentage of U.S.-born versus noncitizen immigrants may be high. However, the reality is that the anti-immigration campaigns of the 1930s swept thousands of U.S. citizens out of the country. Despite the alleged "voluntary" nature of the deportations, many people left because they had no choice.

Ignacio Pina lived through this nightmare. Eighty-one years old in 2006 when he told his story to *USA Today*, Pena recalled plainclothes authorities bursting into his home and taking him and his five siblings. After ten days, they were stripped of their belongings, including the contents of a chest that held the birth certificates for Ignacio and his brothers and sisters proving their U.S. citizenship, and deported to Mexico. Pena's experience was far from unique. Local Los Angeles authorities routinely conducted highly publicized raids in public places. For example, on 26 February 1931 immigration officials closed off La Placita, a Los Angeles square, and then questioned over four hundred people about their legal status. The raids created a climate of fear, and many Mexicans left voluntarily to escape the harassment. By June 1931, Walter Carr, the L.A. district director of immigration, admitted that thousands of alien Mexicans had literally been scared out of Southern California. Forced deportation efforts not only suc-ceeded but drew praise from members of Anglo associations like C. P. Visel of the L.A. Citizens Committee for Coordination of Unem-ployment Relief, who applauded U.S. officials for "the exodus of aliens deportable and otherwise who had been scared out of the community."

Many of those wrongfully forced out of the United States had no idea that their expulsion had been illegal. George Clements, the man-ager of the Los Angeles Chamber of Commerce's agricultural depart-ment, wrote in a memo to his boss, Arthur Arnoll, that Mexican legal status was not a factor: "It is a question of pigment, not a question of citizenship or right." Most of the deportees were told they could return, but Clements admitted that was a lie. Most were given a card that made their return impossible because the card showed the per-son was a "county charity," and even U.S. citizens could not return without a birth certificate or similar proof of citizenship. For people like Ignacio Pena and his siblings, their proof was left behind in the United States when they were forced to leave. Even if they had their documentation, authorities often made no distinction between those who could prove citizenship and those who could not. Those who resisted ended up in the "physical deportation" category: they were taken to train stations in squad cars and placed on trains for Mexico.

One of the enduring images of Depression-era America can be found in books like *The Grapes of Wrath*, where families huddle together in shacks and tents, trying to eke out a living. One of the greatest tragedies of the forced deportation program of the 1930s was that Mexican families found themselves deprived of even one another's comfort. Those able to prove citizenship watched as those who could not went back to Mexico. Many were gone for years, returning, if at all, only after harrowing experiences in Mexico. The effect on families proved devastating. Sadly, the experiences of the Depression remain part of the American cultural landscape today. The world Henry Leyvas grew up in has long since passed, but the struggle between Anglos and minorities continues in the context of the inability of America to control its own borders. Illegal immigration has touched off a debate that pits states against the federal government and communities against one another. Since 2003, deportations have jumped over 60 percent, and every time the massive black gates that divide the United States and Mexico slam shut, as *USA Today* notes, "it wipes out a dream, divides a family, ends a life lived in the shadows of the law." Each side seems to have a compelling argument. One side claims that people living in violation of the law have no rights, no matter how long they have lived in America. Another recognizes that with over 12 million illegal aliens in the country, many of whom have been here for years, simply deporting them is no longer an option.

By the time *People v. Zammora* went to trial, Anglos and minorities in California and Los Angeles in particular had been waging a struggle for power and space that had spanned more than ninety years. The struggle had reshaped Los Angeles, both geographically and socially. Efforts to change the face of central L.A. had worked. Even if those efforts had failed to eradicate the Mexican population and other minorities, it had forced many of them to relocate, leaving only a small community remaining in the Plaza and downtown area. But merely moving the population to a different part of the city did not eliminate the conflict, and on the eve of World War II, Los Angelenos felt the stress.

Some historians contend that the apprehension that fueled the Sleepy Lagoon trial and later the riots in 1943 had much to do with a contest over social space. Los Angeles had tried to create some sense of order in the physical layout of the city, and in the process designate certain areas for its growing and diverse minority population. Mexican Amer-

ican youth served as a constant reminder that the boundaries of physical neighborhoods were not impenetrable, and the most obvious man-
ifestation of that expansion became the pachuco and the pachuco's
unmistakable attire, the zoot suit.

No one knows for sure where the term *pachuco* comes from. One
explanation traces the term to El Paso, Texas, and claims it was a term
for a resident of El Paso, which is still called *El Chuco* in some circles.
As Mexican and Mexican American *traqueros*, or railroad workers,
moved west to Los Angeles, the distinctive style that characterized
the pachuco moved with them. Another explanation ties *pachuco* to the
city of Pachuca, in the Mexican state of Hidalgo. Pachuca is suppos-
edly the town that Mickey Garcia, inventor of the zoot suit, came
from before he arrived in El Paso. Some say the term derives from
pocho, a word used to describe a Mexican-born person in the United
States who has lost touch with his Mexican culture.

Whatever its origins, in the 1930s and 1940s, the term *pachuco*
defined Mexican American young people and the unique style they
embraced. Mexican Nobel laureate Octavio Paz claims the pachuco
culture to be an American counterpart of the *zazou* subculture of
World War II–era Paris. Although there is no confirmed link between
the two, both subcultures defined themselves by clothing style, affin-
ity for jazz, swing, and jump blues, and social attitudes. Pachucos in the
United States also had their own distinctive dialect, a street language
called *Calo*. Pachucos were colorful and bold, and, in a city characterized by an Anglo paranoia toward Mexican Americans in general and
juvenile crime in particular, pachucos provided a constant reminder of
what many people feared. The term *pachuco* became synonymous with
gangster and *gang*. The pachuco's female companion, the pachuca, came
to stand for the same negative images. High coif, heavy lipstick and
makeup, and black clothing defined her style — a style associated with
gang membership, violence, unpatriotic behavior, and sexual promis-
cuity. As open and obvious as pachucos were, pachucas may have been
even more threatening in some respects. In an era that still embraced
domesticity, young minority women out in public and openly enjoy-
ing themselves ran contrary to everything "American."

Exactly how zoot suits, jazz music, and street lingo became the
symbol of crime under the moniker of *pachuco* is not clear. The media
played a part by describing Mexican American juveniles as "pachuco

gangsters" or "zoot suit gangs." These images gave the reading public a negative image to associate with their fear of a culture that seemed to be staking its own claim to the American dream. The connection between zoot suits and crime infected not only the general public, but also made its way into professional circles that one might have thought should have looked beyond the propaganda and been able to distinguish truth from fiction. Almost a year after the Sleepy Lagoon verdict, an article in the December 1943 *Los Angeles Bar Bulletin* entitled "Juveniles and Justice" demonstrated how powerful and pervasive the negative image of the pachuco had become in Los Angeles. Authored by Robert Scott, a sitting judge of the superior court of Los Angeles, the article offered a fair-minded appraisal of juvenile delinquency, addressing both its causes and cures. Absent from its pages is any notion of biological predisposition and the idea that every Mexican youth must be crushed. However, Scott could not escape that connection between appearance and crime. In describing the goal of rehabilitation and preventive programs Scott said, "We want a delinquent boy to become a good boy. We want a 'zoot suiter' to trim his pachuco haircut and his indiscretions, to enlarge the bottoms of his draped trousers, and to enlarge his sense of social responsibility to correspond." It was as if crime and antisocial behavior were embodied in the zoot suit that pachucos wore, and merely by taking it off, they could reject the behavior that was associated with its wearing and become law-abiding citizens.

The pachuco clearly increased Anglo fears of a growing Mexican and Mexican American population encroaching on its way of life. But the phobia that gripped white Los Angelenos and Californians in general went beyond youth culture. This overt presence and intrusion into the physical white sphere by Mexican American youth came at a time when Mexican Americans in Los Angeles and the Southwest United States began asserting rights to other aspects of the American dream: work and education. Without downplaying the struggle for social space by Mexican youths that characterized the post-Depression and World War II eras in Los Angeles, Mexican Americans as a group had and were making serious efforts to carve out a place in the larger arena of American society. If one is looking for reasons why Anglos perceived a threat to the white status quo, labor organization and school desegregation are two examples of Mexican American efforts to make better lives for themselves in a way that Anglos simply could not ignore.

The tendency is to see Mexican Americans as victims, but reality belies this notion. The Mexican agricultural labor movement in the areas surrounding Los Angeles and the drive for equal education present proactive examples of Mexican Americans pushing their way into the mainstream of American life. Pachucos and zoot suits may have provided flamboyant evidence of a minority pushing the social boundaries, but it would have been impossible to ignore these other efforts.

Through efforts to better their working and living conditions in the San Gabriel, San Bernardino, and Pomona valleys, Mexican Americans, led by the efforts of people such as Ignacio Lutero Lopez, openly challenged segregation in a variety of public places. Signs that proclaimed "Mexicans and Dogs not allowed" commonly adorned store windows. Courthouses had segregated bathrooms, and swimming pools in California often declared Mondays as "Mexican Day." The only day Mexicans could use such facilities was also the day of the week when the pools were their dirtiest, and pools were normally drained after the day set aside for Mexicans. Using traditional tools such as strikes and work slowdowns, Mexican labor organized and fought for better work conditions. Meanwhile, on a broader front, Mexican Americans began to use their considerable numbers to force change in the region with the threat of economic reprisals. Mexican Americans constituted significant segments of the population within small towns in what Matt Garcia calls the Citrus Belt of Southern California. For Anglo businesses in the area, a boycott by a significant segment of the consumer market could adversely affect and even destroy a small business. Thus, in the 1930s and 1940s, Anglos in the suburbs began to support Mexican American civil rights efforts because it was in their own self-interest to do so. In just one example, Mexican Americans went on a month-long boycott of the Upland's Grove Theatre because the owner segregated his patrons, putting Mexican Americans in the less desirable seats in the front row. Not only did they successfully carry out their boycott, but the white press lent its support. The 3 March 1939 headline in the *Ontario Daily Report* proclaimed the victory: "No Discrimination Pledge: Mexican

Organizations Win in Controversy over 'Jim Crow' Seat in Movie Theatres." Ironically, the headlines from the inner city that played up the violence and lawlessness of the zoot suit gangs actually helped drive Anglo support for civil rights and labor reform in the suburbs. Boycotts and consumer embargoes provided a far more desirable alternative to Mexican efforts to claim their place in the public spaces of suburban Los Angeles. In the 1930s, Lopez and those who followed his lead advocated an approach to social and labor reform that emphasized education and social responsibility.

More than just the efforts by suburban Los Angeles Mexican Americans to change social conditions, the methods they used showed a people with a firm grasp of the American way of effecting social change. Contrary to the assertions of Mexican youth crime in the city, Mexican Americans in the agricultural suburbs of Los Angeles and throughout the American Southwest used the tools of a democracy to effect change. Boycotts, embargoes, strikes, slowdowns, and the effective use of voluntary associations demonstrated the same understanding and ability to improve basic conditions and gain fundamental rights that disadvantaged whites used to bring about the same goals. In the face of these peaceful, well-organized, and determined efforts, allegations that Mexicans were inherently violent and had no respect for human life proved hard to reconcile. As Mexican Americans organized locally, they also came to realize the fundamental power of their vote. In time, these efforts spawned Unity Leagues, town-based organizations that cut across racial lines and attempted to unify Mexican Americans, African Americans, Asian Americans, and progressive Anglos to fight issues like police brutality and segregation. More important, these leagues organized and registered minority voters and pushed minority candidates. Although much of this occurred in the mid-1940s, years after Henry Leyvas and his friends were tried, the genesis of this activity can be found in the late 1930s and early 1940s. As the Sleepy Lagoon case went to trial, the reality that Los Angeles' white spot was beginning to change color could not have been lost on the jury.

Perhaps the most threatening aspect of Mexican American expression of equality came in an area that not only brought significant penetration into the "white" world, but actually made Mexican Americans legally white. Most Americans look to the 1954 United States Supreme Court case of *Brown v. Board of Education, Topeka, Kansas* as the genesis of public school desegregation in the United States. However, more than two decades before *Brown*, Mexican Americans in the Citrus Belt fought the first successful case resulting in court-ordered school desegregation.

Discrimination in the area of public education took on a variety of forms. First, because whites had been able to segregate neighborhoods, the schools available to Mexican children were those that existed in their neighborhoods. Thus segregation was both de jure, sanctioned by Jim Crow laws, and de facto, a practical result of where Mexican Americans lived. By 1930, a total of 85 percent of Mexican American children attended classes taught in facilities that were either completely separate schools or were in separate classrooms on the campuses of white schools. In agricultural areas, white farmers who employed Mexican labor used their influence on school boards to make Mexican schools mere extensions of crop fields or fruit sheds — places where children could be indoctrinated into being good, subservient workers. Even if one lived closer to a white school than a Mexican American school, Mexican children had to register at "Mexican" schools. Under the guise of language barriers, Mexican children were put in segregated schools with the promise that once they learned English, they would be reassigned. In most cases, Mexican children were not reassigned.

Whether trapped in schools operated within the barrios or in separate structures near white schools, Mexican American children experienced horrific conditions. Poor buildings, broken windows, sagging floors, inadequate heating, and outside toilet facilities represented only the structural inadequacies. The school year was markedly shorter, and because many Mexican American children were older than their corresponding grade level when finally admitted to school, they were classified as "retarded." California offered mandatory education only through age sixteen. Thus, many Mexican and Mexican American children were simply pushed out at sixteen. Even if Mexican American children managed to keep pace, once past the eighth grade, the chances of going to high school diminished. Many rural areas could not afford both an elementary school and a high school. Those qualified to move on to high school ran headlong into the policy of white schools and Mexican schools, and at the high school level, Mexican high schools were few and far between.

At all levels, Mexican American children suffered from a watered-down curriculum often designed to push them into manual labor vocations. In addition, they were more likely to be suspended, expelled, and harassed, and unlike white children, there was no effort to enforce mandatory attendance laws in most states. In a nation where Mexican immigration was driven by a thirst for cheap labor, there was no cheaper labor than the unpaid work of children. Although parents did not sit idly by and watch their children cheated out of the possibility of a better life, outrage had to be tempered. Strong efforts to change the situation in the 1930s provided an excuse for forced repatriation. In some areas, whites admitted a few Mexican children into white schools to quell complaints, but the overall effect on Mexican American education proved minimal.

The beginning of change came in 1931 in the Lemon Grove area around San Diego. The basis of the fight was an 1897 Texas federal district court case, *In Re Rodriguez*, where a federal judge held that for purposes of immigration classification, Mexicans were white. Theoretically this ruling should have afforded Mexican Americans all the privileges of citizenship, but that proved not to be the case. However, armed with legal authority that defined them as white, Mexican Americans began attacking school desegregation on Fourteenth Amendment due process grounds. Unlike African Americans, who were forced to approach the problem from an equal protection basis, Mexican Americans could claim to be white, and thus any state law segregating them was a violation of due process. The first Latino desegregation case, *Romo v. Laird*, came in Arizona in 1925, followed by *Independent Sch. Dist. v. Salvatierra* in Texas in 1930. Both made advances, but in *Salvatierra*, for example, the appeals court diluted the victory by dissolving an injunction against the school district because there was no evidence the district intended to discriminate.

In July 1930, the Lemon Grove, California, school board took up the issue of how to handle seventy-five Mexican students attending the local elementary school. The board elected to build a new school for Mexicans only, but no one told the parents of the Mexican students. Six months later, in January 1931, Jerome T. Greene, the principal of Lemon Grove Grammar School, stood in the doorway of the school and ushered all of the Mexican American children to a building soon to be dubbed *La Caballeriza* — the barn. The students refused to go, and their parents refused to send them to the separate school. Instead, working through Enrique Ferreria, the Mexican consul, they hired Fred C. Noon and A. C. Brinkley, two lawyers with a history of working with the Mexican consul, and filed a suit seeking to prevent the Lemon Grove School Board from forcing their children into an inferior school. Robert Alvarez was chosen as the named plaintiff in the class action suit, and on 24 February 1931 Judge Claude Chambers began hearing evidence in *Alvarez v. Owen*.

The plaintiffs put on witnesses and launched a direct attack on the school board's argument that the Mexican children were segregated because they were educationally "backward." Testimony revealed that most of the students were U.S. citizens who had been born in the United States. One student spoke no Spanish at all. At one point, Chambers questioned a school board witness and got directly to the heart of the matter.

> CHAMBERS: When there are American students who are behind, what do you do with them?
> SCHOOL BOARD WITNESS: They are kept in a lower grade.
> CHAMBERS: You don't segregate them? Why not the same with the other children? Wouldn't the association of American and Mexican children be favorable to the learning of English for these children?
> SCHOOL BOARD WITNESS: (Silence, No Answer).

Chambers ruled against Lemon Grove and ordered the children reinstated. He found Mexicans to be outside the definition of any ethnic group covered by California's education code segregation law. They were not Indians, Negroes, or Mongolians, the three groups that could be legally segregated in California. In effect, he found Mexicans to be white.

The *Alvarez* decision did not end the fight but merely defined the battleground. For almost two more decades, California's Anglo population continued to segregate Mexican American children using *Alvarez* as a guide to avoid legal pitfalls in their efforts to legally segregate children. Not until 1946, in *Mendez v. Westminster*, did California minorities succeed in overturning the state's "separate but equal" school segregation laws. But the fight over schools and equal access made up a portion of the world in which Henry Leyvas and his friends lived. As they went on trial for murder in 1942, the Anglo population, including those who sat on the jury, felt the constant pressure of Mexican Americans and other minorities pushing for their piece of the American dream. While the image of Mexican American youths as gangsters helped stoke the fires of prejudice, the contest in Los Angeles and throughout Southern California was about more than just the zoot suit image.

The pretrial publicity would have been impossible to ignore. The media attention in August immediately after the Sleepy Lagoon incident had been preceded by a series of incidents in the spring of 1942 that enabled both the police and the media to build on racial and ethnic tension to create an anti-Mexican sentiment that provided the groundwork for the media and legal blitz that came in the fall. A series of false allegations by the police, coupled with newspaper coverage, created an image of a lawless Mexican community. In one instance, a young Mexican man served forty-five days for accosting a woman. Upon his release, he was immediately brought before a grand jury, indicted for rape, convicted, and sentenced to twelve years in prison. A quick appeal brought a reversal, but there was no way to undo the negative media attention. That same spring, a group of men at a wedding were arrested for playing a penny craps game. The police had always ignored such harmless diversions as being inconsequential. But this arrest led to a conspiracy indictment by the grand jury and converted a petty misdemeanor into a felony charge. On 21 July 1942 a story appeared playing up a fight between two rival "Mexican gangs," the Belvedere gang and the Palo Verde gang. The article did more than just play up violence; it emphasized the specific Mexican "character" of the participants and laid the groundwork for the racially based "predisposition to violence" argument that dominated the Los Angeles papers leading up to the Sleepy Lagoon murder trial.

The racial tension and paranoia that existed between Anglos and Mexicans in 1940s Los Angeles does not completely explain the social and cultural context in which the Sleepy Lagoon case was tried. The world of *Zammora* was a world at war. Part of what had made the media campaign against Mexican American youths so effective was the presence of another racial group under scrutiny in the early months of 1942: Japanese Americans. Before Pearl Harbor, it was difficult to find newspaper articles or editorials questioning Japanese American loyalty. However, after 7 December 1941 everything changed. Initially, both the press and public officials exercised restraint, but the tone slowly changed. The arguments that emerged in the late summer and fall about the racial predisposition of Mexicans for violence found a precursor in the same type of biological rationale surrounding Japanese Americans. Within two weeks of Pearl Harbor, articles appeared in Los Angeles newspapers questioning the loyalty of Japanese Americans. Tales of secret societies and espionage plots followed earlier suggestions that Japanese immigrant farmers might be poisoning crops and that federal authorities had already closed banks and businesses with connections to Japan.

The environment of fear spread to other racial groups; Filipinos and Chinese began wearing badges to distinguish themselves from Japanese Americans. The newspapers picked up on this desire to distance themselves from Japanese residents by suggesting the badges meant that Japanese Americans could not be assimilated. Japanese newspapers such as *Rafu Shimpo* encouraged people to think of themselves as Americans and to stop emphasizing their particular ethnic background. However, some Japanese Americans, feeling under attack, struck back. Editorials condemning Filipinos as backward and misguided began to appear, as well as articles condemning Filipinos for attacking Japanese Americans. The criticism escalated to depicting Filipinos as unstable, less civilized, knife-wielding individuals. As Asian immigrant communities began to turn on one another, Chinese Americans took steps to ensure that no one mistook them for Japanese. On 6 January 1942 the *Los Angeles Times* reported that Chinese Americans had begun to use specially prepared decals for display on the windows of their homes, businesses, and cars. The stickers depicted both the Chinese and American flags and sent a message that this person belonged in the camp of America's allies.

This distrust between Asian Americans and immigrants suggested that there were particular racial predispositions of Japanese Americans. An unnamed Chinese restaurant owner told the *Los Angeles Times* that he could easily tell Chinese from Japanese, and American-born Japanese from "Natives of Japan": Native Japanese "toe out more" than either Chinese or Japanese Americans, and Japanese Americans talk and walk faster, "seldom strolling along in a relaxed manner." The anonymous Chinaman also suggested that alien Japanese seldom reached heights over five foot three inches tall. He went on to discuss the facial differences among the three groups and suggested that one could easily discern Chinese from Japanese by observing their facial characteristics.

In late January 1942, a letter from a Frank Kelly to the editor of the *Herald and Express* flatly stated that there was no difference between native-born Japanese and Japanese Americans. Kelly claimed, " a Japanese is a Japanese, no matter where he is born. He is taught from infancy the religion of Japan, which is: Be polite and nice to everybody because someday you will help stick them in the back." Strong efforts by *Rafu Shimpo* to refute the allegations in Kelly's letter raised valid concerns about racial generalization, but at this point, public opinion had moved beyond reason. As Japanese American civil servants found themselves without jobs, people within Los Angeles began calling for their forced incarceration. Anglos, unwilling to see any difference between native-born and American-born Japanese, equated true patriotism with a willingness to be incarcerated. In other words, good Japanese Americans would willingly abandon their homes, their businesses, and their lives and allow themselves to be placed in a camp, simply to allay the white population's fears.

What made the wartime situation so dangerous for Mexican Americans was that as Los Angelenos read stories of Japanese disloyalty and the potential for harm, stories of zoot suit gangs and pachucos appeared right next to them. By the time the Sleepy Lagoon trial began in October 1942, the forced relocation of an entire ethnic group was a reality. Henry McLemore, a syndicated columnist, wrote his 29 January 1942 column from Los Angeles and suggested that civil rights had no place in war, noting, "I hate the Japanese, and that goes for all of them." He added, "I know this is the melting pot of the world and all men are created equal and there must be no such thing as race or creed hatred, but do these things go when a country is fighting for its life? Not in my book." In the context of a war, it seemed that the Bill of Rights applied only if it was convenient. McLemore was not alone in his opinion that war could limit civil rights. Writers and politicians had come to regard Japanese as racially loyal to the home country.

26   { *Chapter 1* }

Wartime had justified the total subordination of one race, and now a city at the epicenter of the wartime fear stood ready to turn its attention to Mexican Americans. Henry Leyvas and the rest of his Thirty-eighth Street defendants were in the direct path of the storm. Among some observers, it was almost a foregone conclusion that Mexican Americans would fill the void left by Japanese Americans and become the ethnic scapegoat in Los Angeles. For those who saw a conspiracy to use war and fear as tools, the media attack on Mexican Americans provided proof. The negative press seemed to escalate almost immediately after the forced relocation of the West Coast's Japanese Americans.

CHAPTER 2

Support or Illumination

The Sleepy Lagoon murder case started at a birthday party for twenty-year-old Eleanor Delgadillo Coronado. Jose Diaz mixed with the other guests at the party, drinking a little beer, talking, and doing a little dancing. The twenty-two-year-old Diaz grew up in a house just north of Eleanor's in a neighborhood dominated by Mexican Americans. The son of Mexican immigrants, Diaz had been certified fit for military duty and chose to spend the last weekend before his induction with his parents and friends. Around 11:00 P.M. that night, the party got a little rowdy when some uninvited guests, about twenty boys from the neighboring town of Downey, got upset when the beer ran dry. They were forcibly driven from the party. They left defiantly, some swearing to come back. Meanwhile, a mile and a half away on Williams Ranch, Henry Leyvas and his girlfriend, Dora Baca, hung out with a friend at a reservoir named "Sleepy Lagoon" by the locals. Leyvas, Baca, and their friend, Bobby Telles, were all a part of the Thirty-eighth Street neighborhood located about five miles west of the reservoir.

Leyvas, Baca, and Telles were not alone. Other kids from the Thirty-eighth Street neighborhood had gathered. While the Downey boys were being thrown out of the Delgadillo birthday party, the kids from Thirty-eighth Street drank, talked, and relaxed. Apparently the Downey boys did not take well to being thrown out of the Delgadillo party. At trial Dora Baca testified to what happened after an unidentified vehicle passed by, traded insults, and drove on. She described how a short time later a car returned and the subsequent fight that broke out leaving her, Henry, and his friends from the Thirty-eighth Street neighborhood beaten and stunned. After returning to Thirty-eighth Street to summon reinforcements, Henry and several carloads of his friends returned to the Sleepy Lagoon only to find the place deserted. At that point Henry made the ill-fated decision to look else-where and his search took him to the Delgadillo house up the road.

The party-goers later testified to what happened when the cars from Thirty-eighth Street pulled up to the house. Accounts vary as to exactly what time the Thirty-eighth Street boys showed up, but almost every time line has Henry Leyvas and his friends arrving at 1:00 A.M. or sometime thereafter. The Delgadillo girls danced on the front patio as Leyvas and his friends approached demanding to know where the boys were. The story is unclear as to whether Leyvas wanted to know where the Downey boys were, or the whereabouts of the boys that beat up some of his gang. The girls told them no one was there and that everyone had gone home. Cruz Reyes stood on the patio, watching. It is impossible to know what Leyvas was thinking, but he moved past the girls toward Reyes, and the melee was on. Like many fights, this one was short and intense, with the Thirty-eighth Street boys clearly getting the best of those who remained at the Del-gadillo party. Shouts that the police were on their way broke up the fight. The partygoers were beaten, battered, and bloody, but no one was dead or appeared in danger of dying. The Thirty-eighth Street kids fled the scene and headed to friendlier ground. Hardly jubilant, a somber group made its way back to the Los Amigos Club, with sev-eral, including some of the girls, nursing wounds they received in the fight.

While the Thirty-eighth Street kids assessed the damage, the stunned members of the Delgadillo party did likewise. The fight had spread beyond the Delgadillo home, and everyone began to comb the area to be sure no one had gotten injured and could not make his or her own way back. As they searched, some wandered southwest from the Delgadillo home to a dirt road just below the Avila house and north of a small pond. There they discovered Jose Diaz, face up, pock-ets turned inside out, and barely conscious. Someone called an ambu-lance. Lino Diaz later recalled how he waited in the middle of the road for it to arrive, then rode with his brother to the hospital. Jose could hardly speak, and, an hour and a half after his arrival, he died of a cere-bral concussion, made worse, no doubt, by the two knife wounds to his diaphragm and breastbone.

The LAPD reacted to Diaz's death by rounding up more than six hundred people, virtually every one of them of Mexican descent. In what some termed the "great raid," on the nights of 10 and 11 August, the police moved into Mexican American neighborhoods and blockaded the main streets. All cars entering or leaving the neighborhood were stopped, the occupants removed and searched, and then the car itself searched for weapons and contraband. Most of the six hundred arrests came on charges of "suspicion" of assault, "suspicion" of robbery, "suspicion" of auto robbery, suspicion of whatever. The arrests were a guise, and, of the six hundred taken into custody, the police released more than four hundred almost immediately. One hundred seventy-five remained in custody on charges of possession of some kind of weapon. Among those held in custody were the twenty-four boys, mostly juveniles, who were ultimately charged with the murder of Jose Diaz.

The investigation into Diaz's murder was driven by a clear animosity toward Mexicans and Mexican Americans. Whether predicated on the racial tension that had dominated Los Angeles since the mid-1850s, the fundamental reorganization of the LAPD after Fletcher Bowron became mayor in 1938, or both, the animosity was real. The police became proactive, and that aggressive stance toward crime prevention came with a system of racial profiling that in turn brought a new harshness to the way the police dealt with minorities, most of whom were Mexican or Mexican Americans. Added to the animosity was the belief that the use of violence in police work was both necessary and fair when dealing with young minorities. Angel Padilla, Joseph Valenzuela, Henry Leyvas, Lupe Leyvas, Benny Alvarez, Eugene Carpio, and Manuel Reyes all testified at trial to verbal and physical abuse when brought in for initial questioning. If a confession could not be easily obtained, it was coerced. In an era before *Miranda v. Arizona* and the landmark decisions of the 1960s concerning the rights of the accused, the police felt free to hold uncooperative youths in isolation, unable to call a lawyer or family, until they confessed. In some cases, the police went to extreme measures by booking the accused under a different name, thus preventing anyone, including an attorney, from locating and securing that person's release.

Although the mistreatment was not a matter of public record, the fact that Diaz had been killed and that the police had rounded up alleged Mexican gang members was all over the headlines for every-one to read. Just days after Jose Diaz's death, the front page of the *Los Angeles Examiner* told the sordid story of "vicious gangs of Mexican youths – one group including girls" who "left a trail of death and injury in two forays yesterday." The article went on to describe Jose Diaz being beaten to death at a birthday party, and it also recounted how eleven Mexican youths attacked five white boys at a gravel pit swimming pool in Baldwin Park. Several Mexican boys had allegedly chased a white boy into the pond with a chain, beating him until he disappeared under the water. Whether the Baldwin Park incident was true or not, the report and the Sleepy Lagoon murder inflamed a community and fed the already-existing paranoia toward youth gangs. Reports of these incidents and the subsequent police efforts to find Diaz's killer only added fuel to the fire.

The media frenzy was more than just bad press. While the Sleepy Lagoon case clearly took place in the context of events and racial tension that had its beginnings long before Henry Leyvas was born, he and his friends were on trial for murder because they found themselves in the wrong place at the wrong time, and someone got killed. Granted, the defendants were not blameless in the events that brought the police to the Delgadillo house that night. At a minimum, a clear case of trespass of the Delgadillo home had occurred, as well as multiple acts of assault. But what made it easier to come after Leyvas and his friends for premeditated murder was a perception of who they were, as opposed to any actual evidence of what they may or may not have done. White Los Angeles had developed an image of Mexican youths, complete with a full array of cultural characteristics such as dress, hairstyle, and music. That cultural makeup coalesced in the image of a pachuco, and pachucos could be killers.

In the weeks leading up to trial, Los Angeles' law enforcement leaders played on the pachuco image and tried to assign a set of racial characteristics to the physical image that people had of Leyvas and his friends. Those characteristics portrayed these young people as part of a race that had a biological predisposition to violence. As irrational as this may have been, the explanation had palatability for Anglos, who felt pressure from Mexicans and Mexican Americans no longer content to remain on the fringes of American society. As young people broke down social barriers, Mexican American civil rights efforts made inroads into public schools and other places traditionally off-limits to Mexicans, and the white population felt the pressure.

The reports of more Mexican gang violence had elevated public concern over the gang problem. News that the grand jury had indicted twenty-four members of the "Thirty-eighth Street Gang" served to confirm the fears harbored by many Anglos in Los Angeles. What followed in the next two months leading up to the Sleepy Lagoon trial took the fires of fear and prejudice associated with Mexican youths to a new level. The grand jury did not rest once it indicted the Sleepy Lagoon defendants. Instead, it began an investigation into juvenile delinquency and crime that lasted for the several months leading up to the trial. In the process, government officials not only testified to the extent of the problem, but also offered "scientific" evidence of the Mexican racial predisposition to violence.

Ten days after Jose Diaz died, high-ranking members of the Los Angeles police department and the Los Angeles sheriff's department began testifying before the grand jury. Many had already sent letters to the grand jury foreman, Ernest W. Oliver. The law enforcement testimony provided statistics on the rise of juvenile crime among Mexican youths, but went beyond the numbers by adding opinions as to why crime was on the rise. Captain Vernon Rasmussen of the LAPD blamed the increase on the city's recreational system. He argued that Mexican youths that gathered at the various city recreation centers developed into "a clannish self-centered group and refused to associate with other recreational groups." Rasmussen testified that members of one recreation center would not invite members of other recreation centers to their functions, and this fostered an atmosphere of conflict. According to Rasmussen, he had spoken to directors at some of the recreation centers who described Mexicans as "destructive" and without an appreciation for efforts "put forth for their betterment."

Police chief Clement B. "Jack" Horrall offered his own take on Mexican juvenile delinquency. Horrall, a World War I veteran, joined the LAPD in 1923 and became chief of police in 1941 after Mayor Bowron's reelection. He argued that it was the class status of Mexican immigrants that led their children to join gangs. Mexican immigrants were among the poor class of Mexicans in their own country and had not been able to assimilate American standards of living. Their children educated in the United States noticed the differences between their own standard of living and the majority of people who lived in this country. As a result, the children of immigrants "lost respect for their parents and their parents . . . lost the ability to properly control them."

The testimony offered by Rasmussen and Horrall clearly painted Mexican youths as violent, but neither stopped at the purely environmental factors. Both testified that Mexicans possessed a biological inclination to violence. However, no one expressed the idea more clearly than Lieutenant Edward Duran Ayres. Ayres, who was originally from San Francisco, served in the merchant marine in World War I, joined the L.A. Sheriff's Department in 1924, and served in the robbery and homicide bureaus before becoming the head of the Sheriff's Department's foreign relations bureau. While he conceded the role of both poverty and discrimination as factors in Mexican American juvenile crime, in a written letter titled simply "Statistics," Ayres insisted that the basic cause lay beyond environment and that the main basis was "biological."

Legendary Dodger's announcer Vin Scully once observed that "statistics are used much like a drunk uses a lamp post: for support, not illumination," and nothing provided in the ongoing debate over Mexican youth gang violence fit that description better than Ayres's "Statistics." With nothing to support his position, Ayres argued that human races were as different from one another as animal species. Domestic cats and wild cats may share some common traits, but, in crucial ways, they are completely different; it is these differences that make one domesticable and the other capable of living in civilized society only within a cage. To quote Rudyard Kipling, "East is East and West is West and never the twain shall meet." Ayres told the grand jury that Indians from Alaska to Patagonia "are essentially oriental," at least in their "utter disregard for the value of life." For a country at war with Japan, not even a year removed from the attack on Pearl Harbor, Ayres's testimony not only painted Mexican Americans as violent, but placed them into the same category as one of America's most feared enemies. California had experienced the fear associated with Nisei Japanese American citizens, and most Anglo Los Angelenos felt completely comfortable with the forced removal and incarceration of these people. Now a law enforcement official pur-ported to have scientific proof that Mexican Americans were just like them. Ayres concluded that because "Oriental Aztecs" had sacrificed as many as thirty thousand people in a day, the "total disregard for human life" was universal among American Indians and everyone knew it to be true. Less than 20 percent of Mexicans were white, he asserted; Mexicans as a race were predominately "Indian," and that group was the one that migrated to the United States.

Ayres went so far as to argue that Mexican Americans fought dif-ferently. Whereas Anglos relied on their fists, Mexican Americans resorted to knives or other lethal weapons, and they had no qualms about kicking an opponent when he was down. This method of fight-ing, argued Ayres, was consistent with the inherent desire to kill or draw blood. The fact that Ayres had no real scientific qualifications did not seem to matter. Both Horrall and Rasmussen supported Ayres's argument. But having condemned Mexican Americans as a race biologically predisposed to violence, no one offered any real solu-tion except harsh punishment. Rasmussen argued that the biological tendency toward violence made it imperative that Mexican American violators be punished as harshly as the law provides. According to Ayres, Mexican American lawbreakers interpreted leniency as weak-ness. It was insufficient to just incarcerate the leaders. The only way to break the circle of violence was to put them all in prison until they realized that law enforcement authorities would not tolerate "gang-sterism."

Ayres, Horrall, and Rasmussen never testified publicly, nor were their comments reprinted verbatim in the press. However, that did not mean that what they said did not cause harm and that the gist of their comments did not make it into the public forum. Their argu-ments became the basis of information and legal positions presented by journalists in Los Angeles, and the fact that none of the three had any qualifications to make the biological argument they so zealously advocated did not seem to matter. In the months preceding the trial of Leyvas and his friends, the *Los Angeles Times* hammered away at the themes Ayres, Horrall, and Rasmussen had fed the grand jury, argu-ing that "the community, in self-defense, needs to try the deterrent effect of some severe punishment." Timothy G. Turner, a *Times* reporter, criticized what he called "mush-headed sentimentalists" who thought of "zoot suit gangsters" as naughty boys who should not be punished too harshly.

The most damaging aspect of the law enforcement testimony lay in the perception it left in peoples' minds that juvenile crime had escalated out of control and that such crime was particularly associated with Mexican American youths. In reality, the opposite may have been true. At least some of the information available on immigrant crime in general and on juvenile crime in California in particular revealed a far different picture than the one portrayed by the L.A. law enforcement officials. If one really was looking for a second opinion on the issue of Mexican crime, information existed on a national level all the way down to the city level in Los Angeles. The starting place for anyone in search of the truth was the massive study of immigration and crime undertaken by the federal government in the early 1930s.

The genesis of the Wickersham report goes back to 1929 and the Hoover administration. After a decade, it became clear that Prohibition and the Eighteenth Amendment had failed on many levels. People continued to drink, and the criminalization of the behavior had driven it underground and right into the hands of criminals, providing the ideal setting for the growth of organized crime in America. President Herbert Hoover appointed Charles Wickersham, U.S. attorney general under William Taft, to undertake a comprehensive study of crime and police work in the United States. The United States Commission on Law Observance and Enforcement became known simply as the "Wickersham Commission" and its two-year investigation culminated in fourteen separate reports spanning the full spectrum of law enforcement and crime in America. One of those reports, on "Crime and the Foreign Born," went a long way toward dispelling some of the myths that surrounded immigrant crime and in the process pointed to some of the factors that distorted America's perception of criminal activity within its immigrant population.

An underlying premise of the Wickersham Commission's investigation was the realization that "in attempting to attribute criminality to any particular immigrant group, it is important to remember that there has been in this country in each period of our history much reckless and prejudicial criticism of one or another of our various immigrant groups." Italians had come under attack in the not-so-distant past; before the Civil War it was the Irish; and "at the present time this criticism is directed at Mexico." From the start, Wickersham recognized that his job was to separate the emotion of unchecked passion and prejudice from the statistical reality. His figures reflected crime rates for 1930, a full decade before the Sleepy Lagoon affair, but even then his numbers belie any notion that one race or group was biologically programmed and predisposed to violence.

Gauging crime among Mexican-born residents of the United States presented great statistical challenges. Wickersham's data on Mexican immigrant crime suffered from the fact that 1930 census data were unavailable when his commission did its research and published its report. Rather than producing national statistics, the Wickersham report focused on several main regions with a heavy concentration of Mexican immigrants: California, Texas, Colorado, and Chicago. Without census data, the report used school census information compiled between 1927 and 1930. The proportion of Mexican children in the school census was taken as the proportion of Mexicans in the total population. The term *Mexican* in this context referred to race and thus included both immigrants and U.S. citizens of Mexican descent. The report acknowledged that using schoolchildren to determine total population had several potential problems. One shortcoming was the possibility that the Mexican percentage of the total population might be understated. The report indicated that Mexican children made up 9.4 percent of the elementary school population and the percentage of Mexicans arrested was higher than that. However, even with statistical shortcomings, the results of the report proved enlightening.

The regional treatment of Mexican crime yielded several smaller reports by different individuals. Paul S. Taylor's study on Mexican labor in the United States provided the basis for the California portion of the Wickersham report. Taylor addressed several areas of California: San Francisco, Los Angeles, and the Imperial Valley. San Francisco's Mexican population was small, as was the percentage of arrests attributed to Mexicans. As might be expected, Los Angeles had the highest concentration of Mexicans, whether immigrants or citizens. Using data from the late 1920s, the report concluded that although arrests among Mexicans, or what the report termed the "Red Race," were slightly higher than their proportion to the total population, the difference was not significant.

The Wickersham report clearly had problems in identifying the true extent of Mexican crime in California. However, some of its overall conclusions strongly suggested that the real problem in determining Mexican crime lay in the way law enforcement treated these people. The data relied on arrests and prison population percentages. However, the report surmised that the use of "arrests, or even convictions, to gauge the criminality of Mexicans is open to important objections. Peace officers shared the racial prejudices of the local white communities in which they served." That alone tended to drive up the number of arrests — something Henry Leyvas and his friends discovered in the number of times they were arrested and then released on the basis of "suspicion" of committing some type of crime. Convictions as an accurate basis of criminal conduct presented a slightly different problem. Mexicans as a group were, as Taylor put it, "politically helpless." The combination of poverty and the social prejudice that existed tended to make Mexicans more likely to plead guilty; they were unable to financially mount an extended defense or prosecute an appeal.

Over a decade before Ayres and his cohorts offered their opinions to the Los Angeles grand jury regarding racial predisposition and the need to deal harshly with Mexican crime, the Wickersham report dealt with similar notions and dispelled them as untrue. The idea that Mexicans understood only force or that they encouraged one another to commit crimes so they could benefit from the food and housing afforded in prison were both untrue. Not only did the report condemn these generalizations, but it also viewed them as evidence of the attitude many officials took toward Mexicans in general: "It is clear that Mexicans in the United States, both aliens and citizens, are frequently subjected to severe and unequal treatment by those who administer the laws." Eleven years later, nothing had changed in Los Angeles, and the venom within the statements provided to the grand jury by Rasmussen, Horrall, and Ayres showed just how deep the prejudice ran.

Granted, the Wickersham report came a decade before World War

II. It also did not address crime committed by youth as a subset of the Mexican crime issue. But statistics and reports readily available in 1942 also undermined the notion of a Mexican youth crime epidemic in Los Angeles. More important, this information appeared at the very time that the Los Angeles media campaign portrayed the city as embroiled in a crisis of Mexican juvenile crime.

As the chief probation officer with the Los Angeles County probation department, Karl Holton had a unique perspective from which to evaluate and comment on the juvenile crime situation in Los Angeles. In the fall of 1942, he addressed the Children in War Time Conference held in Los Angeles, and his remarks were reprinted in the November 1942 issue of the *Los Angeles Bar Bulletin*. Holton completely undermined the notion that juvenile crime was on the rise, and he specifically addressed juvenile crime among Mexicans and Mexican Americans.

To begin with, juvenile crime had not simply appeared from nowhere after the start of World War II. In 1940, four thousand sixty-three children came before the Los Angeles juvenile court. That number rose in 1941, but after Pearl Harbor, the number of juvenile cases actually declined. Holton conceded that the decline posed somewhat of a mystery, although increased military enlistment among all young people might have had an effect. Contrary to what Ayres, Rasmussen, and Horrall told the grand jury, Holton addressed what he and others believed were the possible causes of wartime juvenile delinquency. Quoting from a paper delivered by Dr. Martha Elliott at the California Conference on Social Work in April 1942, Holton argued that wartime tends to break down the family and social structures that are so important to effective child rearing. In peacetime, juvenile delinquency results from something that undermines young people's emotional security, such as divorce or lack of acceptance by family or community. In wartime, these factors are exaggerated: the father may go off to military service, the mother may find work in defense-related industries, and the family income may be seriously reduced, while at the same time job opportunities for juveniles may greatly increase their own income levels. All of these factors serve to undermine parental supervision and create both a sense of insecurity and a void in authority among young people. What Holton found interesting, however, was that rather than an increase in juvenile crime, Los Angeles experienced a decline after Pearl Harbor. While the L.A. newspapers depicted a juvenile crime wave, Holton said that juvenile crime in general decreased almost 20 percent in Los Angeles and that virtually every category of crime saw a decline.

Holton then turned his attention to delinquency among Mexican children in Los Angeles. In a tacit recognition of the year-long campaign against Mexican gangs, Holton began by saying, "We have heard a great deal about the problem of delinquency among Mexican children in Los Angeles lately, and I am afraid that many people have an incorrect impression." Holton estimated that thirty-six thousand Mexican children between the ages of six and eighteen called Los Angeles County home. For several years, the L.A. juvenile authorities had dealt with gang fights among Mexican children. Plagued by poverty and raised by foreign-born parents in what he deemed a "disturbing atmosphere of economic stress, cultural conflict, and social isolation," juveniles turned to other means of emotional support, and the gang problem among Mexican children that had plagued cities across America had been acutely present in Los Angeles. Holton admitted that gang violence existed, but he explained that a study performed two years earlier in the Clanton Street area of Los Angeles had made progress in using both public and private agencies in the recreation and delinquency-prevention fields as tools to suppress the gang problem. A committee formed recently at the suggestion of the juvenile courts had bolstered this effort. Holton not only believed that the vast number of Mexican youths had no gang affiliation, but that the county-level efforts he discussed were bearing fruit. The total number of Mexican boys brought into juvenile court in 1942 had shown no increase from the same period a year ago. Auto thefts were down among Mexican youths, and while general theft was up almost 29 percent among other racial groups, the same crime among Mexican youths rose only 6 percent. Holton concluded, "In other words, there is no 'wave of lawlessness' among Mexican children."

Holton admitted "the instances of gang fighting among Mexican youths which has been so publicized have naturally appealed to the imagination of the public (including suggestible youths who might like to see their names in the papers too)." However, he stressed that the causes lay in the environment and that while removing the bad element and leaders from the neighborhoods was a crucial step, rather than openly impugning every Mexican young person, as the newspaper generalizations had done, the city and county needed to embrace these children: "More important is the necessity to let the thousands of American children of Mexican descent know that the courts and social agencies and the people of Los Angeles are proud to have them in the community and guarantee them the full protection of our Constitution and of our American way of life."

Holton listed eight detailed steps that should be taken to help fight juvenile delinquency across the board. This was not a problem that could be solved overnight; it would require a sustained effort on everyone's part. Holton's insights at the conference mirrored the reports he submitted to the courts throughout 1942. Implicit in his conference comments was a belief that comments like Ayres's that helped fan the fires of division and prejudice only hurt the community. As he saw the delinquency issue, it was much bigger than just Los Angeles, but it had to start there: "We talk so much about winning the war. It seems to me that it is time each of us realizes that the job of winning the war begins right here with you and me, and not with the fellow next door or the man across the street."

About the time Holton stepped up to offer a contrary view of Mexican American youth crime, the grand jury proceedings that had begun in the late summer resumed. Although not a public proceeding, the testimony provided by Ayres and the other members of the Los Angeles law enforcement community had indirectly found its way into the public sector through newspapers that picked up on the gist of the arguments and made them part of the growing editorial campaign against Mexican Americans, and the youth population in particular. The second half of the grand jury investigation picked up two months after Ayres, Horrall, and Rasmussen had concluded their testimony. This session provided an opportunity for opponents of the racial predisposition theory to rebut the notion that the "Indian" community, of which Mexican Americans were a part, had a racial tendency toward violence and crime. It remains unclear why this opportunity to respond did not come immediately after Ayres's testimony, but the delay may be attributable to the fact that a rebuttal was not part of the initial plan. Harry Braverman, one of the best-known social scientists of his time and a member of the grand jury, took it upon himself to arrange for the "accused" to present their side. Braverman found the testimony of the L.A. law enforcement community troubling, particularly that of Edward Ayres. He assembled a formidable team of experts who set about to undo some of the damage that had been done.

The responding witnesses cut across the spectrum of the public and private sector. Harry Hoijer, a UCLA anthropologist; Guy T. Nunn from the Minority Group Services of the War Man Power Commission; Manuel Aguilar, Mexican consul in Los Angeles; Eduardo Quevedo, a Mexican American community leader; Oscar R. Fuss, the director of legislation and research for the Congress of Industrial Organizations; and Walter H. Laves from the Office of Inter-American Affairs all attacked the unsubstantiated conclusions offered by Ayres. But of this group, perhaps the most important person to step forward was Carey McWilliams. McWilliams, an author and L.A. lawyer, not only offered his voice to the collective response, but his presence before the grand jury also began an involvement in the Sleepy Lagoon case that spanned over two years and proved crucial to its ultimate outcome.

No one during this rebuttal stage questioned that juvenile crime among Mexican Americans in Los Angeles was on the rise. However, whereas Ayres had been willing to consider racial discrimination as a minor factor, those who testified in response to Ayres pointed to discrimination and prejudice as the most important contributing factor to juvenile delinquency. Whereas it was difficult to see where Ayres found scientific support for his arguments, Hoijer, McWilliams, Nunn, and to some extent Aguilar all cited sociologists and psychologists for authority that delinquency was not a racial problem, but rather a poverty problem. Hoijer systematically dissected Ayres's racial determination argument, citing two prominent studies that demonstrated that differences among the races in any nonphysical sense grew out of environment. He also attacked Ayres's argument that Mexican Americans were descended from the Aztecs, along with the notion that the Aztecs, because they practiced human sacrifice, were indifferent to human life.

Ayres and his cohorts suggested that Mexican Americans did not want to assimilate into American culture. Hoijer and McWilliams argued that Mexican American juvenile delinquency was driven by the inability to assimilate because white society refused to allow them in. Ashamed of their parents' language, culture, and ideals, and yet denied access into mainstream American culture, Mexican American youth found sanctuary by banding together. Contrary to Ayres's suggestion that harsh punishment held the key to controlling Mexican American youth violence, McWilliams and Hoijer suggested "practicing democracy" at home in addition to fighting for it abroad. To end juvenile delinquency, one need only end discrimination. Nunn argued for wholesale changes in American society, including the elimination of housing discrimination and school segregation.

As *Zammora* went to trial, the second round of grand jury testimony had provided a counter to the prevailing belief about Mexican American youths that had been fostered by nine months of newspaper coverage. The testimony must have had an impact. At the conclusion of the proceedings, the grand jury seemed to believe that discrimination against Mexican Americans not only drove juvenile delinquency, but that it would also undermine the war effort. Perhaps influenced by Nunn's suggestion that the social situation that gave rise to the juvenile problem in Los Angeles required sweeping change throughout America, the grand jury took a step in the right direction. Among its posthearing recommendations was a request to the coordinator of Inter-American Affairs to establish the Office of War Information in Los Angeles as a regional office to increase publicity aimed at Spanish-speaking people. In addition, the grand jury requested that the secretary of war make Mexican aliens eligible for defense work. At a minimum, racial equality had become a war aim, if not a larger social aspiration.

The local media provided some coverage of the second round of the grand jury investigation. The press, although limited, was at least more positive and accurate in the depiction of Mexican Americans. The Los Angeles community had a choice: it could use the statistical data and law enforcement opinions as crutches in an irrational assault on a segment of the community, or it could choose to use the same data to gain a clearer picture of what was actually taking place. As the Sleepy Lagoon trial got under way, it appeared that the media frenzy would be too much to overcome. In the end, people wanted support, not illumination. As the trial played out, the prosecution had no real control over what was being printed, but, with public fear of Mexican youth crime at a fever pitch, the prosecution used the images and stereotypes that had become so much a part of the imagination of Anglos in Los Angeles as a key element of its case.

CHAPTER 3

"Laws Are Silent"

The fear sweeping America, and the West Coast in particular, in 1942 and its effect on basic civil liberties come as no surprise. As early as 52 B.C.E., the Roman writer Cicero stated the obvious: *Silent enim legis inter arma* ("laws are silent in time of war"). Napoleon may have put it more succinctly: "War justifies everything." The ethnic tension that existed in Los Angeles in the 1940s found an unfortunate boost from the start of World War II. While the war virtually foreclosed any meaningful judicial relief for Japanese Americans, it also affected the operation of the criminal justice system in Los Angeles. Although the law was hardly silent with regard to the Mexican American population in Los Angeles, the war made the law more difficult to hear at times, particularly when issues of patriotism became intertwined with race. The media attention initially devoted to the relocation of Japanese Americans shifted and began to portray the activities of Mexican American youth as un-American and unpatriotic, and America has a history of turning on those it believes may be aiding the enemy or otherwise subverting the cause.

America's first real war after its independence came in 1812 against its old rival, Great Britain. Most members of the Federalist Party opposed "Mr. Madison's War," and, at the 1814 Hartford Convention, they went so far as to publicly proclaim their opposition — a move that all but destroyed the party. Before that, however, Federalist opposition to the war in its early days brought a violent reaction in Baltimore, Maryland. On 27 July 1812, an angry mob of "patriots" stormed Alexander C. Hanson's *Federal Republican* offices in retaliation for its antiwar editorials. The mob destroyed his press and wrecked his home. The situation became so grave that the Maryland militia placed Hanson and his associates into protective custody. Not to be denied, the anti-Hanson mob reassembled the next night, stormed the jail, and killed one man, severely beating eleven others. Once the Hansonites were subdued, the bodies were dragged outside, where the mob proceeded to mutilate anyone unable to flee or protect himself. The authorities seemed powerless to stop the violence.

The American Civil War once again tested the strength of the rule of law versus the law of necessity. Much like World War II, the main proponent of extralegal means was the government—specifically the Union and its need to suppress dissent. From Lincoln's suspension of the writ of habeas corpus in Maryland in 1861 to the Clement Vallandingham problems in Ohio and the Union institution of martial law that gave rise to cases like *Ex Parte Milligan*, the Civil War provided a precursor to the wars of the twentieth century where civil liberties took a subordinate position to the need to win.

Although there were no significant cases involving the suppression of civil liberties or the attack on a particular racial group during World War I, people of Eastern European and German descent did come under attack, and several significant United States Supreme Court decisions came down after the war. During the war, the government had severely repressed dissent, with its efforts focused on socialists and German Americans in particular. Most of the cases arose out of the enforcement of the espionage acts passed during the war. In *Schenck v. United States* (1919), the Supreme Court affirmed the conviction of a man caught handing out antidraft pamphlets to military personnel. Oliver Wendell Holmes set forth his "clear and present danger test" for limiting otherwise protected speech, claiming the First Amendment did not protect dangerous speech, such as crying "fire" in a crowded theater and precipitating a panic. To Holmes, words lost their First Amendment protection when they were intended to bring about a violation of the law. The cases that followed, *Frowerk v. United States*, *Debs v. United States*, *Abrams v. United States*, *Schafer v. United States*, and *Pierce v. United States*, all involved government suppression of free speech and saw the prosecution of German and/or socialist newspapers and persons upheld. After *Schenck*, Holmes routinely dissented, perhaps having found that his test for unprotected speech had become distorted. In war, laws are silent.

The troubling aspect about war and its effect on justice is that despite clear lessons from the past, the fear of a perceived enemy seems to make it impossible to separate a real enemy from a group of people who share only an ethnic or national similarity. Putting aside for the moment the unfairness of attacking U.S. citizens or even first-generation immigrants simply because they have an ethnic tie to the enemy, Mexican Americans should not have been caught up in the same wave that swept Japanese Americans away. However, Edward Duran Ayres's testimony to the grand jury lumped Indians into a broader group of "orientals." That, coupled with the notion that un-American behavior in peacetime translated to unpatriotic conduct in wartime, added another layer of potential bias to a proceeding already tainted by extreme pretrial publicity. Granted, the courts remained open, but the laws that govern how people are arrested and indicted had already been stretched. The procedures and laws that regulate the conduct of trials provide the safeguards that ensure fairness. If those laws are suppressed or ignored, trials can be reduced to mere form without substance.

Henry Leyvas stood up along with his twenty-one other codefendants as Judge Charles Fricke emerged from his chambers and ascended the bench of the Superior Court for Los Angeles County.

"People versus Zammora and others," he announced.
"The People are ready," announced John Barnes.
"The Defendants are ready," added Richard Bird.

The waiting was over. It had been almost three months since Leyvas and six hundred other people had been rounded up by the L.A. police department in connection with the death of Jose Diaz. Ultimately, twenty-four young people who were at the Delgadillo home near the Sleepy Lagoon that hot summer night were singled out and indicted, and now twenty-two prepared to stand trial for murder. Among the many questions swirling through Leyvas's head had to have been, "How did I get here?" How in the world did the death of one Mexican American in a neighborhood that no one ever really seemed to care about before cause so much attention? It was not as if no one had ever gotten killed before or after Diaz's death, but somehow this was different.

Leyvas sat quietly as the prosecution and defense picked a jury. For a case with so much pretrial publicity, the process proceeded with amazing speed. Within two days, the jury and three alternates had been chosen—and without either side exercising its peremptory challenges. From the record, it appears that the jury was empaneled without any significant examination into bias or regard for attributes that might have proven beneficial, particularly to the defense. Jury selection is crucial. In many instances, the process dictates the outcome of a trial before the trial even begins. Neither side is trying to pick a "neutral" jury. The goal of any good trial lawyer is to get as many members as possible who may be inclined to rule in his client's favor. At a minimum, lawyers seek to exclude people who show an inclination to be adverse to their client. Today, in high-profile cases, lawyers devote extensive time to the process, going so far as to hire experts whose job it is to know how certain people will be predisposed to see certain issues. In some cases, after the jury is chosen, lawyers will pay for a mock jury to sit in the courtroom and at each break, or at the end of each day, question that jury as to how they received the evidence and argument. Nothing remotely close to this occurred in the Sleepy Lagoon case. The makeup of the eight-woman, four-man jury clearly did not bode well for the defendants.

Not one Latino sat on the jury in the *Zammora* case. None had any children in the age range of the defendants. In a case tried in the backdrop of almost a century of racial competition and struggle in Los Angeles, the fate of the twenty-two Sleepy Lagoon defendants lay in the hands of twelve people and three alternates who had no empathy for them—at least, not on the basis of their ethnic background and familial circumstances. Perhaps more important, the record of jury selection reveals little effort by the defense to try and deal with the significant pretrial publicity, which had been driven by a conscious effort to control what the law enforcement authorities and local media called the "gang problem." Jurors come to a case with a set of predispositions based on who they are. This jury's prejudice arose in part from a considerable effort within Los Angeles to deal with Mexican gangs and the symbol of that problem, the pachuco.

In all fairness, it is impossible to completely control passion and fear, whether driven by war, racial conflict, or prejudice. That is precisely why America has courts, judges, and lawyers. In theory, the judicial system is supposed to be above all the furor that characterizes the court of public opinion. However, that is not always the case, and, as the Sleepy Lagoon trial began, the courtroom resembled a sporting event more than a judicial proceeding. The twenty-four defendants represented by seven lawyers created a setting where it was impossible to tell the players without a program.

At the outset, the defendants and their families lacked the means to secure top-flight representation, and the quality of the defense team reflected their economic realities. With the exception of one lawyer, Anne Zacsek, none of the defense counsel had a reputation of any notoriety, and Zacsek's fame unfortunately did not flow from her legal skills but from her former career. Six of the twenty-four defendants could not afford a lawyer and drew an appointed public defender, Richard E. Bird. The remaining eighteen boys hired a hodgepodge of legal talent. The named defendant, Gus Zamora, along with Robert Pena, Benny Alvarez, and Jack Melendez, hired Phillip Schutz. Ben Van Tress, acting on behalf of the Mexican consul, agreed to handle the defense of Joe "Chepe" Ruiz, a Mexican national, as well as Ysmael Parra, Angel Padilla, and John Matuz. Anthony Coviello, a former police officer, represented Manny Delgado. Coviello may have had extensive experience as a cop, but on the eve of the Sleepy Lagoon murder trial, he had almost no courtroom experience. As a result, his name seldom appears in the over six thousand pages of trial transcript. Harry Hunt represented Joe Herrera and Lupe Prosco, and David Ravin defended Danny Verdugo and Joe and Eugene Carpio. The seventh member of the group, and the lone woman, Anne Zacsek, represented Henry Leyvas, Victor Segobia, and Edward Grandpre. Born in Hungary and a former silent film star under the stage name Olga Grey, her claim to fame lay in her supporting role in the 1915 classic film *Birth of a Nation*. But Zacsek's legal skills left much to be desired; they were helped little by her theatrical talents.

Of the seven lawyers, only Bird and Van Tress had real trial experience, and they expressed little confidence in the rest of their colleagues. As a result, they initially took the lead in the defense effort. What is overlooked, however, is that Harry Hunt had been a former district attorney, and his actions in the pretrial stages demonstrated his ability — and ultimately made a huge difference in the outcome for his two clients. Zacsek almost immediately undermined her own clients by informing the court that at least during jury selection, she would be absent from the courtroom to attend to other matters. Richard Bird agreed to represent her clients as well as his own during her temporary absence. Perhaps sensing the potential conflict if Zacsek's absence continued into the trial itself, Bird quickly informed the court that he might have to withdraw from his temporary role as Zacsek's associate.

In contrast to the circus presented by the defense, the prosecution consisted of deputy assistant district attorneys Clyde Shoemaker and John Barnes. Neither man left a legacy of greatness, but both were experienced and competent, and, in contrast to the defense team, they had a clear plan of attack. As prosecutors in the shadow of Hollywood, both men had ample practice at staying focused amid the hoopla while using a defendant's celebrity and notoriety to their advantage.

The task of presiding over the trial fell to Charles W. Fricke. Regarded among the courthouse defense bar as a prosecutor's judge, Fricke frequently enjoyed lunches with prosecutors where he educated them on the finer points of evidence and procedure. Although he came to be known as "San Quentin Fricke" among the criminal bar for sending more defendants to San Quentin than any other judge in the state's history, Fricke was more than just a hanging judge. Originally from the Midwest, Fricke received his LLM, JD, and LLD from New York University by the time he was twenty-one. He practiced briefly in New York, returned to Wisconsin for a short stint, and then made his way to California in the 1920s. After moving to Los Angeles, Fricke served as a prosecutor before becoming a superior court judge. Despite his prosecutorial background and propensity to hand out hard time, in theory, he should have been the perfect judge for this case, because Fricke knew the law better than any other sitting jurist.

Beginning in the 1920s, Fricke began a prolific publishing career that spanned over thirty years. In 1926, he produced his first criminal procedure and evidence manuals, and, by the time of his death in 1958, Fricke had become the acknowledged authority on California criminal law. His treatise on California criminal evidence was in its sixth edition at the time of his death, and the seventh edition came out eight years later. Perhaps because of his academic accomplishments, Fricke had the reputation among the bar as a man who felt infallible. But arrogant or not, Fricke seemed uniquely qualified to cut through the circus atmosphere that dominated the pretrial months and see that justice did not get dictated by popular sentiment. If properly adhered to, the rules of evidence and procedure had safeguards that diluted or rendered impotent the passions of public opinion by objectively scrutinizing both evidence and trial tactics. Even in the 1940s, evidence had to meet certain criteria to be admissible, and basic rules of decorum, although not yet codified into a California code of judicial conduct, existed to ensure the trial process maintained an air of impartiality — at least insofar as the judge was concerned. No one knew these rules in California more thoroughly than Charles Fricke.

The pretrial aspect of the *Zammora* case proved crucial. Not only did the jury selection process fail to yield a panel favorable to the defense, but jury selection yielded a panel that shared little in common with the defendants. Then two specific procedural developments dictated much of what was to follow. One involved the success or failure of defense counsel and the other a decision Fricke made. The Sleepy Lagoon murder trial remains the largest mass murder trial in California history because almost all of the defendants were tried together. However, it did not have to be that way. Although Bird and Van Tress seemed to possess the most experience, it was former district attorney Harry Hunt who stepped up and struck the first significant blow for the defendants when he convinced Fricke to sever his clients from the main suit and grant them a separate trial.

Today, California Penal Code §1098 states that when two or more defendants are jointly charged with any public offense, whether felony or misdemeanor, they must be tried jointly unless the court orders separate trials. Charles Fricke enjoyed the same discretion in 1942. There is no pretrial record, but Hunt was able to have Joe Herrera and Lupe Prosco tried separately from the other twenty-two defendants. A separate trial offers several benefits for the defense in a criminal case involving multiple defendants.

First, it enables a defendant to raise reasonable doubt as to his culpability by arguing "it was someone else" without simultaneously accusing a codefendant. Thus, Herrera and Prosco could argue that they were nowhere near Jose Diaz, that they did not see him, and that they did not see any of their comrades either, thus raising the possibility in the jurors' minds that it was "someone else"; yet that "someone else" was not on trial and could not be convicted in that proceeding. Thus, if the jury trying Herrera and Prosco came to believe that

Henry Leyvas or Gus Zamora killed Diaz, the defendants could be acquitted in one trial without prejudicing Leyvas or Zamora. The second benefit is that smaller trials are more manageable — something that would prove crucial after Hunt got his two clients out of the main trial. Finally, if the trials are held simultaneously, a separate trial secures a different judge.

The potential harm in being tried with a large group of defendants became clear before the trial ever began. As Judge Fricke gave the jury its general instructions, he addressed a problem inherent in multiple defendant trials: possible admissions made by one defendant, and how the jury must treat such statements with respect to other defendants:

> Where we try a case in which we have two or more persons, it sometimes happens there are bits of evidence, and sometimes very substantial bits, which apply to one defendant and do not apply to another. A good illustration of that is, — I am not referring to this particular case, because I do not know whether it exists in this case, but sometimes, let us say, after the arrest has been made, a defendant makes some statement, may make it to an officer, may make it to some acquaintance or other, but that is something which concerns him only. Where a statement is made by a defendant it is not binding upon and does not affect the case of his co-defendant unless it is a statement which was made by him in the course of a conspiracy, in pursuance of the object of the conspiracy, or the other instance is where it has been acquiesced or agreed to by the other defendant or is made in the presence of another defendant and has not been denied by him. In all other instances where the statement of a defendant is evidence against himself alone, you want to be careful to consider that evidence only as to him and not as bearing upon the guilt of another defendant.

The instruction itself could hardly be called clear. In a case where part of the prosecution's case flowed from the acts of alleged gang-related conduct, relying on twelve laypersons to separate the statements and evidence that might apply only to one of twenty-two defendants presented a daunting, if not impossible, task. Why no other defense counsel tried or succeeded in getting separate trials for their clients remains unclear. The failure to do so ensured that Fricke would preside over the case. In addition, because of the sheer number of defendants, the case took a bad turn for the defense almost immediately.

With the jury selected and two of the defendants severed, Fricke made the first in a series of adverse rulings and decisions against the defense. With twenty-two defendants and six lawyers, Fricke decided that the defendants could not sit with their attorneys at trial. Instead, the defendants would all sit together in alphabetical order, unable to converse with their lawyers, and consequently unable to assist them at the counsel table. Fricke reasoned that his courtroom simply lacked the necessary space to seat the defendants with their attorneys. Although that may have been true, the ability to actually sit and converse with one's lawyer as the trial progresses is crucial. Even the most thorough preparation cannot prevent unforeseen twists or turns at trial. A witness may change his or her testimony, or in the course of a witness's examination, something may occur to either the lawyer or his client that needs to be communicated at that moment lest the opportunity be lost. Fricke's seating arrangement allowed for communication only during breaks, and by modern standards, Fricke's first decision in the trial had already deprived the Sleepy Lagoon defendants of their right to effective assistance of counsel. However, in 1942, the right to counsel lacked the clearly defined parameters that criminal defendants enjoy today.

The Sixth Amendment of the United States Constitution provides that

> In all criminal prosecutions, the accused shall enjoy the right to a speedy and public trial, by an impartial jury of the state and district wherein the crime shall have been committed, which district shall have been previously ascertained by law, and to be informed of the nature and cause of the accusation; to be confronted with the witnesses against him; to have compulsory process for obtaining witnesses in his favor, and to have the assistance of counsel for his defense.

The last right of the criminally accused listed in the Sixth Amendment is the right to assistance of counsel. However, without counsel, the other rights provided for in this amendment are either meaningless or almost impossible to enforce. It is significant that the amendment provides for more than simply the right to have an attorney present. Rather, it speaks in terms of "assistance of counsel," and it implies that to pass constitutional muster, an attorney must be able to help his client. Fricke's ruling that physically separated the defendants from their respective counsel seems, even by World War II–era standards, to be a clear violation of the U.S. Constitution. However, judicial interpretation of the Sixth Amendment was still embryonic, and what existed was both sparse and contradictory.

The development of the right to an attorney began with the notion that even the poor should be represented. In *Webb v. Baird* (1853), the Indiana supreme court addressed the right to counsel, stating, "It is not to be thought of in a civilized community for a moment that any citizen put in jeopardy of life or liberty should be debarred of counsel because he is too poor to employ such aid. . . . No court could be expected to respect itself to sit and hear such a trial. The defense of the poor in such cases is a duty that will at once be conceded as essential to the accused, to the court and to the public." The court in *Webb* acknowledged the right to an attorney regardless of wealth and hinted at the importance to the system as a whole in having every criminal defendant represented. However, it would be almost eighty years before the United States Supreme Court confronted the issue.

In 1932, the United States Supreme Court reviewed the convictions of nine young men accused of rape in northern Alabama. The Scottsboro Boys, all African American, stood trial for allegedly raping two white women on a train. The defendants were from two other states and had no opportunity to contact family or friends and obtain counsel. Before the trial, the presiding judge appointed "the entire bar" as defense counsel but made no specific assignment to any one lawyer; nor did he obligate any particular lawyer to defend any or all of the defendants. The only attorney specifically identified was not from Alabama, and he stated in open court that he had no experience with Alabama procedure. From arraignment until the time of trial, the defendants had no specific attorney, and at a time when they could have helped counsel prepare, they were unable to do so.

The Supreme Court, in *Powell v. Alabama*, cited a developing body of state case law across the country for the proposition that the right to counsel in a capital case is a fundamental right of the accused. In their decision, the Supreme Court went back to colonial times to set out how the colonies had rejected any notion that an accused defendant could be denied the right to counsel. The judge's action in appointing "all members of the bar" was merely "pro forma" and provided no effective assistance of counsel. Writing for the majority, Justice Sutherland stated the obvious: "The right to be heard would be, in many cases, of little avail if it did not comprehend the right to be heard by counsel." The decision in *Powell v. Alabama* marks the genesis of the U.S. Supreme Court's quest to define the Sixth Amendment right to counsel.

Powell held that an indigent accused had a right to counsel in a state capital case even if he could not afford an attorney. The case suggests that assistance of counsel is more than just having an attorney present. To be effective, counsel must be able to adequately prepare, which requires interaction with his client before the trial — something the Scottsboro Boys were denied. However, Sutherland and the majority did not really address what it means to have effective assistance of counsel during trial. That issue would go unanswered, and in the ten years leading up to the Sleepy Lagoon trial, the issue of right to counsel became clouded.

In 1938, the Supreme Court built on the decision in *Powell* when it held in *Johnson v. Zerbst* that the Sixth Amendment right to counsel applies in any federal criminal proceeding. However, four years later, in *Betts v. Brady*, the Court stopped short of applying the Sixth Amendment right to counsel in any state felony proceeding, holding that an indigent defendant in state court was not entitled to counsel in all cases and that despite a lack of counsel, the accused might still receive a fair trial that comported with Fourteenth Amendment due process requirements. *Betts* remained the law until 1963, when the Warren Court overturned it in *Gideon v. Wainwright*. Thus, when Fricke separated the defendants from their attorneys for trial purposes, he technically did not break any established legal precedent. The decision in *Powell* held that interaction and communication were key elements of effective assistance of counsel in preparing for trial, but no California or U.S. Supreme Court decision, including *Powell*, had addressed effective assistance during trial. In Fricke's mind, all the defendants had lawyers, the lawyers were present, and they had been given adequate time to prepare. No defendant had requested a continuance arguing that the trial had come too swiftly, and all of these circumstances seemed to comport with the federal and state constitutional protections in place.

The prosecution went right to work as the trial opened on 19 October 1942, calling Bert McAtee as its first witness. McAtee served as the deputy county surveyor for Los Angeles County. A fourteen-year veteran of the office, McAtee's sole purpose was to authenticate and help admit into evidence a map of the Sleepy Lagoon area where Diaz's murder allegedly occurred. McAtee testified he prepared two maps. One was a large drawing of the area, and the second was an inset—a more detailed map of a smaller portion of the neighborhood. There was little to debate. However, during the cross-examination, Judge Fricke addressed the witness, apparently in an effort to clarify a point, but his comments suggested to the witness what the answer was or should be—and even went so far as to tell the jury how it should interpret what McAtee said:

> Q (VAN TRESS): Did they ask you whether or not they wanted certain things represented on that map?
> A (MCATEE): They told me—
> THE COURT: They told you what kind of map they wanted, didn't they?

Later in the cross-examination, a dispute over distances yielded the following exchange:

> MR. BARNES: Before your Honor adjourns may we have the record show that these estimates of distances have been indicated by the witness by using—by estimating with a ruler on the maps, Exhibits 1 and 2?
> THE COURT: A ruler and tape and the witness has, by his manner of testifying and his manner of making measurements, indicated that he is not giving accurate distances but approximate distances only.
> MR. BARNES: That has been done not from memory, but from—

THE COURT: By computation.

MR. BARNES: Yes, your Honor.

MR. VAN TRESS: I think the witness should testify whether or not he is giving accurate distances. I do not think the statement is proper by court or counsel either.

THE COURT: Well, I think it was; I think it was perfectly obvious.

The Court adjourned on the afternoon of 19 October, and the first thing Van Tress did for the defense upon reconvening on the morning of the 20th was to make an oral motion to strike both of Fricke's comments regarding McAtee's estimates of distance. Fricke not only denied the motion without any argument, but he did so in a tone that would come to characterize how he addressed the defense counsel. At one point, he interrupted Van Tress as he tried to point to the precise language he wanted stricken by saying, "Motion denied, Mr. Van Tress. I can read."

Things went from bad to worse as Fricke literally began to critique Van Tress's cross-examination without any objection having been made by the prosecution as to the form of the questions being asked. Fricke suggested the questions were confusing and repeatedly interrupted Van Tress. He broke up the flow of the cross-examination, but from the record, it is also clear that a jury might think that Van Tress did not know what he was doing. Fricke's objections became so persistent that Van Tress tried to make an offer of proof to demonstrate the purpose of his line of questioning. Normally one makes an offer of proof if the opposition is objecting to questions as being irrelevant or inadmissible. The jury is removed, and the attorney explains how his questions relate to the case. Neither Barnes nor Shoemaker had said a word. They did not have to: Fricke had taken over their case — at least insofar as McAtee's testimony was concerned. Van Tress felt compelled to make an offer of proof to demonstrate how basic measurements and distances would be relevant where witnesses would be asked what they saw or heard in the dark of night, amid yelling and confusion. His efforts to establish the basic physical distances and measurements clearly had relevance, but Fricke would hear none of it: "I hope I am talking loud enough so that you can hear. I do not know whether you are doing this deliberately, but I do not want any more of it. You may proceed now."

Van Tress moved on, as did the remainder of his co-counsel. The rest of McAtee's cross-examination and redirect by the prosecution added little to clarifying the place where Jose Diaz died. Fricke continued to spar with defense counsel, and the prosecution began to put on its fact witnesses. Having established the general area where the murder occurred, the prosecution called Jose Diaz's father and brother. The defense moved to exclude the witnesses, which in today's jargon would be called "invoking the rule." It requires witnesses who have not testified to remain outside the courtroom until they are called. The purpose is to prevent one witness from hearing what another says so he or she cannot tailor testimony or perhaps claim to recall something only because someone else has testified to the same fact. Fricke tabled the objection until the next recess, allowing both Teodus Diaz, Jose Diaz's father, and Lino Diaz, his brother, to testify. Teodus spoke only broken English, and, although he asked for an interpreter, none was provided. His testimony added little to the case. Lino, however, had been home, and after members of the Delgadillo party had come to his house, he went out and found Jose at 1:30 in the morning of 2 August 1942 lying face up in a ditch along a road close to the house. His examination lasted longer but did nothing to establish who killed his brother. When he stepped down, Fricke took a recess, dismissed the jury, and ruled on the motion to exclude witnesses, which he granted.

After the recess, the prosecution continued with its preliminary witnesses, calling the coroner, Dr. Frank R. Webb, the chief autopsy surgeon for Los Angeles County. Webb described Diaz's condition, and he speculated as to the cause of his injuries and death. Some of his testimony, particularly regarding the severity of the injuries and the causes thereof, drew defense objections, all of which Fricke overruled. Webb's testimony again offered nothing as to who killed Diaz. However, defense counsel, particularly Leyvas's lawyer, Anne Zacsek, did a decent job of addressing issues as to how intoxicated Diaz was at the time of death, whether his injuries could have been caused by a fall, and whether the bruises and cuts on Diaz's own hands indicated a struggle or fight wherein Diaz delivered significant blows himself, thus suggesting that perhaps Diaz sustained injuries in a struggle where his alleged assailant acted in self-defense.

With the preliminaries over, the prosecution moved into the meat of its case: establishing who killed Jose Diaz. To do so, it turned to the young women who had been with Leyvas and his codefendants that night. Over the next several weeks, ten women took the stand as the prosecution sought to explain how Diaz died, identify his killer, and, in keeping with the months of media propaganda leading up to the trial, establish that his death had been the result of an out-of-control Mexican American youth gang. Barnes and Shoemaker counted on their ability to control and intimidate these young women, who had no reason to cooperate. Both the prosecution and the court were about to discover that these women were not intimidated and that they would not be controlled. Loyalty ran deep in the Thirty-eighth Street neighborhood, and a case whose foundation depended on anyone from that neighborhood ratting out her friends proved fundamentally flawed. The lesson began with one of the youngest members of the group present that night: fifteen-year-old Juanita Gonzalez.

CHAPTER 4

"How Am I Supposed to Know It Is a Gang?"

On the afternoon of 20 October 1942, the prosecution called the first of a procession of young women to the stand. Known as Jeannie among her friends, Juanita Gonzalez was fourteen years old on the night of 1 August 1942. It was late in the afternoon by the time she took the stand, but in the short time before the court recessed for the day, an aspect of the prosecution's strategy appeared to turn on itself. All the twenty-two defendants were young men. Part of that may have been due to the testimony elicited by the grand jury that made the decision to indict the young men. However, from the earliest part of the investigation, it had become clear that the young men who went back to the Sleepy Lagoon area that night looking for some measure of revenge had a fair number of young women with them. No one ever accused a young Mexican American woman of having beaten or killed Jose Diaz, but criminal liability does not require one to have actually done the deed. Assisting in the commission of a crime, either before or after the fact, is a crime. Driving to the scene of a crime, acting as a lookout, helping the perpetrator escape, and hiding evidence are all examples of criminal activity short of committing the underlying crime. As the prosecution began to question Juanita, she came to the realization that she might admit to something criminal, and her direct examination deteriorated.

After establishing her age and the fact she lived close to Thirty-eighth Street in Long Beach, the prosecution began to ask questions related to the Thirty-eighth Street "gang." Juanita answered the first few questions before Clyde Shoemaker's inquiry began to draw objections from several of the defense counsel. Some argued that the questions regarding a gang were irrelevant, but Fricke agreed to allow them as preliminary to a conspiracy argument. At that point, Ben Van Tress cautioned the Court that the prosecution was treating Juanita as somehow outside the gang. But the possibility existed that by answering the questions she could establish her own membership and perhaps some complicity in the crime, and Van Tress pointed out that if that happened, she could be indicted for murder. Judge Charles Fricke did not believe they had reached that point, but as soon as the questioning resumed and Shoemaker inquired as to whether Juanita went to the Sleepy Lagoon on the night of the murder, Juanita began to "take the Fifth" and invoked her right against self-incrimination. Shoemaker immediately asked why, and she told him bluntly, "On the grounds you may charge me for the murder of Joe Diaz, like you done to the boys." Shoemaker pressed on and asked the same question in a similar way. She again refused to answer, and Shoemaker again asked why. Again she told him, "On the same ground I told you, you may charge me with the murder of Joe Diaz as you charged the boys."

Shoemaker then appealed to Fricke for help in controlling his young witness and forcing her to cooperate. Whatever Fricke's predisposition in the case or his feelings toward the defendants or their counsel, he knew the law, and he realized the prosecution was in a bind.

MR. SHOEMAKER: If the court please, we request that the witness be directed to answer the question.

THE COURT: I think the answer is one which may tend to incriminate her on the alleged offense, so directing an answer which would have the tendency of showing a possible association, I do not think the court should force the witness to answer.

MR. SHOEMAKER: At this stage of the case, if your Honor please, without it appearing that this witness is directly or indirectly involved criminally in this case, would it not be proper to require the witness to give testimony and to answer these questions?

THE COURT: I do not think so. The rule is quite definite in that the answer must connect the individual or it would have a tendency to do so, and a question which would merely place the witness upon the scene of an alleged offense would be evidence tending to connect the witness with that offense and that would be one which the witness could refuse to answer.

MR. SHOEMAKER: But if the witness merely seeks refuge from questions to obtain the advantage of refusing to answer questions merely by resort to that usual answer of refusing to answer a question on the ground it might incriminate her, are we confronted with the impossibility of obtaining that testimony?

THE COURT: You are confronted with exactly that situation, if the answer is one which, upon its face, could be used against the witness, in the event of her prosecution for the offense under consideration which would be the crime presented here by this indictment.

MR. SHOEMAKER: Very well. I will ask some other questions.

MISS ZACSEK: I would like at this time, if I may address the court, and request the court, in order to clear this record, to advise this witness as to her constitutional rights.

THE COURT: She has not shown herself in need of advice up to the present time.

MISS ZACSEK: Well, that is not the reason of my question. I would like the record to show, because there will be, of course, continuation of questions and objections, and so forth, and I would like at this stage, — I think that the court's ruling is fine, — I mean it is lovely, — but I would wish the court to address the witness and explain to her, in language she can understand, — after all, she is a child, she is here on the witness stand, she is surrounded by hostile forces to her, at least.

MR. BARNES: That is not a fact, your Honor. She is not surrounded by any hostile forces. The fact she is —

THE COURT: Not only that, but I think it is perfectly —

MR. SHOEMAKER: She is called her —

THE COURT: Gentlemen, please. I think it is quite evident that from some source or other, this witness has acquired the knowledge of her right to refuse to answer if the question is one which tends to incriminate her. I think that is particularly obvious from the fact that the simple question of inquiry as to where she was on a particular evening is one which she refused to answer upon that ground. It is a question which is just on the border line between those questions which the court would say the witness need not answer and those which the witness would be required to answer. I got the impression from the witness' answer that she has been very well informed as to her constitutional rights.

MR. SHOEMAKER: May we inquire by whom she was so advised?

THE COURT: I do not think it is necessary and I do not think it would be proper.

With that, Fricke recessed for the day and left the prosecution mulling its options.

The next morning, the prosecution tried to repair some of the damage to its strategy from the day before by accusing the defense in general terms of witness coaching. Mr. Barnes told the judge that during Juanita's testimony, some of the defense counsel had nodded as she responded to questions. Although Judge Fricke conceded that sometimes nodding is simply an unconscious action to a response or question, he warned the defense that coaching would not be tolerated. He then made it even more difficult for defense counsel to converse with their clients. He gave a standing instruction that at every recess, the prisoners were to be quickly ushered out of the courtroom to the prisoners' room. If counsel wanted to talk to their clients, "they will have to do it at some other time." All of this took place before the jury came back, and, in parting, Fricke warned the defense that he had knowledge that two members of the defense team intended to "interpose obstructive tactics" during the trial, and that he would deal with that when the time came.

The jury returned for the morning session, and the prosecution resumed its examination of Juanita Gonzalez. Aside from the fact that Fricke's language and tone in chambers indicated a level of hostility toward the defense, his new requirement that the defendants would be hurried away during recess served to make a bad situation worse. Already separated from their clients, now defense counsel could not even converse during recess. With the trial in full swing, they now lacked the ability to discuss witness testimony as it unfolded, and even during recesses, they would be hard-pressed to have any meaningful discourse over the particulars of the testimony. The young women on the stand had been at the crime scene, and how much they recalled that night, including the actions of the defendants before, during, and after the fight at the Delgadillo house, was critical testimony. Fricke's latest restriction on client access severely hindered effective cross-examination.

Juanita's testimony wound through the entire morning and into the afternoon. The prosecution painstakingly tried to identify who was present that night and to pinpoint the exact location of people, auto-mobiles, and homes. Juanita had invoked her Fifth Amendment rights on the previous afternoon. Now she adopted a less legal but no less effective strategy: she just could not recall people or events. The prosecution countered by bringing out her grand jury testimony in August and pointing to the contradictions. It claimed to merely be refreshing her memory. But after a short time, defense counsel began to object that the prosecution was "impeaching its own witness." In effect, the defense argued that the prosecution had called this witness in its case in chief. The witness had been assumed to be favorable, and, now that she was not cooperating, they were trying to make their own witness appear to be lying. Although the legal point is an obscure one, and arguably it had no lasting effect on the trial itself, the discussion that followed, which took up hundreds of pages of transcript, revealed the depth of Fricke's knowledge of criminal procedure. At several junctures, Fricke's response to objections and questions from both sides assumed an air of a law school lecture on procedure and trial technique. What is significant is that on issues of fairness, procedure, and evidence, Fricke knew the law, and the depth of that knowledge makes some of his conduct over the remainder of the trial even more difficult to understand.

Juanita's testimony continued throughout the afternoon and finished up midmorning the next day. She offered little to the prosecution's case, and, on cross-examination, the defense confirmed that there had been no knives or chains that night as suggested by the media, and that none of the young men she knew had been fighting that night. It also became clear that some of the questions the prosecution asked used words like *procession*, and she did not know what the word meant. Most of her testimony had been punctuated by a lack of knowledge and a continuing frustration with her inability to properly use the microphone. In the end, a prosecution witness had proven to be far less cooperative and helpful than anticipated, and the trend that began with Juanita continued.

Sixteen-year-old Betty Nunez Zeiss followed Juanita Gonzalez to the stand. Like Juanita, she rode out to the Sleepy Lagoon that night, and the prosecution proceeded down the same line of questioning as it had with Juanita Gonzalez. Zeiss proved a little more cooperative with regard to basic facts. However, before her testimony went very far, the defense used the morning recess to add a new element to the trial. Richard Bird made an oral motion to substitute Mr. George Shibley into the case for him and to take over the representation of Manuel Reyes, Robert Telles, Joe Valenzuela, and Richard Gastelum. The court did not object, and the defendants all agreed to the substitution. Shibley's presence not only marked the addition of more competent counsel, but it brought a new force to bear for the defendants in the case: the Citizens' Committee for the Defense of Mexican American Youth, or CCDMAY.

It is unclear who initially formed the CCDMAY, but there is no debate that LaRue McCormick took the lead in trying to help the Sleepy Lagoon defendants. Born LaRue Manby in La Grange, Kentucky, in 1909, she and her family left the small town outside Louisville and moved to Southern California looking for a better life. Married at age sixteen, the mother of two became actively involved in efforts to effect radical social change. In 1934, she joined the Communist Party and served as the director of the International Labor Defense (ILD) from 1937 to 1950.

The grand jury investigations into Sleepy Lagoon and juvenile crime among Mexican Americans stirred unrest in the local Mexican American community. As the Sleepy Lagoon trial got under way in mid-October 1942, the Spanish-language People's Congress appointed McCormick to investigate the emergence of youth gangs in the community and to organize some type of defense for the Sleepy Lagoon defendants. McCormick applied the boundless energy and organizational skills she had developed as a labor leader and went to work. McCormick saw bigger issues in the case. Before Sleepy Lagoon, she had watched vigilantly for a case on the West Coast that mirrored the Scottsboro Boys' case in Alabama. She wanted some legal forum to demonstrate the effects of racial prejudice on all people of color and to use such a case to rally local support. Sleepy Lagoon had everything she needed to accomplish both goals.

First, McCormick called a meeting of everyone she could muster to discuss the Sleepy Lagoon case. The list included both Communist Party members and people sympathetic to the Communist Party. Among those in attendance were the California president of the Congress of Industrial Organizations (CIO), Phillip M. Connelly; Al Waxman, editor of the *Eastside Journal;* the heads of two CIO labor unions; and several members of the Mexican American community, including screen actor Anthony Quinn. In addition, Carey McWilliams attended the meeting, and, although he played a minor supporting role during the trial, his influence increased dramatically after the verdicts. Although there was some disagreement as to why the Mexican American juvenile delinquency problem existed, the committee members universally rejected the efforts of law enforcement officials to characterize Mexicans as biologically predisposed to violence. Some, like Phillip Connelly, actually rejected the idea that there was a juvenile crime wave at all, claiming, "Crime waves are turned on and off by newspapers like water in a spigot." Differences of opinion aside, the committee went to work defending Henry Leyvas and his codefendants. For McCormick, that meant reaching out to George Shibley, a lawyer she met through the CIO and ILD.

Shibley, a Lebanese American lawyer, graduated from Stanford Law School in 1936 and had spent his entire career advancing progressive issues. A solid defense lawyer, he already had a reputation as willing to take unpopular cases, and Sleepy Lagoon seemed tailormade for his skills. More than anything else, Shibley helped fill the experience void that plagued the defense team, and he began to put pressure on the prosecution merely by challenging their case in a manner that had been lacking in the first week of trial. Shibley's presence immediately invigorated the defense, but, as the case wore on, he also drew the ire of Judge Fricke.

With the substitution in place, the prosecution resumed the direct examination of Betty Zeiss. Unlike Juanita Gonzalez, she had actually seen something. Zeiss found a young man lying face down on the side of the road that night and had rolled him over. He was conscious, groaning, and bleeding from the face and mouth, but she did not say whether his pockets had been turned out. She held his head briefly and then left when she realized everyone else was leaving. She testified to looking back and seeing Joe "Chepe" Ruiz standing over the body holding a board. Ruiz swung the board at him but she could not see if he actually struck the man. The prosecution tried to establish that both the man in the ditch and Ruiz were of Mexican "nationality," making it at least possible that the man in the ditch was Jose Diaz. At this point,

Shibley jumped in and objected to any effort to characterize someone's "nationality," as opposed to their "ethnicity." *Nationality* refers to the status of belonging to a particular nation by birth or naturalization. *Ethnicity* relates to a characteristic of a sizable group of people who share a common racial or cultural heritage. Fricke did not see the difference or did not think the distinction mattered. Shibley had already started to aggravate Fricke, and the insistence by Shibley that all of the defendants deserved to be treated like "Americans" only made matters worse. Fricke countered by telling Shibley that whether American or not, they were entitled to the same rights as Americans, adding that all of this had been covered before he became involved in the case.

As direct questioning of Zeiss came to an end, Barnes returned to the theme: the defendants were part of a gang, as that term had been depicted in the local media over the past year. Shibley and the rest of the defense team continued to object that this assumed something that had not been proven. Before one could call something a "gang," he needed to prove a gang actually existed. As both sides struggled over the issue, the jury could not help but ask itself, who are these kids? What is this "Thirty-eighth Street Gang"?

The Los Angeles police department had a very clear idea of what comprised a juvenile gang. Gangs could be easily identified because they wore the same clothing or a gang uniform. Gangs had leaders and subordinates and were segregated on the basis of sex. All of these characteristics defined an organization dedicated to illegal activity and violence. This is the definition the Los Angeles media embraced, and, in the months leading up to trial, the papers reported the LAPD estimate of fifty pachuco gangs active in the Los Angeles area in 1942. Barnes and Shoemaker pressed each witness to describe the Thirty-eighth Street Gang in terms that white Los Angelenos had come to understand. Not only would the young women refuse to do so, but the facts undermined the notion that Henry Leyvas and his friends were a gang or anything sinister. The testimony depicted a group of young people bonded together by where they lived, went to school, worked, and played. Some, like Leyvas, no longer lived in the neighborhood. Leyvas returned frequently because his girlfriend, Dora Baca, still lived there. Most of the defendants held jobs, many had volunteered for military service, and some had aspirations of life beyond the local neighborhood. But for the time being, they found friendship and security in each other.

Although the Thirty-eighth Street Gang hardly measured up to the standards of a "youth gang," almost all of the young men on trial for Jose Diaz's murder had criminal records. Most of the activity related to petty crimes, and some had police records because they had been suspected of criminal activity or had been sent to juvenile hall for truancy from school. Among the more novel offenses, but apparently not uncommon for the day, was hitching a ride on a freight car. Granted, some of the young men had stolen cars, committed robbery, or been involved in an assault. But the criminal activity that had been part of their lives arose from their individual circumstances, not the kinship and friendship bonds with one another that characterized the social network the prosecution kept calling "the Thirty-eighth Street Gang." However, trials take on their own reality. The truth often becomes what one side or the other can prove or make seem real. The loyalty that Juanita Gonzalez and Betty Nunez Zeiss may have felt toward their friends could easily be seen as something more sinister, and it was the prosecution's intent to do just that. Van Tress hammered away at the lack of any proof of a gang: "We will object to it [prosecution's question] on the ground there is no foundation, in that it does not show this witness is a member of any particular locality or lives in, at or near any such purported headquarters of the gang." Shibley may have just gotten involved, but his objections were already beginning to strike home as he told Fricke, "I further make the objection the apparent reason for such a question is to try to color the minds of the jury by such a suggestion." Fricke overruled both objections, but Shibley was right, and the prosecution would soon admit as much.

The defense did not cross-examine Zeiss. She was unavailable the next day, and the prosecution called Ann Kalustian, known as Ann Cummings. She had heard of the Thirty-eighth Street Gang, but she testified that, as far as she knew, it was not a gang at all, just a group of kids that went by that name. Efforts by the prosecution to get Cummings to define the gang more clearly drew repeated defense objections that this witness denied a gang existed at all; questions asking her to define something that did not exist were improper. What her testimony did reveal was the social nature of the group: she described places like the sweet shop and pool hall as places where "the kids all hang out." The more Shoemaker pressed, the more Cummings resisted characterizing her friends as a gang. He selected one of the defendants, pointed at him, and asked, "Was he known as a member of the 38th Street gang?" Shibley had had enough: he said, "Just a moment, your Honor. I am going to make another objection to a question in that form because there is no evidence in the record as to what constitutes a membership or a member of this so-called gang that counsel refers to." Fricke overruled the objection, commenting that the "best way to answer that is to ask whether or not certain members are members, and that is exactly what is being done." Cummings seemed to sense what was going on, and, without being prompted, she asked the court, "How am I supposed to answer as to this man? How am I supposed to know it is a gang? It has not been organized or anything. No one has told me 'this is a gang and I am the leader.'" Shoemaker changed his question and asked whether the defendant was "associated with the 38th Street gang?" Cummings now understood what was going on and told Shoemaker, "Yes, he did associate with them, but I won't say that none of these boys belonged to the gang, because I don't know."

Shibley and Fricke then began a running debate over the prosecution's continued use of the word *gang*. Shibley insisted it had a sinister meaning, and, until it could be proven that a gang existed, the prosecution should stop using the word. Fricke instructed the jury that *gang* simply meant a group of people, but Shibley would not let it rest. When he renewed his request for a "running objection to the word gang," Fricke responded:

THE COURT: The answer is the use of the word "gang" does not prove a sinister motive. You probably all remember the story of Abraham Lincoln, when Lincoln and a friend of his were looking across the street, and Lincoln said "You see that calf over there. If you would call the tail a leg, how many legs would the calf have?" The friend said, "Five." Lincoln then said, "Calling a tail a leg does not make it a leg." I think that is an answer to the objection. Overruled.

MR. SHOEMAKER: The last defendant I referred to, I believe, was Henry Leyvas.

MR. SHIBLEY: Pardon me. Is that stipulation that was offered accepted, or may it be considered that is a running objection? Otherwise, I feel I will have to interrupt your Honor, which I do not want to do.

THE COURT: I will consider that as a running objection, to the use of the word "gang," yes.

MR. SHIBLEY: Do you accept that stipulation?

MR. SHOEMAKER: We had finished with Melendez.

MR. SHIBLEY: I think there is a question pending. Do you accept that as a stipulation?

MR. BARNES: I think the court stated he would consider it as a running objection.

THE COURT: I will say if that objection is renewed in each instance the court will overrule it. There is no particular occasion to make any further objection merely to the use of the word "gang."

Shibley knew what every experienced trial lawyer knew. Although the court must be given the respect it merits, a lawyer cannot allow the judge to prejudice his client any more than he can allow the other side to do so. Shibley refused to allow the questioning to continue until Fricke acknowledged his running objection. When the questioning of Cummings resumed, she continued to undermine the prosecution's gang theory: she described how some of the group lived in the neighborhood and some did not. They met and congregated at certain places because they were friends. The goal was to enjoy one another's company, not to commit crimes. Almost in response to Shibley's objection to the word *gang*, she steadfastly refused to call the group a gang. When asked whether Joe Ruiz was part of the "gang," Cummings replied, "He did associate with the crowd that lived in the 38th Street district."

Then the sparring between Shibley and Fricke got personal. Cummings became pretty much uncontrollable as a prosecution witness. She had figured out what Shoemaker was trying to get her to do and say, and she resisted. Shoemaker then pulled out her grand jury testimony, as he had with Juanita Gonzalez, and began to compare her testimony to her current answers. Shibley had not been present for the first debate over impeaching one's own witness under the guise of refreshing the witness's memory. He objected and Fricke overruled it, stating the issue had been resolved consistent with the procedure in *People v. McFarland*. Shibley bluntly told Fricke he had read the case, and, when Fricke allowed Shoemaker to continue, Shibley must have been unable to hide his contempt. In the middle of a sentence, Fricke stopped the questioning and addressed Shibley:

THE COURT: Just a moment. I do not want any more of those demonstrations; they have to stop right now.

MR. SHIBLEY: If your Honor please, I was not demonstrating —

THE COURT: I don't want you to contradict me. You were shaking your head and grinning, and I don't want any more of that at the counsel table.

MR. SHIBLEY: I wish to assign your Honor's remarks as misconduct and ask that the jury be instructed to disregard them.

THE COURT: Let the record show —

MR. SHIBLEY: I was not making any demonstration.

THE COURT: Let the record show, in view of the court's attention having been called thereto by the clerk of the court, defense counsel —

MR. SHIBLEY: Mr. George E. Shibley.

THE COURT: (Continuing) — George E. Shibley was grinning, shaking and nodding his head at the time the witness was testifying, my attention being called to it at the time I gave the admonition which already appears in the record.

MR. SHIBLEY: Your Honor, I was smiling at Miss Zacsek in response to a statement that she made to me. I was not smiling or making any demonstration which was an offense to the court. If I have been offensive I apologize. I did not intend anything like that.

Whether Shibley had reacted to Fricke or actually smiled in response to his co-counsel's comment, Fricke now felt personally attacked. His treatment of the defense and Mr. Shibley in particular became increasingly more hostile — a hostility that began to cloud everything Fricke knew about the law and being a judge.

Ann Cummings's testimony revealed just how little she had to offer toward proving who killed Jose Diaz. She had ridden to the Delgadillo house that night, but she spent the entire time inside the car because the emergency brake was apparently broken, and she had to hold it to keep the car from rolling backward. In a repetition of the two previous witnesses, each side asked her to identify all or some of the defendants and state whether they were there at Williams Ranch that night. Cummings simply could not say. Shoemaker asked, "Are you able to tell us, Ann, who all were there that night?" She replied, "I could not come right out and tell you myself, I mean like I told you when they stood up, but I could tell you if they were there or not, as far as I know of. I didn't see even half of them, but I guess they were there, that is why they are here, otherwise they would not be here."

On Friday of the first full week of trial, Betty Nunez Zeiss retook the stand. The prosecution had called her, but her cross-examination was delayed because she was unavailable the next day. As the defense cross-examined her and Barnes took her on redirect, it became clear that the prosecution had no conclusive proof that the person Betty saw lying face down in the road was Jose Diaz. Both sides spent considerable time trying to establish exactly where she found the body, in an effort to compare it to where Lino Diaz said he found his brother laying in the ditch early on the morning of 2 August. In the process of trying to determine where she had found the injured person, the timeline that developed from the time she arrived at the Delgadillo house and got out of the car until she left with the rest of the group suggested that if she had indeed found Jose Diaz, he may well have been there before the fight started. That suggested that the Sleepy Lagoon defendants had no part in his injuries or death.

Zeiss finished her testimony on the morning of 26 October, and Josephine Gonzalez followed her to the stand. Josephine, the older sister of Juanita Gonzalez, listened as Shibley asked Fricke to explain to the witness that she had a constitutional right not to answer any question that might incriminate her. Fricke, no longer trying to hide his disdain for Shibley, asked Josephine whether she had heard what Shibley said and understood it. She said "yes," and that was the extent of Fricke's effort to apprise the young woman of her Fifth Amendment rights. She seemed to understand because she immediately refused to answer and then told Barnes she would not testify. Fricke, however, allowed Barnes to continue to ask her questions under the belief that not every question could potentially incriminate her. Shibley disagreed. The prosecution was trying to prove conspiracy, and every question could potentially make her a part of the conspiracy. Fricke disagreed, and, from that point on, Shibley objected to almost every question by stating, "Same objection, same motion." Fricke began to respond, "Same ruling." Josephine's direct examination became almost unintelligible. Every question brought an objection, and any information that she did have became lost in the legal arguments. The court brought a reprieve to the ordeal by taking its midmorning recess, at which time Shibley took up a matter outside the jury's presence that went directly to issues of fundamental fairness.

The prosecution had apparently advised the sheriff's department that none of the defendants be allowed to change clothes or alter their appearance. Shibley informed Fricke that the boys remained in the clothes they wore the night they were arrested — clothes they wore when they went out, rather than what they wore when they worked, went to school, or went to church. The effect fixed an image in the jurors' minds of the defendants as the very "gangsters" the Los Angeles media had portrayed Mexican American youth gangs to be for almost a year. Shibley placed the blame for such actions directly at the feet of the prosecution, telling Fricke that "Capt. Fitzgerald [of the Sheriff's office] informed counsel Friday it was perfectly all right, it was perfectly all right with Lieut. Prior, and counsel, Mr. Shoemaker, had absolutely forbidden the Sheriff's office to permit these boys to have haircuts or to have reputable clothing in place of their present clothing." Shibley could see only one reason for such an order. By using the word *gang* repeatedly, "Mr. Shoemaker is purposely trying to have these boys look like mobsters, like disreputable persons, and is trying to exploit the fact they are foreign in appearance." The prosecution played on the jury's idea of what a gang member looked like, and, as the trial unfolded, the defendants looked more and more like the very thugs that the prosecution claimed them to be. To make matter worse, Shoemaker admitted that that was exactly what they were doing.

Although he denied that the prosecutor's office had any control over the sheriff's department, Shoemaker admitted to Fricke

> that it is important in the prosecution of this case, for the purposes of identification, that nothing may in any way interfere with the appearance of these defendants, which is distinctive, we feel their appearance is distinctive. . . . [W]e requested the jailer to respect

the situation which was that we felt that it was important in the prosecution of this case, for the purposes of identification, that the appearance of these defendants not be interfered with, particularly in regard to such distinctive matters as their peculiar type of haircut, the way they wear the hair, and that was all. We didn't even mention clothing, and that, if the court please, is the situation which we believe justified our suggestion to the Sheriff that no interference be had with their appearance. There is no more reason, your Honor, for them to have a haircut today or for them to have it yesterday or Saturday than there was last Thursday or last Wednesday or last Monday, but all of a sudden this excitement breaks out for no reason except that it is obvious that counsel realized, perhaps, now, what we expect to prove, that these defendants are distinctive in appearance by reason of their mode of haircut, and possibly their clothing, and that is all there is to it, your Honor.

Rather than sanction the conduct, Fricke went after Shibley again. In a tone that served to reinforce his growing contempt for Shibley, Fricke insisted that he find out what happened before he became involved. The issues of Mexican nationality came up repeatedly in jury voir dire, and was an issue raised by the defense. Shibley did not care. The fact that issues of nationality had already been injected into the proceeding had no relevance to the efforts by the prosecution to prejudice the defendants by fixing their appearance to conform to the case they were trying to put before the jury. The zoot suits they wore triggered a certain emotional response, and the prosecution very much wanted that to continue. Zacsek pointed out that the defendants' hair had not been cut for three months, and that alone had rendered their appearance "scandalous."

At this juncture, the lack of cohesion among the defense counsel became apparent. As Shibley, Zacsek, and Schutz thundered away at the prejudicial effect, Richard Bird got involved in the debate and indicated that changing appearance at this juncture might prejudice the defendants. The jury would notice the change, and the prosecution could comment on any alteration of appearance. Although that may have been true, given the pretrial publicity and ongoing coverage by the media, the rest of defense counsel argued that nothing was as prejudicial as having the defendants sitting in court day after day, clad in zoot suits as their hair and beards grew increasingly more ragged, while the prosecution repeated the moniker *gang*. Personal hygiene alone justified allowing the defendants to clean up. Bird's contribution to the debate undermined the defense case and gave Fricke the out he needed to resolve the issue. The boys could trim their hair and, if needed, change clothes, but there would be no definite change permitted in their appearance.

Josephine Gonzalez's direct examination resumed, but she had become so resistant that the trial degenerated into a discussion between counsel and the court as to whether the prosecution could properly read the witness's grand jury testimony because it contradicted her statements in court. Josephine claimed to be unable to recall anything, yet three months before, she had given clear answers. Had the defense called Josephine or any of the other young women, the prosecution would have been within its right to use the grand jury record to impeach them by showing that they were either not telling the truth then or that they had at least testified differently before. The problem lay in the fact that because the grand jury testimony had looked helpful to the prosecution's case, the women were called as prosecution witnesses. The prosecution assumed that they would testify the same way at trial as they had before the grand jury. When they refused to do so, the prosecution found itself having to call into question the testimony of its own witness, and that is impermissible. Instead of a free-flowing inquiry as to what Josephine saw or heard, any testimony she gave came in broken bits, sandwiched between long arguments as to the propriety of the prosecution's questions and its reading of the grand jury testimony into the record. What did ultimately come out was that Josephine had been arrested on 4 August and remained in the custody of the sheriff's department or juvenile authorities, and that she had been told that if she testified, she would not be prosecuted. The prosecution had such a difficult time getting her to answer that by the end of her testimony, Fricke instructed the jury that grand jury testimony was not evidence, and that all they could consider as evidence was what the witness testified to that day. However, people cannot always forget what they hear. Simply forgetting the grand jury answers would be difficult.

Bertha Aguilar followed Josephine Gonzalez. The same procedure accompanied her testimony. Shibley insisted the court advise her of her Fifth Amendment rights, Fricke refused, and then Aguilar resisted the prosecution's every effort to get her story out. Not only did she fail to recall much, but, at numerous times, she told Barnes and Shoemaker she simply would not answer the question. Dora Barrios took the stand after Aguilar, and her testimony virtually mirrored that of the other young women from Thirty-eighth Street called to testify. Over the course of trying to extract testimony, it became apparent that the prosecution had misjudged the willingness of the young women to cooperate. In a grand jury room with no lawyers and no legal representation, the women had spoken freely. But after months of being exposed to pretrial publicity, being in the custody of the juvenile authorities, and then listening to the heated debate as to their Fifth Amendment rights, the young women simply refused to talk. Fricke explained to Barnes and Shoemaker that there was only so much he could do. The prosecution had had the opportunity to grant immunity before trial and had not done so. Barnes conceded the point but stated he did not see this coming — the grand jury testimony had been clear and forthcoming.

The prosecution had also overlooked another key factor. When the girls testified before the grand jury, the authorities were still trying to put a case together, and most of them were free. While no girl stood trial, several of the young ladies from Thirty-eighth Street that went to the Williams Ranch that night were now in juvenile detention centers. They were already in custody, and the wrong answer on the stand might make a bad situation worse. Ultimately, several of the Thirty-eighth Street girls remained in juvenile detention for several years.

Frustrated by the hostility of the young women he had hoped to use to prove his case, and in an effort to bring the crime scene to life, the prosecution changed gears. It called the county photographer, William Snyder, to the stand. He had taken recent photographs of the roads surrounding the Delgadillo house and that general area. Much discussion had taken place, and the prosecution needed to give the jury some idea of what the area actually looked like. The pictures were admitted into evidence for the limited purpose of showing how the roads ran, but not for proof as to their condition on the night that Diaz died. M. K. MacVine, a deputy sheriff, then took the stand to testify as to the condition of the roads that night. Unfortunately, he could not overcome the presence of other objects in the pictures that had not been present that night, and after trying to expand the use of the pictures, the prosecution gave up, and the pictures were admitted for the limited purpose of showing the location of houses and roads.

After more than a week of futility in trying to use six of the girl-friends and women acquaintances of the defendants to establish part of its case, the prosecution gave up. It had badly misjudged the loyalty these young people felt for one another and the effect on a trial of their inability to extract testimony from an unwilling witness. Between its inability to impeach its own witnesses and the huge impediment presented by the Fifth Amendment, the bulk of the testimony from the six women proved almost worthless. Nothing gleaned from the women had the prosecution one step closer to showing that any of the twenty-two defendants had killed Jose Diaz. The attempts to show a conspiracy ran headlong into the same resistance, as the women followed the lead of the defense's objections to the use of the word *gang* and refused to call their social group a gang. On 2 November, less than two weeks since the trial began, public defender Richard Bird completely withdrew, turning his remaining two clients over to George Shibley. The boys liked Shibley—both his manner toward them and the way he fought Fricke at every turn. It was hard to deny his competence; his trial skills filled a void.

Shibley's importance increased as it became more evident that Ann Zacsek had gotten in way over her head. Although her passion and genuine concern for her clients never wavered, she simply lacked the skills of a trial lawyer. Her questions, both on direct and cross-examination, brought constant objections—objections Fricke routinely sustained as she struggled with the right way to handle a witness. Courtroom procedure has strict rules regarding leading one's own witness, asking compound questions, laying a proper foundation for a question, and, depending on the jurisdiction, staying within the proper scope of both cross-examination and redirect. At times it seemed that she knew that something transpiring in front of her was amiss, but she simply lacked the vocabulary and knowledge to articulate the problem or correct her own shortcomings. More than once, she referred to herself as a mother figure, and her examination of the young women took on the air of a parent trying to coax a story out of her child. Unfortunately, aside from Shibley, she proved more effective than the other men on the defense team. By the end of October, it was clear that the defense's fate lay with George Shibley, and, for all his skills, he had succeeded in alienating Charles Fricke.

As the case moved into November, the defense had one other problem. Although the prosecution's strategy to use the young women as the lynchpin of their case had clearly backfired, there was a derivative benefit of the evidentiary disaster. Loyalty could be perceived as something else. All of the women had been resistant, and a jury already preconditioned to think of Mexican American youth groups as "gangs" could easily see the silence and unwillingness to cooperate as a form of *omertà*, or unified silence characteristic of a gang. The prosecution next called someone who had no incentive to resist and every reason to cooperate: Maria Delgadillo, the sister of the young woman whose birthday party came to a tragic end early the morning of 2 August 1942.

CHAPTER 5

"Baby Mobsters"

Maria Delgadillo began a phase of the prosecution's case that saw it bring to the stand the people at the birthday party that night. The oldest of four Delgadillo sisters, Maria quickly identified her home and the area immediately surrounding it using the photos taken by William Snyder. She also gave a graphic description of the fight that ensued that night and the violence that occurred. One of the boys had knocked her and her brother-in-law, Cruz Reyes, to the ground. Her sister had been knocked down, and her father had also been beaten. She identified both Jack Melendez and Henry Leyvas as having something in their hands and claimed that Leyvas carried a knife that night. She also identified Ysmael Parra and several other boys. But when the prosecution began to go down the list of defendants, Maria recognized only five or six. One of them, Angel Padilla, had been there dancing, although she claimed he was uninvited. She had seen Jose Diaz that night around 11:00 P.M., but not after that. When asked point-blank whether she saw what happened to him that night, she replied, "No, I did not."

When cross-examined, her story became less concrete. It turned out that when she testified before the grand jury, she was uncertain whether Henry Leyvas had a knife; she just thought he had something small. The defense ultimately made her admit that Leyvas had something, and, although it could have been a knife, she did not really know what it was. There was no testimony that anyone got stabbed, and the defense did an effective job of raising the presence of members of the Downey gang earlier that night. When her testimony ended, it was clear that there had been a fight, people had been beaten, car tires had been punctured, and windows had been broken. But no one had seen anyone get killed, and most of the real fighting Maria had seen and been a part of was with other young women — in Maria's case, Delia

Parra, Ysmael's wife. The prosecution was doing a good job proving a fight occurred that night, but no one had tied any of the defendants to the murder of Jose Diaz.

Victoria Delgadillo followed on the heels of her sister. Like Maria, she did a good job describing the fight that broke out that night and putting Henry Leyvas and Jack Melendez at the center of the brawl. Unlike Maria, Victoria could not say that Leyvas wielded a knife that night, only that he had something "black" in his hand. Her sisters, Eleanor Delgadillo Coronado and Josephine Reyes, and Dominic Manfredi, a friend, all corroborated essentially the same story. The party had moved from inside the house to the patio after 1:00 A.M. With the band gone, the patio had the most light for dancing. The Thirty-eighth Street kids showed up around 1:45 A.M., and Henry Leyvas had pushed into the patio area, claiming to be looking for the people who had beaten up five of his friends. The exact language he used is unclear; some heard him say, "the guys that beat up five of our gang." Others heard "some of our boys." Dominic Manfredi testified that Leyvas had a knife and that he had seen the blade but nothing else. Almost without exception, each time a witness went down the line of twenty-two defendants, the most anyone could identify was three or four, in particular Henry Leyvas, Jack Melendez, Ysmael Parra, and Angel Padilla. Padilla, however, had been at the dance hours before the fight. When questioned about the crowd or group that rushed in behind Leyvas that night, the answer was almost always, "Five or six." Finally Eleanor Delgadillo Coronado not only claimed that she saw a knife, but also testified that Ysmael Parra chased Joe Manfredi, Dominic's brother, with it and stabbed him.

Although Gus Zamora's name may have appeared as the lead defendant for the purpose of reporting the case, Henry Leyvas had without question become the most prominent defendant and the apparent leader of the attack at the Delgadillo house early in the morning of 2 August. However, while the prosecution had established the circumstances of the fight, it had done nothing to identify Jose Diaz's killer. Before the examination of the birthday party witnesses had ended, John Barnes and Clyde Shoemaker had stopped asking the money question: "Do you know what happened to Jose Diaz?" Not only did the partygoers have no idea what happened to Diaz, but by the conclusion of Eleanor Delgadillo Coronado's testimony, not one witness at the party that night could place Diaz at the Delgadillo home when Leyvas and his cohorts arrived at 1:45 A.M.

The prosecution then called a series of witnesses who lived in the immediate area but had not been at the party that night. Its most compelling witness, Mary Albino, a young neighbor who lived in the house next door, claimed to have seen several men run out of the Delgadillo house and chase a man down to the road. The pursuers caught up with him and began beating him near the power poles where Jose Diaz's body was found later that morning. However, she could identify neither the attackers nor the victim, and, as the only person thus far to have claimed to have seen any fighting near where Jose Diaz's body was found, her testimony, when combined with that of the people at the party, had two fights going on simultaneously, one on the patio and one at the road. Rather than clear up confusion, in many ways Mary Albino only added to the mystery. No one saw Jose Diaz at the party after 11:00 P.M. At this point in the trial, the only chase that night involved Ysmael Parra chasing Joe Manfredi. Albino offered nothing in the way of what happened to the unidentified victim after the chase to the road. By tracing the chase and beating directly from the Delgadillo home, Albino's testimony virtually eliminated the possibility that the man being chased had been Jose Diaz. At the same time that Albino witnessed the chase, Betty Nunez Zeiss had testified to holding a semiconscious young man's head in her lap.

The prosecution then called Joe Manfredi, Dominic's brother. Joe had allegedly been chased by a knife-wielding Ysmael Parra. What was beginning to unfold demonstrated the unreliability of eyewitness testimony. Caught in a highly charged environment, people remember bits and pieces of what occurred. Manfredi could recall what happened to him, but his recollection of what was going on around him at the same time was less clear. Perhaps the most significant aspect of Manfredi's testimony came in his recollection that only three cars arrived that night. In total, about eighteen people emerged from inside the cars and off the running boards, of whom four or five were young women. There were twenty-two men on trial, but at most, there were six defendants at the Delgadillo house that night who anyone could identify now sitting in the courtroom. It is also significant that Joe Manfredi's rather detailed account of being chased seemed to contradict the chase Mary Albino claimed to have seen. The place Manfredi ran and the route he took would have been beyond Albino's line of vision. More importantly, if the three boys he identified—Leyvas, Delgado, and Parra—were preoccupied with Manfredi, they seemed like unlikely candidates for the alleged assault on Jose Diaz. In fact, missing from all of this testimony was any evidence that identified any of the twenty-two men on trial for Diaz's murder with actually having committed that crime. Everyone's stories unfolded and overlapped, but, in the end, Diaz seems to have been absent from the party. After about 11:00 P.M. on 1 August, no one had seen him. Joe Manfredi had seen him for three or four minutes that night, by the gate at the Delgadillo house, but not again.

It was now 12 November. During an afternoon recess, Fricke sternly reminded defense counsel that he did not want any of them visiting with their clients during recesses. They were to be hurriedly ushered away to the prisoner room, and no visitation would be allowed. The entire situation had been going on since the first day of the trial, and George Shibley had run out of patience. As Fricke admonished counsel to stay away from the defendants during recesses, Shibley stood up and addressed the court:

MR. SHIBLEY: That was addressed, I believe, to me. If your Honor please, I was not here in the case when that first order that your Honor read was made. However, at this time, if your Honor please, I do wish to take exception to it and also make the demand at this time that my defendants, all of them, be allowed to sit with me at the counsel table. And I am going to cite to your Honor the case of Commonwealth v. Boyd, 246 Pennsylvania, page 529, which I believe is followed in this jurisdiction.

THE COURT: That request will be denied. Furthermore, your excuse does not go very far, because the second time I had occasion to mention it, I called your attention to page 213 and requested that you read it. That was directed to you personally. Now, if you did not follow the court's request, I am not responsible for it.

MR. SHIBLEY: If your Honor please, I still make the request, and I do wish to make a showing in the record here, that it is relatively impossible for me to conduct my defense of my defendants without being able to consult with them and sit with them, and talk with them during the presentation of the prosecution's case. I am also going to say this for the record: That the defendants in the position in which they are seated are seated in a column of seats in very much the fashion as prisoners in a prisoners' box, and the jury are looking at them all the time sitting in that prisoners' box. And I say, for the record, that seated as they are, the purpose of it or, at least, the effect of it is to prejudice these defendants in the minds of the jury. And I am going to cite your Honor's action in having them seated there and in refusing them the right to consult with counsel during the trial and talk with their attorneys during the trial in the courtroom, as misconduct, and ask the jury be admonished to disregard the fact that they are seated in the place that they are, and ask your Honor to point out to the jury the fact they are seated there does not impute that they are guilty or that there is any suspicion that they are guilty of a crime.

The courtroom erupted in applause. By this point, anyone sitting through the proceeding could see it becoming a one-sided affair. The defendants sat behind their lawyers in two rows in alphabetical order. They looked in many respects like the very criminals that the prosecution was working so diligently to prove they were. In terms of assisting in their defense, the seating arrangement alone made that impossible. The situation had moved beyond *Powell* and *Betts*. These men all had lawyers, but they had no effective representation because the ability to communicate as matters unfolded did not exist. Shibley was correct: eighteen years before *Powell v. Alabama*, a Pennsylvania state judge in *Commonwealth v. Boyd* held that a defendant should be seated with his or her attorney and be able to effectively consult with him or her. Fricke had made that impossible, and Shibley called him down.

Fricke erupted by first ordering the bailiff to remove and arrest all of the people who applauded and hold them in contempt of court. The bailiff quickly seized two women and ushered them out. Then Fricke addressed Shibley's objection. It had become clear that Shibley posed the main challenge to Fricke's authority, and now Fricke had personalized the matter. The more Fricke insisted that the courtroom could not accommodate the seating arrangements that Shibley demanded, the more Shibley pressed the fact that the right to consult with counsel was fundamental to a fair trial. At one point, Shibley demanded that his clients be afforded the rights guaranteed under the federal and state constitutions, and Fricke responded, "well that is your opinion, I happen to have another one." Shibley pressed harder, then told Fricke that if his clients could not sit with him at counsel table, he would leave the counsel table and sit with them. The notion seemed to so surprise Fricke that the objection-weary judge conceded, then later reneged.

In response to Shibley's objection that the defendants were somehow on display or had been returned to the dock, Fricke launched into an explanation as to how "Italian courts, the French courts, the Spanish courts, the Greek courts, the Scandinavian courts, the German courts as they existed prior to the present World War, and the British courts, every one of those jurisdictions places the defendant in a position far more prominent and distinctive than is done in our American courts." But European practice hardly mattered to Shibley. The point was that this was the United States, and, under the Constitution, judges do not do that kind of thing.

The debate took up the entire afternoon session, and Fricke adjourned for the day. However, the next morning, Shibley took up where he had left off. Fricke denied Shibley's motion to have his clients seated with him, and, after a few more preliminary matters, the morning continued with Joe Manfredi still on the stand. Manfredi's testimony concluded with little else of significance. Cruz Reyes took the stand next. His wife, Josephine Reyes, had earlier testified about what had happened to her husband. But now, in recounting his personal experience, Reyes cast even further doubt that Mary Albino had seen Joe Diaz get chased that night. Reyes described being cut by a knife while standing in the kitchen of the Delgadillo home. As soon as he got cut, he fled the house, ran past the Albino house, and ran down to the ditch where Mary Albino had seen "someone being chased." If Manfredi's recollection of his chase experience caused some confusion as to whether Albino had actually seen Jose Diaz chased and beaten, Cruz Reyes's experience made it seem very likely that Albino had seen Reyes that night. Once again, where was Jose Diaz?

At this point, the case took another strange twist. Absent some radical change in the evidence, there was little likelihood that any of the twenty-two defendants would take the stand in his own defense. That meant that the prosecution would have no opportunity to cross-examine any of them in an effort to help prove its case. The young women from Thirty-eighth Street had been wholly uncooperative. The people at the Delgadillo party painted a picture of a very ugly fight, but no one could identify Jose Diaz's assailant, or even place him at the party on the morning of 2 August. Therefore, in an effort to add badly missing details to their case, the prosecution began to systematically offer into evidence the statements made by the defendants when they were arrested or taken into custody shortly after Diaz's death.

To accomplish this goal, the prosecution called a series of L.A. deputy sheriffs to the stand. The deputies had taken part in interrogating people after the murder and had transcribed over sixty statements. Among those statements were those of the twenty-two defendants. The process began with L.A. County deputy sheriff N. K. MacVine. MacVine testified earlier in an effort to authenticate some of the prosecution's photos. Now he took the stand to read a statement made by defendant Joe Valenzuela on 3 August 1942. The case once again ground to a halt as the defense objected to the statement as either a confession or an "accusatory statement" — in other words, Valenzuela had not admitted to any wrongdoing or confessed to any crime, and his statement should not be admitted. In an effort to keep the statement out, George Shibley insisted that the witnesses be interrogated on voir dire.

Unlike the process of choosing a jury, which is also called voir dire, voir dire in regards to a witness takes place during the course of a trial as attorneys seek to exclude testimony. They must do so in a way that precludes the jury from hearing anything. The practice developed because to exclude testimony that was nevertheless heard by the jury defeats the purpose. Some things are potentially so damning that even if told to disregard what they have heard, few people can do so. Thus, for the purpose of keeping Valenzuela's statement out of evidence, George Shibley took the risk of placing his client on the stand for the limited purpose of establishing that his statement was not given freely and voluntarily. What followed was a tale of police interrogation tactics that combined physical abuse and verbal intimidation.

Shibley had good reason to attack the statement. Even coerced confessions subsequently stricken by the court have been shown to increase conviction rates because people simply cannot put them out of their minds. A judge's admonition not to consider a stricken confession as evidence competes with a juror's own feelings of guilt toward a defendant and causes the juror to look at other evidence differently. For example, if there was some doubt as to an eyewitness identification such that under normal circumstances it would carry little weight, where a juror has heard the defendant confess, now perhaps in the juror's mind that eyewitness really did see the defendant. Shibley moved carefully, questioning Valenzuela only on the interrogation of 3 August 1942. To go beyond that left Valenzuela open to cross-examination by the prosecution for matters outside his statement. Valenzuela testified that several members of the L.A. sheriff's department verbally intimidated him, and, when he refused to cooperate, they punched him. One at a time, the L.A. deputy sheriffs took the stand and denied having punched or in any way intimidated Valenzuela. After a full morning of testimony on 16 November, MacVine retook the stand, and the prosecution once again offered Valenzuela's statement into evidence. Shibley, on the basis of the voir dire testimony of Valenzuela, objected to the statement as coerced. Fricke, as he had done for most of the trial, overruled the objection.

Valenzuela's statement did not rise to the level of a confession. He did not admit to committing any crime, including the murder of Jose Diaz. However, the statement did serve to provide evidence of the procession of cars to the Sleepy Lagoon that night, and it provided the fact that Henry Leyvas had come back to Thirty-eighth Street with a story of how he and others had been beaten. What is interesting is that had Valenzuela taken the stand, he could have been impeached using his own police statement. But since he had a Fifth Amendment right not to testify, the statement became the prosecution's way of getting Valenzuela's own words into evidence. Under modern-day California's rules of evidence, the statement should not have been admitted, because, at the time the prosecution tried to admit the statement, Valenzuela had not testified. However, in 1942, such statements could be admitted if they were limited to evidence against Valenzuela only and if the statements were not the product of coercion. But even if admitted as to Valenzuela, nothing he said should have been used against his other codefendants.

The process of admitting the defendants' statements proved easier, because the allegations by the defendants of verbal coercion and physical abuse did not seem to concern Fricke. After Valenzuela, the prosecution admitted the statements of Victor Thompson, Benny Alvarez, Josephine Gonzalez, and Edward Grandpre. Almost every statement drew an objection from the defense that the statements had been coerced. In each instance, the L.A. police or sheriff's office denied any coercion, either verbal or physical. In most cases, the defendants' statements served to place people at the scene and establish the motive for going out to the Sleepy Lagoon: revenge against the Downey gang. Grandpre's statement had an excerpt of Joe "Chepe" Ruiz bragging that "they got what they had coming." However, no one admitted to killing anyone. In all, the prosecution admitted the statements of virtually every defendant. Every statement drew an objection as having been coerced, and Fricke overruled every one of them. Perhaps the most damning statement in any of them was attributed to Joe Ruiz. Victor Segobia heard him say, "we stabbed some guy, he won't be going to the army." That sounded very much like Jose Diaz. When the court recessed for the day on the 18th, the prosecution had just gotten started with its admission of the defendants' statements. Early that morning, before court resumed, George Shibley picked up three more clients as Mr. Ravin stepped down and Shibley took on Gene and Joe Carpio and Daniel Verdugo. He now had nine of the twenty-two defendants under his wing.

The admission of statements continued into 25 November. In effect, each defendant testified as a prosecution witness through his statement to the police, and the information gleaned from those statements helped put into perspective what happened that night. The wholesale admission of each statement in its entirety clearly violated evidentiary rules. Fricke refused to acknowledge any coercion in connection with the statements. The testimony of each defendant that he had been punched, beaten, or verbally intimidated carried no weight. The testimony of the law officers, on the other hand, served as conclusive evidence that they did not touch or threaten anyone. Once the statements cleared the hurdle of having not been coerced, the court allowed each statement into evidence in its entirety. That too was an error. No statement rose to the level of a confession in the sense that a defendant said that he killed someone. However, although there were some admissions as to fighting, puncturing tires, and breaking glass, there was a great deal of information that qualified as neither an admission nor a confession. There was no legal basis to admit many portions of the statements that applied to any other defendant other than the person who gave the statement. Had the inadmissible portions been excluded, the statements would have been reduced to choppy, incoherent recitations. Instead, every defendant who gave a statement to the police in effect testified as to what they saw and remembered that night through their police statements. Evidence of who chased whom and who might have had a knife, chain, or board all came before the jury. Because the defendants might never take the stand, their statements would go unexplained. Still, nothing pointed to Jose Diaz's killer, or to Diaz's presence at the party when the cars bearing the Thirty-eighth Street boys arrived. But the picture the defendants painted in their own words could only have left an enduring image in the minds of the jury of a Mexican youth gang, out of control and proud of what it had done.

As if the statements to the police had not been enough, the prosecution then called the L.A. deputy district attorney to the stand. V. L. Ferguson handled the grand jury investigation into Jose Diaz's murder, and, by using him, the prosecution offered and admitted into evidence the grand jury testimony of sixteen of the twenty-two defendants. Unlike the statements given to the police and sheriff's department, no one could claim that this testimony had been coerced. Before each defendant testified, Ferguson had explained that they did not have to testify and that what they said might incriminate them and could be used against them. Without the advantage of being able to consult an attorney before submitting to the grand jury, every defendant testified, and, in so doing, they waived any immunity or Fifth Amendment protection they might otherwise have had. Almost every one of them believed it was necessary in order to clear himself.

However, simply because the testimony had been voluntary did not make all of the grand jury testimony per se admissible. If someone had confessed, that would have been grounds to admit the statement. If someone made an admission against his own interest short of a confession, that would also have been grounds for admitting that portion of the statement. However, absent one of those two situations, prior statements, even under oath, are governed by strict rules of evidence, and were so governed even in 1942. Prior statements are used to impeach. They come into play when someone is testifying and says something inconsistent with what he or she said in a prior proceeding. None of the defendants was testifying, and therefore there was nothing to impeach. The statements came into evidence in lieu of their testimony. Some of the material had no bearing on what happened to Jose Diaz but under the circumstances proved extremely prejudicial.

In grand jury proceedings, the jurors are permitted to ask questions. Some of the questions asked were of a general nature, and the answers varied. A popular question was whether "anyone in the gang used marijuana." The grand jury also asked general questions about the Thirty-eighth Street Gang. None of this material served as an admission or confession, but, without a doubt, testimony given in August 1942 that by law was secret now became quite public and was used to serve the prosecution's purpose of depicting the defendants as drug-using hoodlums. Fricke knew better than to allow the statements into evidence outside the parameters of the evidentiary rules, yet each objection from the defense received a quick and cursory "overruled."

The two-week period from mid-November until early December must have seemed like an eternity for Shibley, Zacsek, and the rest of the defense team. Every day mirrored the day before as they struggled to exclude police statements and grand jury testimony using the same arguments and strategy and getting the same result. After Joe Valenzuela testified as to his treatment by the police, the defense team put on every defendant for the limited purpose of describing their experience of verbal intimidation or abuse. The boys testified to being beaten, placed in small rooms with several officers, and verbally threatened that "things would go hard for them" if they did not talk. The prosecution countered by calling the law enforcement officials, and, faced with two competing stories that could not be verified, Fricke sided with law enforcement every time. Despite the abuse, not one boy admitted to killing Jose Diaz, nor did he point to any of the others as having done so. However, everything the prosecution failed to accomplish with the Thirty-eighth Street girls and the people at the Delgadillo party, it made up for by using the police statements and grand jury testimony. If one is looking to piece together what happened that night and is willing to take the time, they can reconstruct the night using the words of the defendants themselves as they appear in the trial record.

The boys from Thirty-eighth Street experienced the full brunt of a custodial interrogation, not only in the looming presence of multiple law officers, but also in the threats of physical abuse that for some became reality. On voir dire, Shibley repeatedly asked the police officers to describe their size and weight, trying to convey to Fricke the great physical disparity between most of the defendants, who were mere boys, and the police. The prosecution objected each time, and, each time, Fricke sustained the objection, cutting off any effort to prove the intimidation. In the end, because all of this occurred outside the jury's presence, the jury panel heard the complete statement of each defendant and then an objection at the end that it lacked a proper foundation.

Without any drama or notice on the record, the prosecution rested its case on 2 December 1942 after almost six weeks of testimony. Not one witness ever identified any defendant as having struck Jose Diaz. In fact, after six weeks and dozens of witnesses, no one could place Diaz at the party when Henry Leyvas and his friends rolled up early in the morning on 2 August. However, despite the lack of evidence tying anyone to Diaz's murder, the prosecution had done a commendable job of depicting the defendants as a "youth gang" gone wild on the morning of 2 August 1942.

The defense began its case by calling Leyvas's girlfriend, Dora Baca. She recounted how she and Leyvas had been attacked on 1 August at the Sleepy Lagoon and Leyvas's reaction to the attack. On cross-examination, the prosecution hammered away at Baca's bias on the basis of her loyalty to Leyvas. They also repeated their theme of the Thirty-eighth Street boys as a gang. Consistent with the other young women from the neighborhood, Baca resisted any notion that the young men were part of some "gang." At one point, Ben Van Tress asked her where she had heard of the Thirty-eighth Street Gang. She replied, "I heard it here in court by Mr. Shoemaker and in the papers." Baca's brief statement raised a component of the trial that proved every bit as troublesome for the defense as its ongoing battle with the prosecution and the judge. Unlike the grand jury proceedings in August, once the trial began, the Los Angeles press covered it closely.

As the trial progressed, the media coverage increased, and none of it cast the defendants in a positive light. The prosecution spent six weeks hammering away at its theme that the boys from Thirty-eighth Street were a gang and that Henry Leyvas stood at the top as its leader. Part of the problem lay in the fact that Leyvas possessed real leadership skills, and, although some of the defendants denied that anyone followed him, to someone looking on in court, he seemed to be the leader. Members of the press routinely attended the proceedings, and news photographers took advantage of the recesses to ply their trade as well. Leyvas and his codefendants had no experience with this type of publicity and media scrutiny. Isolated in jail, they had little idea of the degree to which they were being tried, both inside Judge Fricke's courtroom and in the court of public opinion. The separation of defense counsel from their clients made the situation even worse. Counsel could not advise their clients, because they were unable to see them; thus, controlling the defendants' demeanor in front of the jury and press proved almost impossible. Eduardo Pagan recounts an instance where the younger boys, many of them confident that they would be acquitted, acted flippantly in trial, sometimes to the point that Fricke commented on their actions. A photographer took a picture of Leyvas — dirty, hair uncut, apparently trying to hide his own laughter. The subsequent publication showed a cocky young hoodlum who stood accused of murder, apparently unfazed by the proceedings.

In December, as the defense presented its case, an article appeared in *Sensation* magazine. Published over the signature of Clem Peoples, chief of the criminal division of the L.A. sheriff's department, the article described the defendants as "baby mobsters," "young wolves," "cruel young gangsters," and a "blood-thirsty mob." The jury in the case had not been sequestered. Every night, they went home, and, with no effort to insulate them from the media onslaught, they heard and read any trial publicity they wanted. Not only did the adverse press serve to reinforce what the prosecution claimed, but knowing that the general public already saw the defendants as murderers made it virtually impossible to view the evidence in an unbiased manner. How could any of the panel explain to friends and neighbors how they had acquitted boys who everyone knew had to be guilty?

An anonymous writer likened the minds of a jury to "twelve test tubes" and asked, "What scientist would commence an experiment with twelve test tubes, soiled and discolored by the deposits of repeated experiments?" The answer to the rhetorical question was "none," but, he suggested "this is precisely the condition of the minds of the jury exposed to a barrage of pictures, previous criminal records, confessions, purported testimony, theories of the case, diagrammatic reconstruction of the crime, liberally sprinkled with 'X' marks the spot, interviews, and discussions prior to the trial of a capital or colorful felony case in any American jurisdiction today." Before his death in 1938, the legendary Clarence Darrow offered an even more direct analysis of the effect of news coverage of trials: "Trial by jury is being rapidly destroyed in America by the manner in which newspapers handle sensational cases. . . . [A]s the law stands today, there is no important case where the newspapers are not guilty of contempt of court day after day." Darrow insisted that there was no need for a new law to remedy the problem. Judges, he argued, had full authority to stop newspapers from influencing decisions, but "everyone is afraid to act." Darrow handled some of the most celebrated trials of the early twentieth century, and his comments, made years before the Sleepy Lagoon trial, showed that little had improved in the intervening years: Fricke had allowed the media to take over his courtroom and the case.

Canon 35 of the judicial ethics of the American Bar Association, published on 30 September 1937, provided as follows:

> Improper Publicizing of Court Proceedings: Proceedings in Court should be conducted with fitting dignity and decorum. The taking of photographs in the courtroom, during sessions of the court or recesses between sessions, and the broadcasting of court proceedings are calculated to detract from the essential dignity of the proceedings, degrade the court and create misconceptions with respect thereto in the mind of the public, and should not be permitted.

California did not officially adopt its own canons of judicial ethics until 1949, but, when it did, the canon related to trial publicity was based on the 1937 ABA canon. Fricke saw himself as a judicial scholar. His extensive rulings on points of evidence and procedure throughout the case took on the condescending air of a law professor lecturing first-year law students. Even if the ABA canons did not impose a legal duty on his conduct in court, they represented the aspirations of the American bar as to its expectations of those who sit on the bench. The press coverage, including photographs like the one of Henry Leyvas, and the almost carnival atmosphere that characterized the *Zammora* case, existed because Fricke took no steps to protect the rights of the accused.

The article in *Sensation* magazine provides but one example of the media being allowed to virtually dictate the outcome of a sensational trial. The article came out after the close of the case but before the jury retired to decide the fate of the defendants. Even without the ABA canons, a legal scholar — which Fricke saw himself as — would have known that the conflict between the freedom of the press versus the right of an accused to a fair trial had been debated for some time before the Sleepy Lagoon trial. A respect for prior judicial opinions, some of them United States Supreme Court decisions, should have resulted in some effort to control the media circus that characterized the *Zammora* trial. The problem was that despite an effort by the courts to address the issue in the decades preceding *Zammora*, the most recent United States Supreme Court opinions on the matter served to cloud the situation rather than make a judge's path clear.

In December 1941, the United States Supreme Court decided a pair of cases that grew out of fact situations in Fricke's own backyard. In *Bridges v. California* and *Times Mirror Co. et al. v. Superior Court for State of California, In and for the County of Los Angeles*, the Supreme Court overturned two California supreme court decisions, one holding a union leader in contempt and the other doing likewise to members of the *Los Angeles Times*. In *Bridges*, a union official sent the U.S. secretary of labor a telegram that found its way into the local newspapers in California. The telegram, sent while the ruling on a motion for a new trial in a labor dispute was pending, conveyed a threat from Harry Bridges to have his union strike if the judge's "outrageous" decision in a labor dispute was enforced. The lower appellate courts upheld the leader's conviction for contempt as an interference with the "orderly administration of justice." In the *Times Mirror* case, the *Los Angeles Times* published a series of editorials while a decision was pending in the sentencing of two union members convicted of assaulting nonunion employees. The editorials called the defendants "sluggers for pay" and described the men as people "who commit mayhem for wages." The editorials opined that the judge risked committing a "serious mistake" if he granted probation. The judge held the newspaper in contempt, and subsequent appeals to lower appellate courts and the California supreme court affirmed his ruling.

The U.S. Supreme Court analyzed the problem as first and foremost a restriction on First Amendment rights and drew on its recent decisions in cases like *Cantwell v. Connecticut.* Of particular concern was the absence of any declaration by the California legislature of the degree of conduct necessary to punish someone for pretrial publicity. In other words, what conduct was so egregious that it threatened a defendant's right to a fair trial? Writing for the majority, Justice Hugo Black tried to define the conduct necessary for pretrial suppression of media-generated publicity. Relying on *Gitlow v. New York*, he stated that "it must necessarily be found, as an 'original question' that the specified publications involved created such likelihood of bringing about the substantive evil as to deprive [them] of the constitutional protection." The problem lay in determining how much likelihood, and, for that issue, he went to the "clear and present danger" cases of the post–World War I era: *Schenck, Abrams*, and *Debs.* Although he admitted that those cases did not provide a guideline for when a danger was "clear and present," something Oliver Wendell Holmes pointed out in later cases where the majority applied the standard, Black concluded that the clear and present danger cases provided a working principle that the substantive evil (of pretrial or predecision publications) must be extremely serious and the degree of imminence extremely high before utterances can be punished. Applying that standard, the majority held that although legal trials are not like elections, to be won through the use of the meeting hall, the radio, and the newspaper, the publications under scrutiny in the *Bridges* and *Times Mirror* cases did not rise to the level of harm necessary to abridge First Amendment freedom of the press.

Thus, had Fricke demonstrated a willingness to suppress the pretrial and trial publicity, he faced the possibility that his actions might not pass constitutional muster. The statements in both the *Bridges* and *Times Mirror* cases seemed harsh and clearly designed to influence the outcome, yet under the majority decision, they did not rise to the level sufficient to punish the conduct and presumably did not rise to the level sufficient to have suppressed those statements. However, both those cases involved one or a few utterances of limited duration, while the press coverage in *Zammora* involved numerous publications over several months that built on one another and in effect conducted a trial in the court of public opinion. *Bridges* had not been a unanimous decision. In his dissent, Justice Frankfurter, joined by justices Roberts and Byrnes, provided a good argument as to why First Amendment freedom of the press should not prevail in matters of justice: "A trial is not a 'free trade in ideas,' nor is the best test of truth in a courtroom 'the power of the thought to get itself accepted in the competition of the market.' " Rather, a court is a forum with

> strictly defined limits for discussion. It is circumscribed in the range of its inquiry and in its methods by the Constitution, by laws, and by age-old traditions. Its judges are restrained in their freedom of expression by historic compulsions resting on no other officials of government. They are so circumscribed precisely because judges have in their keeping the enforcement of rights and the protection of liberties which, according to the wisdom of the ages, can only be enforced and protected by observing such methods and traditions.

A strong argument, but as Fricke might have surmised, still not the law. A suppression of the media coverage would have been difficult. Subsequent U.S. Supreme Court cases such as *Craig v. Harney* (1946) and *Maryland v. Baltimore Radio Show* (1950) stood for the proposition that a trial is a public event and what transpires in the courtroom is public property. Judges have no right to suppress, edit, or censor events that transpire in proceedings within their courtroom. Only by knowing what goes on in court can the public judge whether it was fair. However, even under the rule in *Bridges* and the subsequent decisions that secured the right to report on trial proceedings, Fricke could still have limited some of the media frenzy. The press in *Zammora* was not reporting events in a strict sense. Had the press been reporting, then articles should have appeared citing the prosecution's inability to prove Jose Diaz was even alive and present on the morning of 2 August 1942. Witnesses such as Deputy Sheriff Clem Peoples had been allowed to publish comments on the defendants against whom he testified in a manner totally inconsistent with any objective reporting of the case. However, the real problem went beyond the negative press. Even if outside publicity had been curtailed, Fricke had become the defense's biggest opponent. Even with the law and the mandates of the ABA canons, Fricke's general demeanor toward the defense began as less than favorable and escalated to obvious contempt, and the jury saw most of it take place right before their own eyes.

California's canons of judicial conduct did not become effective until 1949. They define the judiciary's obligations toward the parties and counsel. Even without state mandates, the ABA canons existed in the 1930s, and California's code drew heavily from the ABA rules. Fricke knew this, and he knew that the ABA canons specifically addressed a judge's conduct in trial: they mandated that he "be patient, dignified, and courteous to litigants, jurors, witnesses, lawyers, and others with whom the judge deals in an official capacity." The notion that judges had obligations to attorneys and litigants existed as a matter of common knowledge. To find the timelessness of such rules, one need have looked no further than the *Los Angeles Bar Bulletin.* The August 1942 issue contained a reprint of "Rules for Judicial Conduct: Things Necessary to Be Continually Had in Remembrance," by Sir Matthew Hale. Hale served as lord chief baron of the exchequer from 1660 to 1671 and lord chief justice of England from 1671 to 1676. Among his eighteen points included maxims such as, "That in the execution of justice I carefully lay aside my own passions, and not give way to them, however provoked," and "That I never engage myself in the beginning of any cause, but reserve myself unprejudiced till the whole be heard."

By December 1942, Fricke's conduct toward the defense had become so hostile that even to a casual observer, he demonstrated an ongoing bias. He was courteous to the prosecution but short and abrupt with defense counsel, unless he chose to be purposefully condescending toward someone — conduct he routinely demonstrated with Anne Zacsek. At one point, Zacsek objected and Fricke snidely remarked that he would not know what to do if she did not offer some exception to his rulings. As bad as the publicity and negative conduct from Fricke had been, his evidentiary rulings began to hurt the most. By allowing police statements and grand jury testimony into evidence in their entirety, the defendants, or at least most of them, had in effect already testified. Now, in an effort to explain some of that testimony, Shibley, Zacsek, and the rest of the defense team had to decide whether to put their clients on the stand. By doing so, their clients would waive the Fifth Amendment right of self-incrimination, opening the defendants up to cross-examination and the possibility that they might say something that could put them behind bars for the rest of their lives. If they did not testify, they risked being convicted on slanted and coerced testimony. The defense stood on the horns of a dilemma and could lose, no matter which choice it made.

CHAPTER 6

"Running into a Blank Wall"

Immediately after Dora Baca, the defense called two other witnesses: one was a volunteer worker familiar with the Thirty-eighth Street neighborhood, and the other was a young man, Phillip Del Pozo, who testified by way of a deposition taken in September 1942. Del Pozo also knew the neighborhood and some of the young men in it. He had not been indicted despite having driven to the Delgadillo house that night. The defense tried to use Del Pozo's testimony to refute the notion that the Thirty-eighth Street boys were a gang, and the defense tried to establish that no one had seen Jose Diaz that evening or seen anyone do anything to him. Dora Baca had testified to Henry Leyvas's auto accident the week of 25 July 1942 and his limited ability to walk. Leyvas had become the lead figure in the fracas that night, and the defense had hinted at an automobile accident during the prosecution's case. The accident had apparently forced Leyvas to walk with a limp, and, if true, it certainly undermined the notion that he tore into the Delgadillo house that night in the manner the prosecution depicted. To bolster Baca's testimony, Anne Zacsek also called the hospital x-ray technician to the stand in an effort to admit Henry Leyvas's leg x-rays. Unfortunately, that effort only reinforced the limits of Zacsek's trial skills as she struggled over the prosecution's objection to accomplish a basic authentication of medical records. In the end, she simply gave up.

From 3 December through 14 December, the defense called thirteen of the defendants, including Henry Leyvas. The admission of the police statements and grand jury testimony forced the defense to rehabilitate or explain some of that testimony. The jury had heard none of the defendants testify as to the coerced nature of their statements. Without some rebuttal, it appeared that they spoke freely and voluntarily, adding to the damage of some of their statements. However, as the defense quickly discovered when it put Manuel Delgado on the stand, trying to clean up the damage done by the prosecution created damage of its own.

Delgado testified for almost two days and not only tried to clarify his grand jury testimony, but also called into question whether certain portions had been properly transcribed. He also took issue with some of what he said both before the grand jury and in the statements made to the police after his arrest. However, he added nothing in the way of coercion or abuse. The gist of his testimony on direct refuted any notion that he saw Jose Diaz that night or saw anything happen to him. The fireworks began when Barnes took Delgado on cross-examination. Barnes attacked Delgado on everything from bias and an effort to protect his friends, to the recurring theme that the Thirty-eighth Street kids were a "gang." Defense objections only made matters worse. At times, Barnes simply argued with Delgado, and an objection from the defense not only got overruled, but Fricke also began to comment on Delgado's testimony, calling it evasive and pointing out to the jury that Delgado was "quibbling" with Barnes. Before his cross-examination ended, Delgado actually conceded that Leyvas told him he had "cut" someone that night.

Perhaps the most damaging aspect of Delgado's testimony came in the way it was presented. There is no record that sets out the defense's strategy going into trial, but, from hearing Manuel Delgado testify, it seems clear that he was unprepared to take the stand. His attorney had some clear points he wanted to make, but Delgado's answers reflected a client unsure as to how he was supposed to respond. Whether the defense never intended to call Delgado, or whether Fricke's limitations on attorney–client contact made trial preparation difficult, Manuel Delgado seemed unprepared. When the other defense counsel asked him questions, Delgado appeared confused and often resisted their efforts. When Shibley tried to suggest that the deputy sheriff lied to Delgado by telling him that cooperating would bring leniency, Delgado denied it, instead insisting that he testified before the grand jury and gave a statement to the police because he was innocent and did not kill anyone. While Delgado's answer clearly came from an earnest belief as to his own innocence, he did not understand the importance of establishing that his statements may have been coerced.

Another aspect of the case became evident as the Sleepy Lagoon defendants presented their case. While the prosecution tried to present the boys as a unified gang, the individual defense counsel seemed to realize that the interest of their clients may have been inconsistent with those of their other codefendants. With twenty-two boys on trial for the murder of one man, the attorneys used each of the codefendant witnesses as an opportunity to help clear their client or clients. What had to have been even more disturbing, however, was that defense attorneys did not accept representation of their clients on the basis of the common aspects of their defense or the similarity of their involvement that night. Rather, each family had secured their attorneys on their own, with cost as the major factor. Shibley now had nine of the codefendants. Although the prosecution had completely failed to prove that anyone had killed Jose Diaz that night, the prospect nevertheless existed that, if one boy had killed Diaz by himself, that evidence alone might exonerate some of the other defendants; thus, each defense attorney felt obligated to explore that possibility. However, they also had to tread carefully, because they could not prejudice one of their clients in order to save another. With the defendants in a position to incriminate one another, the failure at the pretrial stage to sever more of the accused began to bolster the prosecution's case. Unable to provide any evidence of how Jose Diaz died or who had killed him, the prosecution could now benefit from one defendant inadvertently incriminating another in an effort to exonerate himself.

Late in the afternoon of 4 December 1942, almost one year from the attack on Pearl Harbor, Henry Leyvas took the stand in his own defense. Leyvas had become the focal point of the entire trial. Already perceived as the leader of the so-called Thirty-eighth Street Gang, Leyvas seemed to be the one person everyone at the Delgadillo party remembered. Zacsek stumbled through the opening part of his testimony but managed to clearly establish the auto accident that injured Leyvas a week before the Sleepy Lagoon murder. She then tried to establish that after surrendering himself to the police on 3 August 1942, Leyvas's interrogators beat and abused him during the four days between his arrest and his grand jury testimony. Fricke refused to allow the line of questioning, pointing out to Zacsek that without a confession, his state of mind when he made the statement and testified before the grand jury was irrelevant. Zacsek kept trying, the prosecution kept objecting, and finally she simply asked Leyvas, "When you went into that Grand Jury room did you tell the truth?"

A: No, I didn't.

Q: Did you have any reason for not telling the truth?

A: Yes, I did.

Q: What was that reason?

A: The officers had beat me up.

MR. SHOEMAKER: May I have that answer, please?

(Answer read.)

Q BY MISS ZACSEK: Had anything else occurred to you?

A: Yes, I was incommunicado.

Q: Did any officer tell you anything about testifying in front of the Grand Jury in respect to being held incommunicado?

A: They says as soon as I would talk — if I would refuse to talk they would keep me incommunicado, and if I did some talking in there, well, they would take me out of it.

Q: You said you talked and told a lie because you had been beaten up. When had you been beaten up?

A: When I first — when they first picked me up at the Firestone sub-station.

Q: That was on August 3rd?

A: It was.

Shortly after arriving at the Firestone station, the deputy sheriffs moved him to the Seventy-seventh Street station. Leyvas testified to hearing them speaking in Spanish about letting a prisoner loose and then shooting him in the back. Then, over the next hour, Leyvas described in detail what happened to him that afternoon after he arrived at the Seventy-seventh Street station. Handcuffed and sitting in a chair with as many as seven law enforcement men around him, Leyvas refused to talk, and, after a short time, his questioners lost patience and began to hit him. Despite being struck in the neck, head, and chest with both open hands and closed fists, Leyvas steadfastly maintained his silence except to tell the police he had a lawyer and had been instructed not to speak. At one point, Leyvas began to bleed from the mouth, and, at several junctures, two of his codefendants, Henry Ynostroza and Victor Thompson, came into the room. The goal was to have Leyvas identify them and perhaps implicate one or both, thereby turning the young men on one another. Leyvas identified them only as his friends, and his unwillingness to do anything else only further upset the police. At one point, his injured leg became the focus of the physical abuse. Leyvas then specifically identified Deputy Sheriff Clem Peoples as one of his interrogators. When word came that Anne Zacsek had come to see her client, Peoples gave Leyvas some pills and told him not to tell his lawyer what had occurred. When it became apparent that Leyvas had nothing to say despite the physical abuse, he was taken to a cell, and on his property slip was written, "Incommunicado until further orders from Capt. Kunou."

All of these issues had come up earlier in the case as the prosecution put the defendants' statements into evidence. When it came to physical abuse, there was not even an issue of knowing one's rights. The police knew better. Earlier testimony on voir dire revealed that some of the boys resisted, knowing that they did not have to talk. In Leyvas's case, his lawyer, Anne Zacsek, told him to be silent before he ever surrendered to the police. He even repeated his lawyer's advice to the police as they escalated the interrogation. However, Leyvas's abuse went beyond the beating and the extended isolation; the exposure to the steady pressure of the interrogation eventually wore him down, although neither he nor any of his codefendants ever confessed. But even in 1942, that kind of abuse was impermissible, and there was good law to support Leyvas's allegation that his Fifth Amendment rights had been abused.

Today, anyone looking to define the rights of a criminally accused person undergoing a police interrogation begins with *Miranda v. Arizona*. Although the decision established the duty to apprise a person of his right to remain silent and created what we know today as "Mirandizing" an accused person, *Miranda* did not spontaneously create protections against abusive police interrogation methods. The Warren Court's creation of a clear procedural rule in *Miranda* built on a body of law that had been in existence for seventy years—and was on the books and well established in 1942 when the L.A. police department and Los Angeles sheriff's department set out to find Jose Diaz's killer at any cost.

The limitations on police conduct designed to elicit involuntary statements or confessions finds its constitutional genesis in two late nineteenth-century Supreme Court cases, *Counselman v. Hitchcock* (1892) and *Brown v. Walker* (1896), and neither were police cases. *Counselman* involved the grant of immunity to a witness who nevertheless refused to answer. The case itself stands for the beginning of transactional immunity in a criminal setting—immunity that covers all crimes related to the specific matter under inquiry. However, the case is also significant for its analysis of the Fifth Amendment right against self-incrimination. *Brown* came six years later and involved a federal action for violation of the Interstate Commerce Act. Brown refused to answer questions that tended to incriminate him on charges of illegal gaming; a lower court ordered him to do so and fined him for contempt when he failed to answer. Brown had been granted statutory immunity, and the Supreme Court held that was sufficient to protect him from self-incrimination. However, in arriving at its decision, the Court explained the evolution of the Fifth Amendment and where it stood in the fabric of American jurisprudence:

> "Nemo tenetur seipsum accusare," had its origin in a protest against the inquisitorial and manifestly unjust methods of interrogating accused persons, which has long obtained in the continental system, the British throne in 1688, and the erection of additional barriers for the protection of the people against the exercise of arbitrary power, was not uncommon even in England. While the admissions or confessions of the prisoner, when voluntarily and freely made, have always ranked high in the scale of incriminating evidence, if an accused person be asked to explain his apparent connection with a crime under investigation, the ease with which the questions put to him may assume an inquisitorial character, the temptation to press the witness unduly, to browbeat him if he be timid or reluctant, to push him into a corner, and to entrap him into fatal contradictions. . . . So deeply did the iniquities of the ancient system impress themselves upon the minds of the American colonists that the states, with one accord, made a denial of the right to question an accused person a part of their fundamental law, so that a maxim, which in England was a mere rule of evidence, became clothed in this country with the impregnability of a constitutional enactment.

The Court in *Brown* did not even address physical abuse, but rather looked to the evils of nonphysical abuse and verbal intimidation. Physical abuse was so beyond the pale of any civilized society that no one questioned its impropriety. However, as Justice Blatchford stated in *Brown*, other unjust methods of interrogation did not pass constitutional muster either.

One could argue that without a rule like *Miranda* a court simply cannot realistically apply broad constitutional concepts to the day-to-day reality of criminal prosecutions and police work. However, the opposite is actually the case, and, again, someone like Fricke, who prided himself as a legal scholar, should have known that it was his duty to look beyond his own disdain for the defendants or their counsel and give meaning to the Constitution. Three decades before the Sleepy Lagoon case, in *Weems v. United States* (1910), the Supreme Court had in effect articulated the obligation of every judge:

> Therefore a principle, to be vital, must be capable of wider application than the mischief which gave it birth. This is peculiarly true of constitutions. They are not ephemeral enactments, designed to meet passing occasions. They are, to use the words of Chief Justice Marshall, "designed to approach immortality as nearly as human institutions can approach it." The future is their care, and provision for events of good and bad tendencies of which no prophecy can be made. In the application of a constitution, therefore, our contemplation cannot be only of what has been, but of what may be. Under any other rule a constitution would indeed be as easy of application as it would be deficient in efficacy and power. Its general principles would have little value, and be converted by precedent into impotent and lifeless formulas. Rights declared in words might be lost in reality.

In the hands of the Los Angeles law enforcement community, the Constitution had indeed become an "impotent and lifeless formula," and Fricke's unwillingness to give even a passing credence to the allegations of Henry Leyvas and his codefendants had ensured that for those on trial for Jose Diaz's murder, "rights declared in words" had become lost in reality.

Total disdain for improper police tactics found a voice not only in the judiciary of the day but in the investigations of the United States Congress. The conclusion of the Wickersham Commission report specifically addressed the kind of verbal and physical abuse Leyvas had described in detail and stated, "To the contention that the third degree is necessary to get the facts, . . . [we say] it is not admissible to do a great right by doing a little wrong. . . . It is not sufficient to do justice by obtaining a proper result by irregular or improper means. Not only does the use of the third degree involve a flagrant violation of law by the officers of the law, but it involves also the dangers of false confessions, and it tends to make police and prosecutors less zealous in the search for objective evidence." Quoting a New York prosecutor, the report concluded, "It is a short cut and makes the police lazy and unenterprising. . . . If you use your fists, you are not so likely to use your wits. . . . [T]he third degree brutalizes the police, hardens the prisoner against society, and lowers the esteem in which the administration of justice is held by the public."

The allegations raised by the defendants during the prosecution's case should have alerted Fricke to the possibility that law enforcement had greatly overstepped the boundaries of proper police conduct. The evolution of the Fifth Amendment rights of an accused, coupled with the Wickersham report on crime that came out in 1931, provided more than enough legal support for Fricke to limit the admission of the police statements, even exclude them altogether. It is important to remember that Fricke had been a prosecutor, and that experience alone provided some insight into how the LAPD and the sheriff's department operated. If it was specific legal authority permitting him to act, he had more than enough, and it came in the form of a United States Supreme Court decision rendered less than three years before the Sleepy Lagoon trial began.

In February 1940, the Supreme Court handed down its decision in *Chambers v. Florida* (1940). In an opinion written by Justice Hugo Black, the Court directly addressed police brutality and nonphysical interrogation techniques. In facts with an eerie similarity to the police conduct alleged by Leyvas and his friends, the Supreme Court struck down the criminal convictions of three black men on the basis of how the police conducted the investigation. *Chambers* involved the killing of an elderly white man in Broward County, Florida. The night of the murder, the police rounded up almost forty men, all black, without warrants and put them in jail. The next day, the Broward County sheriff's department took several of the prisoners, including two of the men ultimately convicted, to Miami, making it clear to the prisoners that they feared some kind of white mob action against the men. The evidence indicated the suspects were questioned repeatedly, day and night, for several days. During that time, they were held incommunicado and denied access to an attorney, friends, or family. When questioned, they were in a room alone surrounded by between four to ten men. After days of questioning, one of the men broke and confessed. Ultimately, three men stood trial and were convicted, including Chambers.

On appeal, the defendants alleged the confessions were coerced and violated their Fourteenth Amendment rights of due process. In his short but carefully crafted opinion, Black conceded that there was a dispute as to the use of physical violence and mistreatment. But the record showed "without conflict" the "dragnet arrests" on suspicion alone, without warrants, and the protracted questioning and cross-questioning of the young, black tenant farmers under circumstances where they had no access to family or counsel. The Court concluded that the methods used were designed to break the young men down, and did so. For five days, they refused to confess, and then, under constant pressure, one of the young men broke. Black's analysis of the evolution away from tyrannical and dictatorial governments and the methods of an inquisition sounds very much like the Court's language in *Brown v. Walker*. Unmoved by the assertion that law enforcement methods such as the ones used were necessary to uphold the law, Black concluded, "To permit human lives to be forfeited upon confessions thus obtained would make the constitutional process of due process of law a meaningless symbol."

Even if Fricke properly discounted the allegations of physical abuse, the dragnet arrest of more than six hundred persons without a warrant, coupled with the lengthy incarcerations that not even law enforcement denied, should have been sufficient for Fricke to act on the basis of the analysis in *Chambers*. Yet confronted with persuasive, if not compelling, evidence of abuse, Fricke could have done something. His failure to act seems curious when viewed in light of Hugo Black's admonition to the judiciary in *Chambers*: "Under our constitutional system, courts stand against any winds that blow as havens of refuge for those who might otherwise suffer because they are helpless, weak, outnumbered, or because they are nonconforming victims of prejudice and public excitement." According to Black, it was up to

Fricke to protect the Sleepy Lagoon boys from the prejudice and fear that dominated the community and the media coverage.

Henry Leyvas spent four days in police custody and went directly from there to the grand jury room. His days of interrogation, even though they did not yield a confession, tainted what he told the grand jury — not only factually, but also in his admission that his testimony had been given voluntarily. In effect, the police coerced him into waiving his Fifth Amendment rights. To say that his interrogation left a bad taste in his mouth would be accurate: in response to Zacsek's questions on direct examination, Leyvas testified that he was still bleeding from inside his mouth when he testified before the grand jury.

Leyvas remained on the stand until 9 December. His cross-examination became a running debate as to why he testified one way before the grand jury and another on direct examination. At one point, Barnes asked Leyvas why he "perjured" himself before the grand jury, trying to completely discount his testimony of police abuse. Lost in the efforts of the prosecution to get Leyvas's past criminal record into evidence and the fact that he lied to the grand jury was the fact that nothing Leyvas said, either on the stand or before the grand jury, tied him or anyone else to Jose Diaz's death.

The defense called eleven other defendants, but the ordeals of Manuel Delgado and Henry Leyvas altered strategy. The remaining defendants testified only to their age at the time of the incident to show the jury that each was a minor on 1–2 August 1942. Efforts to establish police abuse fell to friends or relatives who saw them sometime after their arrest. For example, Joe Valenzuela's mother testified to bruises on his face when she finally got in to see him on 7 August 1942. In retrospect, the decision made sense. From a purely evidentiary standpoint, the defense had to know that the prosecution had presented nothing that established how Diaz had died that night or that managed to tie any defendant to Diaz's death. As damaging as the police statements and grand jury testimony had been in terms of casting the defendants in an unfavorable light, none of it identified Diaz's killer, or even established that he had been at the party the morning the young men from Thirty-eighth Street showed up.

The prosecution called three rebuttal witnesses that added little to the evidence, and, on 15 December 1942, both sides closed. The court then adjourned for three weeks, reconvening on 7 January 1943. Charles Fricke gave the jury its instructions before going into deliberation. The jury deliberated for five days, and, on 12 January 1943, they returned verdicts of guilty for seventeen of the twenty-two defendants. Henry Leyvas, Robert Telles, Manuel Delgado, Johnny Matuz, Jack Melendez, Joe "Chepe" Ruiz, Angel Padilla, Ysmael Parra, and Manuel Reyes were all found guilty of murder. Henry Leyvas, Robert Telles, and Joe Ruiz stood convicted of murder in the first degree, or premeditated murder. Eight other boys stood convicted of assault with a deadly weapon with intent to commit murder. Five of the boys were acquitted on all charges.

George Shibley immediately made a motion for new trial and asked for time to prepare his argument. The other defense counsel joined his motion, and Fricke set the hearing for 25 January 1943, which was then continued until 1 February. Motions for new trial are almost always made by a nonprevailing party but are rarely granted. They serve two functions in most jurisdictions. First, they are a procedural prerequisite to an appeal and generally extend the period of time for filing an appeal until the motion is heard. Second, they allow the party making the motion to present the grounds justifying a new trial in an organized, coherent manner. For almost two months, Shibley and his colleagues unsuccessfully fought a host of issues that they believed prejudiced their clients to the point of justifying a new trial. Now they would have the opportunity to present their objections to Fricke and in the process provide a road map for the ultimate appeal.

Shibley led off the motion proceeding and immediately drew the ire of Judge Fricke. Fricke intended to conduct the hearing in his chambers—not an uncommon practice, but someone had subpoenaed all twelve of the jurors, thereby making it impossible to do so. Fricke wanted to know who brought the entire jury to the hearing, and Shibley calmly told him, " I subpoenaed them." Fricke immediately wanted to know why, and, before Shibley could complete his explanation, Fricke cut him off. Unless Shibley intended to impeach the jury by showing they arrived at their verdict by "lot or chance," the subpoena would be quashed. Shibley said no, he intended to use them to show that the verdict in the case had been the result of "public hysteria and public opinion." Shibley came into the case after it began and took no part in the jury selection process. He believed the defendants could never have received a fair trial in Los Angeles County, and he wanted to use the jury testimony as proof of that. Fricke refused to allow it, correctly pointing out that community prejudice rising to the level Shibley described should have been raised by a motion to transfer venue, to move the case to another county where the press coverage and public opinion had not poisoned the jury pool.

Although Shibley's instincts were correct, procedurally, Fricke was right. Shibley's colleagues had botched the jury selection and pretrial process beyond his ability to correct it weeks before he ever became involved. Although the pretrial record did not reflect the degree to which the defense counsel had simply acquiesced to the jury panel, the transcript from the motion for new trial laid bare the extent of the oversight. Between the eight defense attorneys present when the case began, they had over a hundred unused peremptory challenges. The defense could have stricken more than a hundred potential jurors without cause, then stricken jurors thereafter by showing bias or prejudice driven by pretrial publicity. The defense never tried this tactic, and, as vigorously as Shibley pressed the issue that they did not fully appreciate the degree of the pretrial prejudice against "Mexican boys," he was not going to win this argument: although compelling, it came too late. He had a fifty-five-page exhibit prepared that had over three hundred fifty magazine and newspaper articles on the case before it went to trial. He had statistics on the extent of the daily circulation of the Los Angeles newspapers that numbered in the hundreds of thousands. Shibley concluded that no juror anywhere in Los Angeles County could have been immune. Fricke had other ideas:

THE COURT: I prefer to draw a very much different conclusion. My own conclusion would be I do not believe that twelve intelligent, law-abiding, American citizens, as considerate as this jury was, would violate their oaths as public officials and return a verdict upon the basis of prejudice or influenced by prejudice. The answer to the proposition, basically, as a matter of law, however, is just simply this: There is nothing to show that any juror saw any one of those things you have referred to.

MR. SHIBLEY: I beg your pardon?

THE COURT: I say, there is nothing at the present time which indicates that any one of the jurors saw any one of these articles or newspaper or magazine clippings you have referred to. If they did not see them, of course, they could not have been influenced by them.

Factually, it would be hard to argue the jury did not see the articles Shibley tried to admit, but, legally, Fricke was correct. For all intents and purposes, Shibley's effort to correct a huge oversight by the defense at the outset of the trial died there. He and Fricke argued for a few minutes longer, but Fricke refused to budge. As it turned out, he did not want to hear much of anything else either.

Ben Van Tress began on behalf of Joe Ruiz and limited his entire argument to insufficiency of the evidence. Before he even got started, Fricke cut him off, saying, "During the entire course of the trial I kept very close notes . . . and I haven't the slightest doubt in my own mind not only that the evidence fully sustains all of the verdicts but would sustain the conviction of offenses of higher grades than those cases in which the jury returned verdicts of less than first degree murder and less than assault with a deadly weapon with intent to commit murder." Fricke concluded, "I am willing for you to argue but I am afraid you are running into a blank wall." Van Tress seemed at a loss for words. He asked Fricke if by not arguing his motion, he waived anything on appeal. Fricke assured him that he did not. Van Tress sat down and Zacsek stood up. Although she saw the act as futile, she could not be silent on Henry Leyvas's conviction.

Zacsek challenged the whole premise that the jury had convicted on a conspiracy argument. The evidence showed Leyvas never left the patio. He could not have killed Diaz, particularly when no one could place Diaz at the scene. If the defendants acted as part of a conspiracy, why did five of them escape any conviction at all? She hammered away at the grand jury testimony and insisted it should not have been allowed in. Fricke not only denied her motion for new trial, but he also denied her second motion to reduce the degree of the crimes from first degree to second and from murder to assault. Fricke remained unmoved by any of her argument. In his opinion, the five men acquitted should have been convicted.

Phillip Schutz stood up to argue on behalf of Manuel Delgado and several others. In recognition that his argument was preordained to failure, he began by telling Fricke, "*Morituri te salutamus,*" "we who are about to die salute you." Schutz's statement proved to be a fitting epitaph to a doomed motion. From the defense perspective, Fricke had presided in a dictatorial Caesarlike manner for the entire trial. Now he turned a thumbs down to pleas for mercy and justice before they were even made. Schutz attacked the failure to sever the defendants into separate trials, arguing that any one of these young men would have been acquitted on all charges if tried alone or in groups of two. Schutz nevertheless could not understand how, under any theory of conspiracy, one could be held guilty of a crime simply because he was in the same place as someone who might have committed a crime, particularly when no one was ever able to testify to who actually killed Diaz or how it happened. In effect, the young men were all there, some were angry, Diaz turned up dead, one of them must have killed him, and thus sixteen others are also guilty. Fricke responded that sometimes juries do that kind of thing. Realizing the futility of any further argument, Schutz preserved his appellate grounds for appeal and sat down.

Fricke openly admitted that the fate of these young men had been reduced to a matter of time and convenience. He was so convinced of their guilt and of the sufficiency of the evidence that nothing could sway him. With everyone else done, Shibley stood up to conclude his argument. He also acknowledged the futility of the insufficiency of evidence argument, asked that his points of error on that ground be preserved, and then moved on to his other basis of appeal. Up to this point, the motions for new trial had been anything but coherent. Now, however, Shibley began to take apart other aspects of the trial, many of which involved Fricke's rulings. Unfortunately, Fricke had heard it all before and proved no more receptive now than he had during trial.

First, Shibley attacked the reading of the stenographic statements taken of the defendants during their interrogations. He cited case law that, to everyone's surprise, Fricke denied having read. The gist of Shibley's challenge was that the transcript was admissible to impeach the person who transcribed it — in this case, the stenographer — and only after it was established that the transcript was accurate could it be used to refresh the memory of the person who made the statement. As Shibley pointed out, the stenographer did not testify, and when the statements came into evidence verbatim, none of the defendants had even testified. The evidence itself had been damning, and most of it had been pure hearsay. Shibley believed that given the nonexistence of any real evidence as to the defendants' guilt, the jury had relied heavily on these inadmissible statements.

Shibley then moved on to the issue of effective counsel at trial. The defense had challenged Fricke repeatedly over the course of the trial regarding his decision to physically separate the twenty-two defendants from their counsel during the proceedings, thus making it impossible to effectively represent them. Shibley returned to the ruling as the basis of a new trial. Fricke dismissed the objections during trial on logistical grounds. As far as he was concerned, there was not enough room to accommodate the defense's demands, and that ended the debate. For Shibley, the debate never ended. The defendants, seated behind their counsel in rows, looked guilty. More important, effective communication did not exist. The objections and discussion during trial had not revealed the extent of the handicap, but, now, arguing for a new trial, Shibley recounted how in the midst of witness questioning he had been reduced to passing oral messages back to his clients, often by way of some of the other defendants. The response came back in the same manner: through other defendants, to other co-counsel, and then to Shibley. Fricke stood on his belief that it was not possible to seat the defendants with their counsel. Shibley argued it might have been hard, but an acceptable seating arrangement could have been provided. He again cited Fricke to *Commonwealth v. Boyd* and this time read directly from the decision:

> In every criminal trial the accused has a common law right to counsel, and this right may not be abridged by any rule or regulation which would operate to hinder and obstruct free consultation between the accused and his appointed counsel, especially at the critical moment when his alleged guilt is being made the subject of inquiry by the jury sworn to make a true deliverance. At such a time the accused has a right to sit with his counsel where he can have equal opportunity to hear the testimony of witnesses, absolute freedom to assist by suggestion and information in his own defense.

Shibley had no problem articulating the harm. Numerous items of evidence adduced at trial had been missed because Shibley's clients could not point out omissions or errors in what was being offered until well after the opportunity to do so had passed. The only effective access to the defendants required counsel to go to the county jail. But those visits occurred long after the opportunity had passed, and even then, the court recessed at 4 P.M. and dinner came at 6:30, thereby ending all visitation rights. Fricke rejected the argument, just as he had during trial, and Shibley moved on, having made his point and preserved the issue for appeal.

Finally, Shibley reasserted his contention that the prosecution had been guilty of misconduct throughout the trial by referring to the defendants as "Mexicans" or making a point of their "Mexican" nationality. Fricke argued that the defense had raised the issue of nationality when picking the jury and the prosecution had every right to pick up on the theme. Shibley argued that it should have ended with voir dire. Whereas any item of bias is fair game when choosing the jury, once the jury has been selected and the case begins, the use of nationality should have been stopped. Shibley pointed to how the prosecution read into the record a statement by one of the defendants as to what a police officer had told him during questioning, specifically, "Well, that is the way you Mexicans are. You never fight fair. You are a bunch of cowards." Then Barnes had said, "There is more than a smidgen of truth to that statement." Shibley emphasized how Clyde Shoemaker had insisted that the boys be left in the same zoot suits they wore when they were arrested, and how their appearance proved central to the prosecution's case. In Shibley's mind, the jury had been allowed to convict these boys on who they were perceived to be — a perception fostered by the prosecution and sanctioned by Fricke. Fricke saw no harm in using terms like *Mexican* or *gang*. When Shibley tried to cite cases in support of his argument, Fricke curtly replied, "Put them in your brief."

Shibley had fought the good fight, but, by late afternoon of 1 February 1943, he had endured enough. After one more try at getting his media exhibit into evidence, Shibley sat down. Fricke overruled every motion for new trial and every motion to reduce the sentences. The defense asserted that they would all appeal both the verdict and the sentence, and then Fricke asked if there was any legal cause why sentence should not be passed. There was none. The seventeen boys convicted of either assault or murder stood and received their sentences. Those convicted of simple assault got six months in county jail. However, for the group that would become known as the San Quentin boys, Fricke sentenced each to the "term prescribed by law." For Henry Leyvas, that meant life.

The prosecution called forty-two witnesses to the witness stand, used the grand jury testimony of sixteen of the defendants, and used every transcribed statement made by any defendant to the police. Not one word of testimony in the more than six thousand pages of trial transcript served to tie any person to the death of Jose Diaz. In fact, every witness who had seen Jose Diaz that night could not recall having done so after around 11:00 P.M. on 1 August 1942. Yet seventeen boys stood convicted, nine of them for murder. Although they might prevail on appeal, for now, the system had failed. The courtroom, a place that in Hugo Black's words was supposed to be a haven from the winds of prejudice, had become exactly the opposite. It seemed to Shibley and his colleagues that the state had used the judicial system to sacrifice seventeen young men to fear and bigotry. The defense had done all they could. Granted, some of them lacked the skills required for the job, but none had been short on passion or effort. In retrospect, it might not have mattered. Whoever defended the Thirty-eighth Street boys was in for a beating. It remained to be seen whether those convicted of murder would ever see freedom again. None had the financial means to continue the fight, and the meager resources available to their families had been exhausted. Cicero may not have been right. To say that the laws had been silent in time of war might be a stretch. However, for those on the defense side of the docket, it seemed as if the rules that governed evidence and procedure and that ensured fundamental fairness had been suppressed.

CHAPTER 7

Alice's Boys

Twenty-five-year-old Alice Greenfield had wanted to be there from the start, but sickness intervened. Diagnosed with pleurisy, she spent the early stages of the *Zammora* case recovering in a hospital bed, but she was never out of touch. Greenfield knew George Shibley through the Congress of Industrial Organizations, where she volunteered, hoping to catch on full-time, until her sickness intervened. However, Shibley made sure she got copies of the daily trial transcripts, and she spent her hospital days summarizing the testimony for him until she recovered. Once back on her feet, Greenfield attended the trial every day, and what she saw appalled her. As soon as the verdicts came down, she volunteered for the Sleepy Lagoon Defense Committee (SLDC).

Born 5 April 1917 in Calgary, Alberta, Canada, to Russian immigrants, Greenfield came to the United States in 1922 when her family relocated to Los Angeles. She attended both junior and senior high school in Los Angeles, and, although she grew up in predominately white neighborhoods, she had a strong sense of fairness that drove her into activist work at an early age. Her realization that the racial situation in America was drastically skewed came while she attended Los Angeles Community College, where for the first time she had an opportunity to meet and interact with people of color. For Greenfield, the Sleepy Lagoon trial served as a reminder that America was far from fair, that color mattered, and the racism she saw all around her in Los Angeles knew no boundaries. Years later, Greenfield, now Alice McGrath, conceded, "I came to the Committee having no recognizable skills for doing anything except running the mimeograph machine, stuffing envelopes. . . . But I dealt myself in. I just wanted to be part of this." As it turned out, she would be a big part of what followed.

Before the Citizens' Committee for the Defense of Mexican American Youth (CCDMAY) had changed its name to the Sleepy Lagoon Defense Committee (SLDC) or found new leadership and new counsel, the old committee formed during the trial began the effort to cultivate public opinion, both to engender sympathy for the cause and to help kick-start the fund-raising effort. Almost immediately after the verdicts, it issued a release entitled "We Have Not Yet Begun to Fight." Although the trial was over and the jury had been dismissed, the struggle had only shifted from one court to another. The release traced the evolution of the trial from the fight at the Delgadillo house that night to the verdict. In addition to stressing the issues of local prejudice and uncontrolled hysteria over Mexican crime, the release began a theme that placed the Sleepy Lagoon trial in a larger context: "The effect of these convictions, like the effect of the long series of mass arrests, persecutions, and police brutalities against the Mexican-American people, may have very serious consequences. Unity for all-out production and military aggression may be badly impaired; mistreatment of minorities is an Achilles' heel vulnerable to all manner of Axis insinuation." The release concluded by reasserting the committee's goal of raising money from a broad range of community sources.

On 2 March 1943, a month after the young men had been sentenced, the committee put out an untitled press release that continued to tie the Sleepy Lagoon case to larger issues of Mexican American discrimination at home. Denouncing the notion that juvenile delinquency was somehow endemic to Mexican Americans, the release pointed out that no race had a monopoly on juvenile crime and the real problem lay in poverty, overcrowded housing, and social discrimination. After tracing the evolution of Mexican immigration into the United States, the release described how the media assault on Mexican youths in 1942, coupled with the mass arrests in August after Diaz's death, had stigmatized Mexican Americans as a people. Aside from the inherent injustice of racial discrimination and prejudice, this concerted attack in Los Angeles actually threatened the war effort, and the press release provided specific details on the connection between the trial and the war.

The Latin American press had expressed hostility to full pan-

American cooperation in the war effort. Newspapers in Mexico and the rest of Latin America seized on the publicity of the mass arrests as a means of persuading Latin Americans that they could expect nothing but abuse from the United States. Proponents of disunion known as the Sinarquistas were purportedly closely modeled after the Falange of fascist Spain. Organized in 1936 by the Hitler government, Sinarquistas allegedly maintained direct contact with the Fichte-Bund in Hamburg. At one time, the movement claimed a membership of two hundred thousand in Mexico, and it still had important bases of operation in the southwestern United States—California, Texas, Arizona, and New Mexico. In Los Angeles, the organization had an admitted membership of eight hundred under the leadership of Pedro Villaseñor. The trial of the twenty-two Mexican American youths for the Sleepy Lagoon murder emboldened the Los Angeles Sinarquistas movement and aided its cause by creating an atmosphere of hostility and distrust toward the Mexican American population. Sinarquistas pointed to the trial as proof that "Mexican-Americans cannot get a fair break in 'gringo' courts, therefore, why should they support the 'Yankees' war?"

Discord and racial prejudice at home had become tools for Axis propaganda efforts in the western hemisphere. The press release argued that America could not afford to provide fuel for its enemies to drive a wedge between itself and its Latin American neighbors. The broader theme offered the opportunity to take the committee's fund-raising and education efforts beyond the Los Angeles area. Patriotism demanded tolerance by Americans of one another's differences, regardless of color or creed. By 1943, it became clear that America had to carry the war effort both in western Europe and the Pacific, and the committee's approach to the Sleepy Lagoon case depicted the trial and the verdict as a hindrance, both to unity within America and between the United States and its Latin American allies.

The committee's suggestion that the verdicts undermined national and regional unity repeated a theme that began before the young men were convicted. In November 1942, the committee published a general petition suggesting that the Axis powers played off the treatment of minorities in the United States to stir unrest. The petition made specific suggestions to local, state, and federal authorities designed to ameliorate the intolerable social conditions that led to juvenile crime and to embrace the Mexican American community as a resource to help win the war at home by opening up war-related industry jobs. Some of the suggestions actually found their way to the L.A. grand jury and became included in its posthearing recommendations.

On 14 March 1943, the committee held a conference at Belmont Studios in Los Angeles, California. With no permanent leadership in place, local attorney Clore Warne served as chairman for the conference. The meeting had been scheduled for the Unitarian Church in L.A., but Assistant District Attorney Clyde Shoemaker apparently took steps to make that site untenable. The committee minutes provide no insight into what happened, but the first resolution passed that Sunday called for a formal protest with District Attorney Fred Howser and the mayor's office. Carey McWilliams was there, and, although he was not yet a leader, he nevertheless had a clear opinion. He spoke out against Shoemaker's efforts, claiming that, if he believed the trial was fair, he would not only have allowed the meeting to proceed but would also have appeared and defended the verdict. McWilliams had already begun to see the larger issues. Much like the "Hate the Japanese" campaign that had surfaced in 1942, the efforts to turn the fear of zoot-suiters into the same kind of hatred directed at Japanese Americans only divided the Los Angeles community.

Warne read a letter of support from Orson Welles, who apologized for his absence, and a telegram from the Spanish-language section of the International Workers Organization pledging its support. The Pan American Committee from New York sent a letter expressing regret for the convictions in January. Both Mexican consuls in Los Angeles attended in person, and Ignacio Lopez from the office of the Coordinator of Inter-American Affairs came as an "interested observer" to learn the facts in the case. R. Bentley Strather spoke for the Negro Victory Committee and the Civil Liberties Committee, and he urged all minorities to work in unison. George Shibley addressed the conference and explained in detail what happened at trial; he echoed McWilliams's sentiments that the anti-Mexican campaign undermined the war effort.

The conference then got down to nuts and bolts. Robert S. Morris, treasurer of the committee, reviewed the work of the committee since its inception, crediting LaRue McCormick as its originator. He summarized the work of the committee to date, including the selection of George Shibley as attorney on a go-forward basis to prosecute the appeal and assuring the parents that there was a group interested in their young men. Some members of the committee met with the boys after the verdict to assure them that they had not been abandoned. Morris's parting suggestion recommended expanding the committee. To win, it would be necessary to carry on a broad educational program and to raise funds. The conference then broke up into three panels: trade union; church, university, and civic organizations; and youth. Forty-five minutes later, the panels reconvened.

The trade union panel stressed publicity and the need for a subcommittee devoted to potential speakers. CIO radio would help spread the word, and the committee had already lined up both the CIO's and AFL's union publications with a special edition on the Sleepy Lagoon case slated for 5 May 1943. The panel agreed that engendering support within the community might be difficult if the tone of the local press remained the same as it had been for all of 1942. In an effort to change the tenor of local reporting, the panel advocated that committee members be appointed to visit local publishers. Someone needed to go to the *Los Angeles Daily News* and try to get it to report on the D.A.'s action with the Unitarian Church. Visits to both the mayor and the D.A.'s office were a must, and efforts had to be made to solicit real support from the Office of War Information (OWI). The panel collected $93.50 in donations. This initial collection was far from what would be needed, but at least it was a start.

The church, university, and civic committee echoed Morris's suggestion and recommended a larger committee under the supervision of the central committee. Initially, mass meetings would be needed to discuss the plight of the seventeen convicted boys in detail and connect their plight with other cases of discrimination. Large meetings allowed for fund-raising among the attendees and the opportunity to get the local press to attend and report on the efforts to free the boys. The youth committee also reported and planned a countywide youth conference to not only work on freeing the boys incarcerated in San Quentin, but to build unity between national groups going forward. The recommendations from the three panels were accepted by the conference.

Following the panel reports, various smaller subcommittees formed in 1942 took the stage and reported on their efforts. The credentials committee gave a summary of the total membership. Fifty-four organizations had stepped up in the effort to free the young men; they comprised twenty union locals and thirty-four churches and fraternal and youth groups. In total, one hundred twelve delegates from these organizations attended the conference. LaRue McCormick suggested that each group select one person to represent it on the new committee, and, before adjourning, the conference delegates passed a number of resolutions "urging all democratic organizations to unite to demand immediate correction of this injustice and by their concerted efforts guarantee permanent freedom from persecution of all Spanish-speaking people in the Southwest." At 6:00 P.M., the conference adjourned.

As the delegates left, they had to have been both encouraged and concerned. The fact that people from a variety of different community organizations still cared about the case and the boys themselves had to bolster their spirits. However, of some concern had to be the daunting task that lay ahead and the cost involved in mounting a successful appeal. The speakers and panelists at the conference kept returning to the same theme: the need to broaden the base of support. As the conference broke up, the ad hoc Citizens' Committee for the Defense of Mexican American Youth that began in October 1942 was about to change. Now, in the wake of the Sleepy Lagoon verdicts, it reorganized and became the Sleepy Lagoon Defense Committee (SLDC). It had one main goal: do what was necessary to overturn the convictions of the seventeen defendants, and particularly the twelve that now sat in San Quentin. Alice Greenfield would become its workhorse, but, to succeed, it would need leadership. Carey McWilliams joined the CCDMAY in October 1942, when the Sleepy Lagoon trial began, and his comments at the conference reflected a desire to continue the struggle. Now he put a prolific career as a writer on hold and agreed to take the helm of the SLDC as its national chairman.

Just who was Carey McWilliams? His biographer calls McWilliams the most important American intellectual you have never heard of, especially if you were born after 1960. An author, attorney, social activist, and eventually the editor of *The Nation* from 1955 to 1975, McWilliams was born in Colorado and grew up in Steamboat Springs.

He came to Los Angeles as a boy after his father, Jerry McWilliams, lost everything he had, including his life, after World War I. Once a wealthy rancher and a state legislator from Steamboat Springs, the elder McWilliams lost his fortune investing in cattle when the beef embargo ended after the war. Broke and distraught, he died in a Colorado mental institute while his son was still in high school. His father's death proved life-changing for McWilliams because it forced him to come to grips with why his father had died. Faced with blaming his dad or the system, McWilliams blamed the system, and, for the rest of his life, he looked with a jaded eye on capitalism and free enterprise.

McWilliams got both his bachelor and his law degrees at the University of Southern California. The law served as a means to making a living while he indulged in his true passions: writing and activism. Although he was hardly a zealot in the 1920s, the Great Depression of the 1930s energized his existing feelings about the system and free enterprise. He saw everyone as a potential victim, but minorities, immigrants, and manual workers appeared particularly vulnerable to exploitation. He used his legal skills in representing workers and focused on agricultural labor issues. In 1939, his first book, *Factories in the Field*, put a real face on the fictional characters portrayed in John Steinbeck's *The Grapes of Wrath*, which came out the same year. As an ally of the farm worker, McWilliams became California's chief of immigration and housing in 1939, and he used that position to help raise wages and secure better housing for the growing numbers of migrant farm workers who had come to California and remained. In a short time, California growers were referring to McWilliams as "Agricultural Pest Number One—worse than pear blight or boll weevils." Earl Warren ran for governor in 1942 and pledged to Central Valley voters that, if elected, firing McWilliams would be his first official act.

The Sleepy Lagoon case ended at roughly the same time that McWilliams's tenure as a public official came to a conclusion. McWilliams quickly saw the larger ramifications in what happened to Henry Leyvas and his friends. He accepted the daunting task of freeing the Sleepy Lagoon defendants, but he did so under three conditions. First, the SLDC's books had to be audited after the appeal. Second, the committee had to be broader and more inclusive of other groups. Third, new counsel had to be retained. The audit requirement served as a means to protect McWilliams and the SLDC from the inevitable attacks that would come, claiming the SLDC was nothing but a front for the Communist Party. Although McWilliams was not a communist, he had friends who were, and, by 1942, J. Edgar Hoover had McWilliams on the FBI's security index, making him subject to detention in the event of a national emergency. Broadening the committee served to ward off allegations that the committee was nothing but an effort by the radical left to advance social issues. McWilliams's insistence on new counsel was an obvious goal for a variety of reasons.

The audit would have to wait until the end, and broadening the SLDC's base became an ongoing project. But finding new counsel emerged as an immediate need. For one reason or another, trial counsel simply melted away after the verdicts. In some cases, the defendants no longer needed an attorney, because they had been acquitted. However, even the seventeen now in county jail or imprisoned at San Quentin needed new counsel. By the end of the trial, George Shibley represented nine of the defendants. He had performed very well, and his efforts, although apparently futile at the time, would prove crucial to the success of the appeal. He had come to the Belmont conference ready to continue his effort, but, shortly after the conference, Shibley fell victim to the nation's manpower needs and, within weeks, found himself in the military, stationed in Wyoming. Anne Zacsek and the other attorneys with convicted clients had no interest in the appeal, and they frankly lacked the skills required for what lay ahead. What the SLDC needed was a top-flight appellate lawyer. They found such a man in the person of Ben Margolis.

Margolis was born to Russian immigrants on 10 April 1910 in New York City. He was diagnosed with asthma at age seven, so Margolis moved to California in 1917 as his parents sought a climate more amenable to his respiratory condition. He grew up in Santa Barbara and attended Santa Barbara State College before moving on to the University of Southern California, where he graduated in 1929. From there, he went on to law school at Hastings, graduating in 1933. He received his education during the depths of the Depression, and the apparent lack of social consciousness on the part of his fellow law students struck a nerve in Margolis. Shortly after graduating, he went to work in San Francisco and became involved in cases involving the legality of the 1935 landmark labor law, the Wagner Act. Labor law appealed to Margolis for a variety of reasons, not the least of which was the ability to effect some kind of social change.

Margolis spent ten years in San Francisco, and, by the time he agreed to take on the Sleepy Lagoon case, he had the experience and reputation as a top-tier labor lawyer. His connections to labor drew him into the landmark press cases of *Bridges v. California* and *Times Mirror v. Superior Court*. Margolis had also been a member of the National Lawyers Guild since its inception. In 1943, while he was in the process of relocating his office from San Francisco to Los Angeles, he received a call from Clore Warne, the L.A. lawyer who chaired the Belmont conference. Warne told Margolis about Sleepy Lagoon, Carey McWilliams, and the importance of the case. He explained that the SLDC had already begun fund-raising for fees and expenses for the appeal and needed a good lawyer. McWilliams, also a guild member, knew Margolis was relocating and was a law school classmate of Margolis's L.A. law partner, Charlie Katz. It seemed to be a good fit, and Margolis agreed to take the appeal. Shortly after Margolis settled into his Los Angeles office, the trial transcript arrived, all six thousand pages of it, and the long process of reviewing and briefing the case began. It took almost a year before the brief was ready to file. As Margolis reviewed the trial, one thing became apparent to him: George Shibley's trial skills and his courage in never backing down from Fricke despite the verbal abuse and constant frustration created a record that could sustain an appeal.

With new counsel in place, McWilliams and the SLDC went to work trying to raise money and spread the word. Aside from not wanting to be perceived as just a tool for the radical left, McWilliams fought to broaden the SLDC's base because he knew that the committee as it was structured during the trial lacked the base to effectively raise money. He needed more labor people committed, more people from the Jewish business committee, and broader representation from other minority organizations. Although actor Anthony Quinn had already stepped up, McWilliams sought to broaden the Hollywood membership as well. Years later, McWilliams credited Josefina Fierro de Bright, the wife of screenwriter John Bright, with helping to bring Hollywood people like Orson Welles, Joseph Cotton, and Rita Hayworth into the fold. Not only did these people have access to the public as movie stars, but they also had money. The SLDC made excellent use of house parties among the Hollywood crowd, bringing the stars and others together and pitching the need for funds. Although all of this came about under McWilliams's direction, he would be the first to admit that the workhorse of the SLDC was Alice Greenfield.

True to his word, McWilliams went about broadening the SLDC's base. On 3 April 1943, the CIO's California executive committee passed a resolution endorsing local efforts to support the appeal. In Los Angeles alone, three hundred thousand Mexicans and Mexican Americans went to work every day. Thousands were already CIO members, and many thousands more were eligible for membership. The attack on the Sleepy Lagoon boys represented an attack on union brothers, or potential brothers. On 30 April 1943, CIO local chairman J. L. Marty circulated a release to all state CIO union locals. Endorsed by CIO president Phillip Connelly and the state executive committee, Marty called for every local to set aside a small contribution each month to cover the cost of the appeal. The release, using the theme of national unity, pointed out how Hitler came to power by attacking minorities. This case was similar: the Sleepy Lagoon trial was being used as fodder for radio broadcasts into Latin America attacking democracy, and America's so-called good neighbor policy in particular. The CIO's attorney had reviewed the case and found it unjust, and the executive committee believed the appeal had merit and a good chance of success. With Ben Margolis on board, the appeal had begun in earnest. Marty estimated it would take $20,000 to win.

While the CIO mobilized its membership, Alice Greenfield began an SLDC publication that spanned the next twelve months. The *Appeal News* began as an SLDC vehicle to let the young men in San Quentin know the progress of the appeal efforts being made on their behalf. The first issue came out on 7 April 1943, and Greenfield encouraged the boys to send in their suggestions and to write letters back. No paper, she claimed, could call itself a paper without letters to the editor. Greenfield reported that new groups had joined the effort and that she had received a letter from Brooklyn, New York. The letter contained a small monetary contribution and a note indicating that the writer hoped that "this will do some good." Greenfield told the young men that this meant the word had begun to reach beyond Los Angeles to people across the country who were going to support the fight. At the bottom, Greenfield wrote a short editorial and told the boys that in this fight, they too had an obligation. "YOU CAN, YOU MUST, YOU WILL help us on the outside by what you do on the inside." The effort by the SLDC to bring attention to the boys and the injustice done them brought with it a heavy responsibility. With the country watching, they had to be as strong as the effort to free them, and this meant that

> YOU CAN NOT be satisfied with just getting along. It is the most essential thing in your life to make a DEFINITE EFFORT to have an OUTSTANDING record. Don't gamble minutes against years. AND . . . don't forget . . . what you do reflects on the others . . . you have no control over that. BY WHAT you do every minute of every hour of every day . . . let us be PROUD to show the record when the time comes.

The obligation Greenfield spoke of ran to one another and to the community at large that had undertaken the tremendous task of freeing them. What was not apparent yet, but soon would be, was that they owed her the obligation to do right, to be strong, and to not undermine the effort on the outside. The young men imprisoned in San Quentin became important to her, and she became important to them. To see the relationship develop, one need look no farther than the pages of her newsletter and the letters the young men sent back to her.

One of the ramifications of placing Sleepy Lagoon in a broader context—of seeing it as an important battle in a much larger fight—was that the individuals themselves got lost in the midst of the social crusade. Although the battle to free the young men demanded sacrifice and effort from a great many people across the social spectrum, Alice Greenfield's earnest plea that the boys step up was no small request. Lost in almost every story of a landmark criminal appeal is that the central figure spends the time between trial and appeal in prison. Prison means hard time, and for eleven of the Sleepy Lagoon boys, prison meant San Quentin. And for Henry Leyvas, prison ultimately meant Folsom.

California prisons before 1940 had the reputation as being among the most oppressive systems in the nation. When newly elected California governor Colbert G. Olson took office in 1939, he wasted no time in turning that reputation around. He appointed John Gee Clark, his pint-sized state chairman, as chairman of the Board of Prison Terms and Paroles and later as the director of penology. In turn, Clark brought in Kate Richards O'Hare to be his assistant director of penology. O'Hare, known as "Red Kate," had no formal training in crime, justice, or penology, but she had spent the last twenty years of her life in prison reform. Her extensive experience included fourteen months of incarceration in a federal prison for resisting the draft laws. Working with Clark, Olson's insight and efforts helped revolutionize the California penal system in a few short years.

Within months, Clark filed charges with Governor Olson against the Board of Prison Directors after several food riots at San Quentin. In October 1939, hearings convened within San Quentin's walls, with the governor presiding. Listeners heard guards testify as to the beatings of at least forty-one inmates for refusing to remain silent in the twenty-two-inch circular cells used for solitary confinement, and known within the prison as "Siberia." Many other examples of mistreatment came out, and, as a result of the hearings, significant changes took place. Officials abolished "Siberia," and California newspapers gained access to the prison. Plans were implemented to reorganize the prison system, eliminate overcrowding, and segregate hard cases and incorrigibles into one place. Unfortunately for Henry Leyvas, that one place would be Folsom Prison.

San Quentin benefited from the efforts of its new warden, Clinton Duffy. Hired in September 1940, Duffy had grown up in the shadow of San Quentin as the son of a prison guard. His promotion from assistant warden marked the attainment of a dream job for him. Unlike his predecessors, Duffy saw his job as much more than simply a zookeeper. The recidivism rate among male prisoners when he took over exceeded 80 percent. No one was being rehabilitated; most became more hardened criminals, and some did not survive prison, falling victim to a fellow inmate armed with some kind of homemade weapon. Criminals were thrown in together regardless of their crimes, and no allowance was made for the mentally ill. Duffy described a mentally ill inmate who happened to be a mathematical genius, but his untreated condition had him standing over a urinal, dipping his fingers in the water and slicking back his hair.

Duffy made changes in almost every area. First, he fired Ralph New, the notorious prison guard who oversaw much of the cruelty inflicted on inmates by guards. He also did away with the so-called dungeon, an area equipped with whips and straps almost as medieval as its name. The quality of food greatly improved, and Duffy took a meal with the prisoners three times a week to ensure the quality. Instead of the saltwater pumped from the ocean for showers, Duffy saw that freshwater flowed into San Quentin. Working with O'Hare and Clark, Duffy helped sponsor new prison legislation passed in 1941 that financed educational, recreational, and even some leisure activities. Inmates could now develop basic reading skills and get a high school equivalency diploma. Radio was allowed in the cells via headphones, and, once a week, a prison-based radio show was broadcast to the general public. A prison newspaper, the *San Quentin News*, came out once a week and included a column written by Duffy. Within four months, the paper had a subscription base of readers on the outside. The inmates began various glee clubs, and Duffy encouraged their growth.

By the time Olson left office in 1943, California's state prison system had been transformed, and San Quentin, home of eleven of the Sleepy Lagoon boys, now had the reputation as a model institution. Governor Earl Warren recognized Kate Richards O'Hare's significant contribution to the transformation of California's penal system by inviting her to sit in on the state crime commission meetings. O'Hare became a regular at the meetings until her death in 1948.

Good fortune had all but abandoned the young men from the time they left the Delgadillo house that hot August morning in 1942. But as they settled into their new surroundings, at least prison had become less brutal. The letters coming back to Greenfield from the young men over the next two years served as a testament to some of the changes, but none of them was free, and, unless Alice Greenfield, Carey McWilliams, Ben Margolis, and the growing number of supporters rallying to the cause could get the verdicts overturned, some of the young men stood to be in prison for a very long time. Despite all the changes, prison remained a dangerous place. Even after Duffy's appointment, convicted gaslight killer Caryl Chessman described inmates as having "enough knives hidden among them to stock a cutlery warehouse." What the boys needed more than anything else was hope, and, as important as everything that Greenfield did from the time she began work for the SLDC, perhaps the most crucial was her remarkable ability to sustain the boys' morale.

The relationship between Greenfield and the young men began before they ever went to prison. By the time the trial ended, Greenfield had become a fixture in the courthouse, and the boys knew who she was and the strength of her commitment to their cause. The relationship had apparently developed to the point that Henry Leyvas felt comfortable writing to Greenfield on 13 January 1943, the day after the verdict. He did not hide his disappointment: "Did you ever make a castle out of sand or mud when you were a very small girl in pigtails and took much pain and trouble to erect it, and all of a sudden a bigger kid came over and destroyed it for you? Well my feelings are somewhat similar. It seems like the whole world just folded up on me, and there is nothing I can do about it." Leyvas hoped their friendship would not change and that she would write and come see him. Greenfield had to have known by now the gravity of the task that lay ahead insofar as sustaining any hope of overturning the verdicts.

From April 1943 to March 1944, Greenfield produced at least one issue of the newsletter a month, and sometimes two. The newsletter not only contained the latest information, but it also had a personal quality about it. In her first issue, she asked the boys for letters, and in the next issue, she thanked them for their letters, telling them all, "In answer to a most flattering demand the editor's picture will appear in the next issue of the NEWS." The effort alone seemed to help. Henry Ynostroza wrote from San Quentin on 11 April 1943 and told Greenfield, "I had gave up hope but when I received this letter I said if the people are trying to help well I got to have hope." He also assured her that the boys got the message about being strong: "I know that all of us up hear will try and make a good record." The response to her picture could not have been better: Ysmael "Smiles" Parra told Greenfield, "It was nice of you to send your picture in the Appeal News. You really came out fine." Judging from the newsletter and the letters back from the boys, Greenfield visited the boys as often as possible, and they appreciated her trips.

In the pages of the dozens of letters that they sent back and forth,

Greenfield and the boys shared in the accomplishments of the SLDC and the young men's efforts to make a good record. They volunteered for war industries, played baseball, and boxed. Warden Duffy, San Quentin's progressive warden, embraced their cause and made an effort to help them on the inside. All of this made Greenfield happy, and her letters reflected a sense of pride in their accomplishments and efforts. In turn, she reveled in telling the boys about the fund-raising efforts, the new contacts that came in every day, and the appeal schedule. Granted, there were down times. In January 1944, the appeal was postponed, and the boys' letters reflected their disappointment. Hope sometimes faded, even if briefly, and, reduced to the routine of prison day after day, anger surfaced. Angel Padilla must have succumbed in 1944 while Alice was visiting. His letter in February of that year reflected a heartfelt regret at having hurt someone he cared about:

Dearest Alice,

Writing to answer your letter which I was more than glad to received. Alice I'm really sorry about the way I acted and talk to you when you came up here. It was really all my fault. I'll hope and pray that you will forgive me because Alice you're one of [the] finest person I ever met. Alice I don't know what happen to me that day, I was just mad at somebody and when you came up I just took it out on you. I hope you understand what I'm trying to say, in other word I did'nt mean what I said to you that day. I'm only too glad that you still want my friendship Alice, because I really do care for you alot.

Well chick I think that make everything reet! so until you come up, drive slow Good looking.

With all my love
Angel

Through the ups and downs over almost two years, this young Jewish woman and twelve guys from Long Beach forged a relationship based on friendship and a mutual need. The letters always had a sense of familiarity, and, although the times were different and perhaps expressions carried different meanings than they do today, the letters bordered on intimate. Early on, Greenfield assured them that she printed some of what they wrote so people could know how they were doing, but she told them that she would not print anything they did not want shared. Of course some news was too good not to share, like when some of the boys got transferred to Chino, which was closer to L.A. Chino was designed for younger offenders, and it offered better food, better conditions, and a safe environment. Greenfield even announced that she would send the newsletter to both places. But throughout the highs and lows, nothing was as bad as the day Henry Leyvas got sent to Folsom.

Initially, all twelve boys were at San Quentin. In July 1943, Smiles Parra wrote Greenfield and apologized for not writing: "I'm really sorry about Henry L. Thats the reason I hadn't written, because I didn't want to be the one to tell you. I only hope that he makes good at Folsom, and, so he can straighten out his record." Leyvas's transfer from the confines of the progressive San Quentin to the maximum-security prison about twenty miles outside of Sacramento resulted from his inability to avoid the dangers inherent in prison. He had gotten involved in a knife fight at San Quentin and had come to be considered a difficult prisoner, and problem inmates went to Folsom. As a result, Leyvas's road got immediately harder, and his friends at San Quentin and Greenfield knew it. Greenfield saw him on 8 November 1943 as part of her trip north to San Quentin. She could not be alone with him without a guard present, and that compromised the visit somewhat, but Leyvas seemed glad to see her. He had reached an acceptance of his fate; he told Greenfield that he could not let himself hope for a reversal, then suffer a disappointment like the one he felt when the verdicts came back. Greenfield had spoken to the warden, Clyde Plummer, at Folsom, and, although he was friendly, Plummer told Greenfield that the SLDC was no different than the group that defended "them dynamiters," and he saw no benefit to sending Leyvas back to San Quentin. Greenfield redoubled her efforts for Leyvas. The newsletter did not always get through to him, and she made a recommendation that the letter-writing campaign to Leyvas pick up. She did not think that anyone from the outside had tried to undermine his faith in the SLDC, but she wanted to be sure he knew about all efforts to get him and the others freed.

Greenfield went from Folsom to San Quentin and spent several days there. She met with each young man individually and got a good sense of how they were doing. Not only did their morale seem high, but reports from prison officials reflected genuine surprise at how well they had comported themselves in prison. One official said that he expected those "zoot suiters to be kind of rough," and he was surprised when they turned out to be no trouble at all. All the boys expressed their gratitude at the SLDC's efforts, but, like Leyvas, they felt that too much optimism might lead to a disappointment too difficult to overcome. Greenfield apparently felt the need to be sure no one undermined the SLDC's efforts by alienating the boys. The only weak link she saw was Delia Parra, Smiles Parra's wife. Apparently Delia had contacted a local priest in L.A., Father Arthur, and had convinced him that the SLDC was ineffective. Such comments threatened the boys' morale; also, the SLDC had reached out to numerous religious groups, and having someone on the outside undermining that effort instead of trying to support it only hurt. Greenfield recommended Delia Parra be included in more of the committee activities so she could see the SLDC in action.

Greenfield had become mother, sister, girlfriend, and confidante to the young men. From assuring them that all was being done, to praising their accomplishments, to pressuring them to write letters to members of the public who were making efforts to help them, Greenfield did everything she could. She also stayed in close contact with their families and helped them when possible. Thus, although Delia Parra's comments did not help the cause, too much had passed between Greenfield and the boys by the end of 1943 for any one person to undermine the strength of the relationship and their mutual commitment to see this ordeal through. Although the twelve remained someone's son, brother, boyfriend, or husband, by the end of 1943, they were all "Alice's boys."

CHAPTER 8

The Riots and Beyond

Although Delia Parra's lack of faith hardly dampened the boys' morale or the Sleepy Lagoon Defense Committee (SLDC)'s zeal, what had to be a little disheartening to Alice Greenfield was the degree to which Parra was wrong. Although keeping the boys' hopes up remained an ongoing priority, unless the committee could pay for the appeal, some of them would never leave prison. From the time Carey McWilliams and Greenfield came on board in the spring of 1943, the SLDC had made huge strides. In both its professed aims — raising money and gaining positive publicity — the committee had excelled, even if it had yet to achieve its goals. The early success came despite two major events that threatened to undermine the SLDC's effectiveness. One involved an attack against members of the committee by a congressional oversight body; the other was an explosion in the streets of L.A. that no one really saw coming.

After the April endorsement by the CIO, the committee pressed its labor connections as a source of both income and publicity. On 5 May 1943, Cinco de Mayo, CIO radio DJ Tom Van Dyke interviewed CIO local labor leader Joe Marty on the weekly edition of *Our Daily Bread*. In a well-scripted discussion, Marty hit on every main theme advocated by the SLDC. After describing the factual background of the arrests and trial, he discussed the negative press coverage, the lack of any substantive case on the part of the prosecution, and the fact that the verdict had become a tool of the Axis powers to undermine both cohesion at home and the unity between America and its Latin American allies. After Marty's interview, the efforts to garner support from labor continued to succeed. In response to the CIO broadcast, the SLDC began receiving small but steady donations from local unions throughout the state. While it pushed the labor front, the SLDC turned its attention to developing other ways to get the story out.

Hollywood screenwriter Guy Endore offered his services, and, as spring turned to summer in 1943, Endore diligently worked on a pamphlet designed to publicize the trial and vilify the media that many believed had tried and convicted the boys.

While Endore worked, the SLDC had to overcome two potentially damaging events, one virtually right after the other. The first came in early June, and, although it would have been impossible to ignore the racial tension in Los Angeles at this time, it would also be hard to find anyone that could have predicted the violence that spread into the streets of L.A. Aside from the general level of racial tension that existed, wartime Los Angeles teemed with U.S. servicemen, either stationed there or traveling to or from the Pacific theater. For many of these men, L.A. meant liquor and women — and brawling inevitably followed. The war made some Los Angelenos more tolerant of the behavior, but not everyone demonstrated a willingness to put up with the military invasion of the city. People in some of L.A.'s ethnic neighborhoods proved less tolerant, and Mexican American kids in particular resisted what they perceived as the arrogant attitudes of the predominately white servicemen. Drunken sailors found themselves targets as they stumbled back to base. In turn, they routinely hurled insults at Mexican Americans as they made their way through the neighborhoods. Rumors on both sides began to circulate. The word on the street had U.S. sailors targeting Mexican American girls; stories circulated on base of reprisals against sailors for dating Mexican American women. Sailors complained that Mexican American youths routinely insulted their wives and girlfriends when they passed through ethnic neighborhoods. By the end of May 1943, the situation had reached a boiling point, and, on the night of 30 May, the top blew off.

In his work Eduardo Pagan recounts a story of about a dozen U.S. servicemen strolling downtown, doing what young men routinely do: looking for beautiful women. On the other side of the street, they saw several young Mexican American women, and they changed course to intercept them. Standing in their path was a group of young Mexican American men in zoot suits. As the soldiers and sailors passed through the zoot-suiters, the apprehension must have become overwhelming. Whether his fear was real or imaginary, one of the sailors, Joe Dacy Coleman, thought he was going to be struck and grabbed the arm of one of the boys. Coleman immediately got hit in the back of the head, and the servicemen found themselves outnumbered and under attack. After a fight that lasted only a few minutes, the sailors in the group managed to escape. They carried Coleman back to the naval armory. Word of the attack spread, and, on the evening of 3 June 1943, about fifty sailors left the armory specifically bent on revenge.

The sailors, some armed with homemade clubs and other weapons, made their way through downtown L.A. looking for Mexicans. Unfortunate victims were assaulted, beaten, and stripped of their zoot suits in plain view of onlookers—and often to cheers from the crowds. Rather than satisfy the need for retribution, the events of 3 June drove an even greater set of reprisals on the night of 4 June. Over two hundred servicemen, many of them in rented taxis, cruised up and down Whittier Boulevard, harassing and beating Latinos. Some struck back, and, for the next several days, servicemen continued to prowl east L.A. and Boyle Heights, storming into bars, cafés, and movie houses in search of Mexican Americans and other minorities, whether clad in zoot suits or not. The headlines screamed out "Sailor Task Force Hits L.A. Zooters," "Zoot Suit Chiefs Girding for War on Navy," and "Zooters Plan to Attack More Servicemen." Some of the same papers that covered the Sleepy Lagoon trial now aggravated an already dangerous situation as news of the violence actually brought thousands of servicemen and onlookers downtown. The L.A. police department did little to curb the violence, and, when they did intervene, it was to arrest a local boy. One young man was pulled from a theater by U.S. servicemen, beaten, and then stripped, and when the police arrived, they arrested him, not his assailants.

McWilliams saw a connection between the police inaction and the trial of Compton Dixon, a police officer accused of kicking a jail inmate to death. The ongoing riots distracted the public from the trial and drew attention back to the Mexican youth problem. While national observers, like *Time* magazine and first lady Eleanor Roosevelt, blamed the LAPD, local authorities went back to blaming Mexican Americans. The city council went so far as to make wearing a zoot suit a crime punishable by thirty days in jail. The entire incident embarrassed the governor, Earl Warren, and the press only made matters worse. Aside from what the Mexican American community saw as yet another example of injustice, McWilliams realized the riots could hurt the SLDC's efforts. As the violence escalated, he took advantage of his political connections to try to end the riots and suppress the negative publicity.

First, McWilliams used his own media connections: he actually reported on the disturbances for a national liberal newspaper, the *New Republic* and *PM Magazine*, a magazine based out of New York. Then he led a meeting of several hundred local residents after the second night of rioting in an effort to try and cool down the situation. Right after the meeting, McWilliams contacted his friend, Robert Kenny, the state attorney general, and suggested that Governor Warren appoint a committee to investigate the disturbances in L.A. Kenny did so, and Warren followed the suggestion and appointed a five-member committee, four members of which McWilliams claims to have handpicked. The committee compiled a report — a report McWilliams had already drafted — and with only a few minor changes, they released the report as their official findings and recommendations. The committee called for press restraint, suggested the police take a more evenhanded approach in dealing with such matters, and called for the U.S. navy to make Los Angeles off-limits to its personnel.

The report worked, and the press took a more restrained stance. A general sense of calm prevailed in the streets, and some local officials expressed the belief that the committee formed by Warren was a dispositive factor in ending the riots. On 9 June 1943, Rear Admiral D. W. Bagley declared L.A. off-limits to naval personnel, effectively ending the riots. On the heels of this effort to not only end the rioting but also to effect damage control over public opinion, McWilliams turned his attention to what he believed was the real culprit: the L.A. police department. In a short report for the *Guild Lawyer*, the publication of the L.A. chapter of the National Lawyers Guild, McWilliams called on the U.S. Department of Justice to investigate the L.A. police department. He specifically cited federal civil rights violations involving Mexican American youths detained by the police without preferring any charges. McWilliams contended that the Hearst press jeopardized the war effort with a distorted and biased presentation of the situation. He forwarded his report, along with a telegram to the U.S. attorney general, Francis Biddle, requesting that the matter be given prompt attention.

By moving quickly, McWilliams turned a potentially disastrous public relations event into an opportunity to improve the racial situation in Los Angeles. He used his skills and connections to help end the riots and to present what happened in a way that did not undermine the SLDC's publicity and fund-raising efforts. At the same time, he extracted a measure of restraint from the local press. The riots had a troubling effect on the young men in prison, and their letters to Greenfield reflected a deep sense of disappointment that this kind of thing could really happen in America. Manuel Reyes told Greenfield, "It sure is terrible, what going on in L.A. I never dream that, that thing's like that would happen in the U.S.A., a land of Freedom. I tought it alone happen in Germany and Japan." Manuel knew two of the boys who had been beaten up, including one with a prosthetic leg who was beaten for resisting arrest because the police refused to tell him the charges being made against him. Greenfield managed to help the boys get through it by reporting on the SLDC's progress and keeping them focused on the present and future.

McWilliams had no time to rest on his solid work. Two weeks after the riots ended, he faced yet another crisis that had the potential to undermine the SLDC's efforts. On 22 June 1943, McWilliams appeared before the Fact-finding Committee on Un-American Activities in California. Initially formed in 1941, by the time McWilliams testified, the committee had become the forum for its chair, state senator Jack Tenney, to investigate left-wing organizations. Before 1940, Tenney would have seemed like an unlikely candidate for such a committee. A former songwriter and bandleader, Tenney earned a law degree at night, and, by 1936, he had served in the California assembly as a Democrat. In 1937, he became president of Local 47 of the American Federation of Musicians, and, for the next several years, he supported numerous left-wing causes. He fought for the dissolution of the House Un-American Activities Committee, and he sponsored bills to repeal California's criminal syndicalism act and to prohibit school boards from inquiring into teachers' political, religious, or economic beliefs. But everything changed for Tenney in 1940, when he lost reelection as president of Local 47. He blamed the communists, and his political slant changed completely. He began serving on committees specifically investigating communists, and, in 1941, he became chair of the California Un-American Activities Committee (CUAC).

When McWilliams accepted the role as national chairman for the SLDC, one of his demands was to broaden the organization so that it did not appear to be a tool of the radical left. The CUAC's activities validated his instincts. Tenney had been investigating a number of organizations McWilliams belonged to, including the American Civil Liberties Union, National Lawyers Guild, and the American Committee for the Protection of the Foreign Born. Over time the Tenney committee became far more inquisitorial than investigational, and "unfriendly" witnesses could expect to be harassed and cut off if their testimony did not meet with Tenney's expectations. Spectators in the gallery reacting negatively to Tenney's antics drew sharp criticism, with Tenney openly accusing them of being communists. To make matters worse, by the time McWilliams took the stand, the CUAC had already heard testimony from Rena Vale, a local writer. She claimed to have met McWilliams as a fellow Communist Party member and that "Comrade Carey McWilliams" had provided legal services to the party.

McWilliams denied any membership in the Communist Party, although several friends within his social circle were party members. The questioning initially focused on his affiliations and acquaintances, but the inquiry gave him an opportunity to delve into the environmental reasons behind the recent zoot suit riots and to almost repeat verbatim the points he raised in his recommendations to the U.S. attorney general and in the report he drafted for Governor Warren's committee investigating the riots. The focus then moved into McWilliams's beliefs on a more fundamental level. In response to a suggestion that racial segregation somehow served a legitimate social purpose, McWilliams declared that "segregation of any type is fundamentally at variance with the American Constitutional law." It violated the Fourteenth Amendment, and in McWilliams's words was "productive of a great deal of harm and mischief."

Then Tenney turned to the issue of interracial marriage, a topic McWilliams touched on in his book *Brothers under the Skin.* Tenney wanted to know whether McWilliams favored abolishing miscegenation laws. McWilliams told him point-blank, "Yes." Such laws were the product of racial prejudice, and, more important, they did not work. Tenney struggled to force McWilliams to advocate interracial marriage, but all he could get was a firm response that to prohibit such conduct was wrong. In the words of McWilliams's biographer, the whole discourse "resembled a zoologist being interrogated by apes."

All of this led back to Vale's affidavit and testimony tying McWilliams to the Communist Party. McWilliams denied Vale's accusations, and in fact denied knowing or talking to Vale at all. He characterized himself as a "Liberal New Deal Democrat" and a supporter of all of the reforms of the New Deal administration. In truth, McWilliams was probably a little left of Roosevelt, but he insisted that his social beliefs were consistent with the present administration and by no means communist.

McWilliams acquitted himself well, but his problems with Tenney and the CUAC continued. Tenney's committee report, published in 1945, claimed that McWilliams had a "long record of communist front affiliations." Tenney rejected McWilliams's description of the causes of the zoot suit riots and instead blamed the violence on communists who hid "behind the shield of housing, food, and all that sort of thing in the advocacy of overthrowing the Government by force and violence." For now, however, McWilliams had again demonstrated an ability to turn potential adversity into an advantage. By the time Tenney's report came out, the Sleepy Lagoon case was over and the SLDC had disbanded. McWilliams had used the CUAC hearings as a forum to push the SLDC's message and to publicly respond to Tenney's misinformation campaign. Despite the terrible events, June 1943 had been a good month for the SLDC. It had gone on the offensive and had begun to take control over some of the forces that had been instrumental in influencing the outcome of the Sleepy Lagoon trial — specifically, the way the press reported events and how it perceived minorities in general.

The two July issues of *Appeal News* let the young men know specifically what the SLDC was doing and its progress; the most important news involved the appellate brief. Although Margolis had yet to be paid and had spent money out of his own pocket for expenses, the work on the brief continued unabated, even though it was taking longer than anyone expected. Fund-raising activities postponed by the riots, like Al Jarvis's dance, finally came off. Jarvis was a good example of how much mileage the SLDC got from its supporters. In addition to being a singer and performer, Jarvis was L.A.'s first radio DJ, and he allowed his weekly radio show to become a platform for the SLDC's message. One of his guests would be Guy Endore, and perhaps the SLDC's biggest accomplishment to date was the completion and release of Endore's first pamphlet, *The Sleepy Lagoon Case*. By 9 September 1943, all ten thousand copies of the first printing had been sold, and Endore's second pamphlet, *The Sleepy Lagoon Mystery*, was in the works. One man, Eliseo Hernandez, had sold five hundred copies in one day, most of them to Mexican people whom Hernandez claimed were learning for the first time what was really going on and how the newspapers had been lying to them. Letters from domestic and international groups as well as from individuals poured into the SLDC office applauding the message, pledging monetary support, and promising to spread the word.

Who was Endore, and what exactly did he say that had given the SLDC's message such a boost?

Born Samuel Goldstein on 4 July 1900, Guy S. Endore grew up the son of a coal miner in Pittsburgh, Pennsylvania. Life was difficult for his father, and making ends meet often proved a challenge. When Guy was four years old, his mother committed suicide, perhaps no longer able to handle the strain of her life. His father changed the family name and placed Guy and his siblings in a Methodist orphanage as he struggled to provide for them. As fate would have it, he sold some type of invention, and, with his newly acquired means, he sent Guy and his other four children to Vienna to be educated. They stayed there for five years under the supervision of a Catholic governess. When their father disappeared, the funds for their education dwindled, and the children returned to Pittsburgh. Endore managed to work his way through Columbia University, graduating in 1923 with a B.A. and a master's in 1925. In 1930, he married Henrietta Portugal, moved to Los Angeles, and embarked on a long and prolific career as a novelist and screenwriter.

Endore enjoyed a fair amount of success and actually had a screenplay, *G.I. Joe*, nominated for an Academy Award in 1945. However, for much of his career, he fought the consequences of his political beliefs. An admitted member of the Communist Party, he endured the witch hunts of the 1940s and '50s. Although he was never called before any committee or arrested for his beliefs, he suffered the fate of so many others in Hollywood during the McCarthy era, and he found himself blacklisted. Endore's writing skills and political beliefs made him an ideal candidate to recast the Sleepy Lagoon trial into story form. Perhaps even more important, this would not be the first time Endore had put pen to paper in an effort to undo a legal injustice. He worked with the International Labor Defense (ILD) and the Communist Party in the 1930s to help overturn the convictions of the Scottsboro Boys. His pamphlet *The Crime at Scottsboro* publicized the injustice that took place in Alabama and served as a tool to raise money for the appeal.

Endore wrote two pamphlets, and, although both were designed to advocate the SLDC's position on the trial, they were different. The first, *The Sleepy Lagoon Case*, was a short, straightforward depiction of the trial and the racial aspects that yielded what the SLDC believed was such an unfair result. The thrust of the pamphlet was the degree to which the case had been and was continuing to be used by America's enemies to undermine the war effort. The pamphlet enabled the SLDC to clearly and concisely explain to the public what happened and how the boys had been tried, including the racial context and the media frenzy both before and during the trial. However, the more ingenious work was the sequel that followed several months later, *The Sleepy Lagoon Mystery*. In his second work for the SLDC, Endore took the facts as he knew them and wove them into a tale of intrigue and conspiracy. Rather than simply depicting the Sleepy Lagoon boys as people in the wrong place at the wrong time, which, factually speaking, they were, Endore presented what happened to them before and during the trial as part of a larger plan. The mastermind of the conspiracy: William Randolph Hearst. Endore, claiming to have interviewed an "honest reporter," described the entire campaign against Mexican Americans as orchestrated from high atop San Simeon, Hearst's castle retreat. According to Endore's source, the Mexican crime wave began with a "teletype message from Wintoon." Wintoon was the post office address of San Simeon. The teletype suggested that L.A. editors survey crime reports looking specifically at the numbers of Mexican, Negro, and/or alien bookings. The L.A. editors were supposed to then transmit their findings to all other Hearst editors. The message was signed, "Colonel Willecombe." The reporter knew nothing of Colonel Willecombe's identity, but Joe Willecombe had been Hearst's executive secretary for years.

According to the reporter, the investigation into Mexican American crime turned up nothing spectacular or unusual—findings consistent with studies of immigrant and minority crime from the Wickersham report to the L.A. probation department. However, the teletype message carried an implied directive: investigate Mexican crime and find it, whether it existed or not. After the teletype message, the Mexican crime wave exploded. L.A. editors then went down their "stooge lists," people willing to be quoted by the Hearst press on any subject so long as they got their names in the paper. For Endore, this is where the Sleepy Lagoon Mystery began. After almost eight months of creating a problem that did not exist, Jose Diaz was found dead. The Hearst press then shifted into high gear. From the arrests and indictments to the conclusion of the trial and beyond, the L.A. press stayed with its theme of Mexican American youth crime out of control. As the trial progressed, Endore argued that the media literally dictated its outcome. Granted, there was sufficient blame to go around, and he put a fair amount on Judge Charles Fricke. One of the strengths of Endore's pamphlet was that he used actual excerpts from the trial record; rather than simply state that Fricke acted unfairly or that he treated defense counsel with disdain, Endore quoted the transcript.

The key to the pamphlet lay in its ultimate message. Endore argued that the trial went beyond being unfair; it was the product of a design by people who used their power to not only convict the boys, but indict an entire race. The end result not only imprisoned seventeen innocent boys. It created a tool whereby America's enemies could undermine national unity and destroy the cohesion between the United States and its Latin American allies. The Hearst campaign fostered a fascist fifth column within the United States that continued to use the discord engendered by the media. The result of the trial went beyond injustice and unconstitutionality; it was un-American. But perhaps the most intriguing part of the story lay in the message that what happened to these young men and this ethnic group could happen to anyone. Endore's closing message foreshadowed the words of Martin Neimöller, first published in 1946, but a truism that had come to pass in Germany long before the boys went on trial:

In Germany, they came first for the Communists, And I didn't speak up because I wasn't a Communist; And then they came for the trade unionists, And I didn't speak up because I wasn't a trade unionist; And then they came for the Jews, And I didn't speak up because I wasn't a Jew; And then . . . they came for me. . . . And by that time there was no one left to speak up.

The underlying message of the pamphlet was that the attack on Mexican Americans succeeded only when people stood by and did nothing. To do nothing meant risking that the something might happen to you someday.

Endore's second pamphlet was clearly a propaganda piece designed to go beyond merely informing the public. But what made it effective was that it contained enough verifiable facts in the form of newspaper articles, trial transcripts, and other contemporary documentary evidence so that anyone reading it could not simply dismiss the story as unfounded. The portion that lacked hard evidence still had an air of believability. The "friendly reporter" can only be characterized as a literary creation. There is nothing to substantiate his identity or even his existence. The "reporter" provides the crux of the piece in the allegation that Hearst orchestrated everything that happened to the young men. However, from what is known of Hearst, both then and now, even without direct evidence of a conspiracy, people who wanted to see a conspiracy could believe that Hearst possessed the power to affect the outcome of the trial.

Hearst had a track record of using sensational journalism to achieve a desired result. The Spanish-American War, today acknowledged as the first press-driven war, stands as a testament to the power of yellow journalism. Hearst, then the owner of the *New York Journal*, used spectacular stories to fire up public sentiment against Spain, the same way Endore argued that his papers created the sense of a Mexican crime wave out of control in Los Angeles. When the U.S.S. *Maine* exploded in Havana Harbor, Hearst blamed Spain when in fact there was no evidence whatsoever to support such a claim. Nevertheless, an aroused U.S. public demanded intervention, and the rest, as they say, is history. The death of Jose Diaz and the subsequent indictment of twenty-four Mexican American youths served as confirmation of what Hearst and his newspapers had been preaching. The Sleepy Lagoon case and the negative press campaign of the preceding seven months had a familiar Hearst ring to it.

There is also some support for the proposition that Hearst carried a grudge against the Mexican people in general. There are wild stories that during the Mexican revolution, Hearst lost eight hundred thousand acres of land he owned in Mexico to the man Hearst referred to as the bandit Pancho Villa. Although there is no objective proof of a causal connection between losing land and Hearst's alleged hatred of Mexicans in general, Hearst and other American entrepreneurs had significant investments in Mexico that did not survive the revolution. Hearst's Mexican ranch fell under siege from the revolutionary armies in July 1912 and again in October 1912. Overrun at one point in 1913, Francisco Madero recaptured the spread, only to lose it again in 1913, when he was overthrown by General Victoriano Huerta. Thereafter, not only did Hearst lobby newly elected president Woodrow Wilson to intervene, but, just like with the Spanish American War, he used his newspapers as tools to stir up support for intervention in Mexico. Parker H. Sercombe, a former bank president in Mexico City, privately told William Jennings Bryan, Wilson's secretary of state, that Hearst's property holdings in Mexico, if unaffected by the revolution, could yield profits of up to $10 million. It was not hard to understand why Hearst wanted U.S. intervention in Mexico. Even if his loss of investment property did not fuel an animosity toward Mexicans, Hearst's own words suggest that he saw Mexico and Mexicans as less than equals.

In 1914, Wilson accepted an offer from neutral Latin American countries to arbitrate the United States–Mexico dispute. Hearst accused Wilson of making "the ruling power of this continent . . . the plaything of cunning, unscrupulous Mexicans and their South American sympathizers." Although he thought Mexicans might be "far enough advanced to govern themselves under ordinary conditions," they were "not far enough advanced to give themselves as good a government as the United States could give them." In Hearst's opinion, Mexicans were inferior, and the size of investment by U.S. citizens in Mexico demanded U.S. intervention to protect American property. Paraphrasing William Sherman, Hearst concluded, "War is hell, but anarchy is also hell."

Hearst's losses in Mexico were by no means small, and they came at a time when he stood to make a fortune through his collaboration with American industrialists like Lammot du Pont. Du Pont had developed a method to make paper from wood pulp, and the loss of the forestland alone cost Hearst significantly in what he might have made by combining his forestry assets with du Pont's new methods. Motive aside, perhaps the most compelling argument in support of Endore's conspiracy theory lay in Hearst's own character. His biographer points to a key trait of Hearst's that Endore hoped would make the existence of the "honest reporter" somehow believable. Even as Hearst got older, he remained very much in control. Into his late seventies, every editorial had to be reviewed and edited by Hearst, then set in type only after he approved the final text. Major articles and features also had to be cleared through Hearst. In 1939, he criticized the editor of the *San Francisco Call-Bulletin* for a series of unapproved articles that condemned the invasion of migrant workers from the Midwest. The gist of Hearst's criticism was that the migrants should be welcomed as good Americans who had fallen on hard times: they were better for California than "the Chinese or the Japs or the Filipinos or the Mexicans." The message was clear. These articles did not reflect Hearst's beliefs, and they should have been approved before their release. In April 1943, Hearst celebrated his eightieth birthday. Henry Luce's *Time* magazine reported on Hearst's condition and described him as "no longer nimble, [but] he still stands impressively erect and is remarkably healthy." As for his newspapers and the journalism they practiced, it was "still wide-eyed, red inked, and impulsive."

Whether true or not, Endore's second pamphlet increased both revenues and general publicity. The SLDC sold thirty thousand copies of the first pamphlet and fifty thousand copies of the second. In addition to the small charge for each pamphlet, the message brought other supporters and contributions. Endore's pamphlets did more to broaden the committee's base than anything else because it enabled the SLDC to reach people with no direct tie to the case within Los Angeles and beyond. In September 1943, the Citizens' Committee for the Defense of Mexican American Youth (CCDMAY) formally changed its name to the SLDC, a move that in part reflected one of McWilliams's initial goals of broadening the committee's base. Part of the goal was to make membership synonymous with patriotism and to give the SLDC the appearance of mainstream American support. As the Tenney hearings demonstrated, it was impossible to separate the SLDC's connections from left-wing groups that the government deemed subversive. But the loss of these groups would have severely hampered the committee because it was the ILD and other such organizations that helped get the committee started and had done much of the heavy lifting in the early stages. However, the constant effort to publicize the case and to bring in new members and supporters reflected a reality that everyone recognized: for some people, membership in the SLDC carried risks, and the pitfalls could be severe.

To no one's surprise, some of the families of the young convicted men immediately stepped up to help the CCDMAY. Alice Greenfield described family participation as roughly equal to the responses of the defendants themselves, "all the way from enthusiastic participation and down to rather, maybe suspicious, bare acceptance of our presence and work." Among the families, Henry Leyvas's sister, Lupe, and Margaret Telles, Bobby Telles's mother, stood out in their efforts to help educate the community and raise money. Lupe was a conspicuous presence at home fund-raisers, including those held in Hollywood homes, and helped raise hundreds of dollars at each event. Margaret Telles traveled the state to get the word out. Able to reach both English- and Spanish-speaking audiences, she worked tirelessly on her son's behalf. Leyvas and Telles, and the other family members who contributed time and effort, had a personal stake in the outcome of the appeal, and, at a certain level, the fight had nothing to do with larger issues of injustice and social change. However, those larger issues were very much present, and yet, despite the potential benefit to the Mexican American community as a whole, Mexicans and Mexican Americans did not immediately flock to the aid of the families and the committee.

The Mexican community remembered all too well the forced deportations of the early 1930s. Although the deportations lessened after 1931, agricultural workers endured harassment from immigration officials at all levels for the remainder of the decade. By 1942–1943, the Mexican community was appropriately intimidated by a sustained campaign of harassment. Many people had seen labor leaders and protesters jailed and later deported for speaking out. During the entire time the SLDC operated, the ILD spent significant time and resources fighting deportations. Even Mexicans of some means and importance hesitated to get involved. Even Anthony Quinn resisted his mother's efforts to get involved with helping Henry Leyvas and his friends. Quinn knew the CCDMAY had communist connections, and those connections could not only jeopardize his acting career but also his residency in the United States. He told her flat out, "Mama, I can't become involved in a murder case. Jeez, you've read the papers. Everybody who has come to the defense of the kids is being called a Communist. That's all I need mama, we could be run out of the country." Quinn's fears were legitimate. McWilliams had already been called before the CUAC, and America's struggle against communism and subversive organizations never let up. As McWilliams pointed out later in his life, for people on the left, there was no postwar hiatus between World War II and the cold war. The scrutiny and harassment from the government continued unabated. Quinn finally gave in when his mother pointed out that they might not be in the United States but for the help that the Leyvas family provided on their journey from Mexico.

Aside from the intimidation factor, the Mexican community was for the most part conservative. The Sleepy Lagoon kids were both *pochos*, culturally adulterated Mexicans, and *pachucos*, gangsters. The term *pachuco* had a negative connotation for white Los Angelenos, and, in addition, the Mexican community considered these kids an element that degraded the community as a whole. An unidentified man wrote attorney Manuel Ruiz claiming to be stationed at the Victorville Army Flying School and described Leyvas and the other defendants as "goddamn Mexican punks." Reputation proved crucial in the struggle. Greenfield preached to the boys every month about the need to be exemplary in prison. She became more than a little distraught when Delia Parra not only questioned the effectiveness of the committee, but also shared her doubts with a local priest. The local parish priest within the Mexican community had publicly denounced the SLDC. The church remained an important community institution, and the opinions of its priests carried weight among parishioners. To make matters worse, another important community institution, the Spanish-language daily newspaper *La Opinion*, initially voiced its opposition to the SLDC's work.

The sum of all of these factors made the Mexican community wary of helping the boys and the predominately white SLDC that had stepped to the forefront of the effort. However, the SLDC needed the local Mexican community, and it continued to lobby for local support.

The conference at Belmont in March 1943 helped bring the local community and local churches into the committee. Alice Greenfield also began publishing the *Appeal News* in both English and Spanish, and the committee made a concerted effort to develop relationships with the Spanish-language newspapers. The SLDC hired Maria Lerma and Adelina Olguin, who enabled the SLDC to translate and edit their publications into Spanish, thus more clearly articulating the Sleepy Lagoon case to a purely Spanish-speaking audience.

As the SLDC worked to solidify ties with the local Mexican community, it continued to draw support from a variety of other sources. Labor unions, from longshoremen to the United Auto Workers, mostly CIO affiliates, continued to join and to contribute. Individuals like Anya Goldberg of West Los Angeles enabled the SLDC to reach into the local Jewish community. Goldberg organized fund-raising events within her circle of social contacts. Over the course of nineteen months, her social network enabled Goldberg to make regular contributions to the SLDC, with one donation in excess of $1,000 — no small sum by 1940s standards. As the SLDC moved into the autumn of 1943, its momentum increased, and it got a boost in October 1943 when, after almost six months of work, Ben Margolis filed the appellate brief on behalf of the Sleepy Lagoon defendants.

The brief represented a major victory for the SLDC and the young men. The fund-raising had generated money, but not nearly enough to pay anyone in full for his or her efforts. However, the committee's effort and commitment demonstrated a growing momentum, and that had been enough to keep Ben Margolis and his staff working. The fruits of six months of hard work poring over the six thousand pages of trial transcript had come to fruition. The appellants' brief in *People v. Zammora* was itself over five hundred pages long. Shortly after filing the brief, Margolis spoke at a fund-raising event and described what he had seen. He described over one hundred instances involving evidentiary or procedural matters where Judge Fricke had ruled in favor of the prosecution over a defense objection, and then in an identical situation had ruled against the defense in response to a prosecution objection. He described Fricke's conduct as the worst case of discrimination he had ever seen in the state of California. Margolis's brief built on Shibley's tireless efforts in objecting to the deprivation of counsel and the repeated instances of racial profiling. However, the heart of the brief lay in the complete absence of any proof that connected any defendant to the death of Jose Diaz.

Over the course of preparing the brief, Margolis had met with the boys four or five times. His main purpose in visiting them was to show them that they had a chance. Initially, Margolis sensed a belief on their part that what had happened at trial would happen on appeal. He also felt they distrusted him personally and Anglos in general. They had grown up in the local community and had seen what happened to other people, and they initially thought that Margolis had gotten into the case for his own sake, and for the publicity that came with it. They had grown to like George Shibley and had become accustomed to his style, and it took a little time to warm to Margolis. The one exception was Henry Leyvas: Margolis not only got to know Leyvas fairly well, but he also felt Leyvas was crucial to the fight and in keeping the others emotionally invested.

In 1984, almost forty years after the appeal, Margolis gave an interview. His memory of certain aspects of his life and the Sleepy Lagoon case in particular varied, but he had a very clear recollection of Henry Leyvas. Margolis saw natural leadership qualities in Leyvas. Under different circumstances, he thought Leyvas could have been a leader. Although uneducated, Leyvas was bright, and his correspondence during his time in jail reflected a young man with depth and the ability to express his emotions. But for what Margolis sought to accomplish—the release of the seventeen boys from jail—Leyvas provided a key element that made his young clients stay invested in the fight, even given their skepticism of the system and their slim chances of success. The other boys looked up to Leyvas. Notwithstanding what some of them testified at trial, he was the leader, and with all of them in jail or prison, his leadership manifested in another important way. Leyvas understood at a fundamental level what had happened. He had the greatest sense that he and the others had been discriminated against, and that meant a fight. Leyvas was not backing down from a fight, and he would carry on, no matter where he was—the street, San Quentin, or Folsom. Leyvas's mind-set worked well with Alice Greenfield's efforts, and Margolis believed that, in the end, the combination of all these factors helped sustain his young clients while the appeal made its way through the legal system.

With the brief on file, the SLDC and its supporters could only wait for the oral argument. Originally set for January 1944, it was postponed until May. However, the hiatus between the brief and the oral argument did not signal a slowdown in the efforts of the SLDC to generate publicity and raise money. In October, the SLDC held two fund-raising functions. One was at the home of a Hollywood celebrity. The other was a reception for a writer studying discrimination in America. The first, on 15 October, held at the home of Ira Gershwin, had both Carey McWilliams and Margolis speaking, along with Leyvas's sister, Lupe. Rita Hayworth joined the effort, as did Joseph Cotton, and the event raised about $600. Two days later, Mr. Joseph North spoke at a reception in his honor. North had traveled the United States and spoke on the task of fighting discrimination in America. Alvah Bessie, an author and screenwriter for Warner Bros., also addressed the group. The small effort raised another $250.

By the end of November 1943, the SLDC had raised $1,793.44 toward its goal of $25,000. This modest sum represents about $17,000 in present value. Most of it had come in small increments, spread out across a widening base — exactly what McWilliams had wanted. On 12 December 1943, the SLDC held a huge gala buffet at the Mocambo in Hollywood attended by some three hundred celebrities paying $5 each for a ticket. Anthony Quinn made the keynote address. Other celebrities had joined the fight, including Katherine DeMille, John Garfield, Gene Kelly, Hattie McDaniel, Dooley Wilson, Morris Carnovsky, Lena Horne, Gale Sondergaard, Gloria Stuart, Mary McCall Jr., Harold Nichols, and Roman Bohnen. A week later, Alice Greenfield reported the event had raised between $1,500 and $1,750, matching the SLDC's efforts up to that point. More importantly, a check for $1,450 was now on the way to the legal team that had prepared the brief. The effort had begun to show results, and December had been the culmination of nine months of hard work by people across a wide spectrum of social classes at the local, state, and national levels. As 1944 began, the SLDC looked to build on its efforts. The coming year would determine whether the hard work would bear fruit or merely yield a repeat of the disappointment everyone experienced in January 1943, when the jury convicted the seventeen Sleepy Lagoon defendants.

CHAPTER 9

"With the Haste of the Mob"

The Sleepy Lagoon Defense Committee (SLDC) began 1944 the way it ended 1943: by raising money. After the successful event at the Mocambo, two more events followed in January and February 1944. The first, held at the Philharmonic Auditorium, offered supporters an evening of jazz and featured Buddy Rich, Nat King Cole, and Benny Carter. The second, on 20 February, had a Latin music theme and saw Rita Hayworth speak on behalf of the cause. The Hollywood connection had really begun to pay dividends. From October 1943, when the events held at celebrity houses began, until March 1944, immediately after the third large fund-raiser in as many months, the SLDC raised $19,000—a huge sum for the time. The funds not only bankrolled the legal effort, but also financed intense letter campaigns and advertising. Although the SLDC spent slightly more than it brought in, the goal was not to make a profit but to finance the campaign to free the boys. To that end, Carey McWilliams and the committee had decided that proceeds would not be used for familial support but for the legal effort.

The beginning of the year also marked the start of another effort to get the boys out of prison. The SLDC pushed the boys hard to start applying for parole. Henry Leyvas, Joe "Chepe" Ruiz, and Bobby Telles had been convicted of first-degree murder, but the remainder of the boys stood convicted of lesser charges, and parole presented a real option for them. In the January *Appeal News*, Alice Greenfield implored, "READ THIS CAREFULLY! It is a matter of great importance: Application for parole does not affect in any way the legal appeal. If parole should be granted, the appeal would continue just the same for the purpose of clearing the record." Aside from Henry Leyvas's problems that got him reassigned to Folsom, the boys had done as Greenfield had insisted and built stellar records on the inside. Now she wanted them to use those records to get them out as soon as legally possible.

The SLDC had organized the effort on the outside, and Greenfield told them that they needed to be organized on the inside. Ysmael "Smiles" Parra agreed to serve as the informal chairman for those at San Quentin. They needed what she called a "communications secretary," someone who would be sure they all saw correspondence coming in, ensured that newspaper and magazine articles would be shared, and that outgoing correspondence, particularly letters sent from the young men to SLDC supporters, would be signed by all of them. The boys had become an important asset in their own cause, and Greenfield and the SLDC tried to make sure they realized their full potential.

While Ben Margolis waited to argue the case — a wait extended beyond January by the state's request for an extension of time to file its brief — the SLDC began circulating a petition directed at Robert Kenny, Carey McWilliams's friend and the attorney general of California. Kenny's office now had the appeal, and at least in theory, he could examine the facts of the case and decide for himself whether the verdict had any merit. The petition requested that he take any and all necessary steps within his power to help set aside the verdicts. Kenny did not have the authority to simply dismiss the case or otherwise unilaterally drop the appeal. However, he did have the ability to independently analyze the case and make a recommendation as to how to proceed. McWilliams also knew from the zoot suit riots in June 1943 that Kenny could be a valuable ally; his voice carried influence with Governor Warren, who had the power to pardon the Sleepy Lagoon defendants.

Meanwhile, efforts of a more subtle nature had begun to reap benefits. A central aspect of the Sleepy Lagoon trial had been the media hype before and during the trial. Although the smaller and ethnic presses and labor newspapers and radio had supported the SLDC cause almost from its inception, particularly the Jewish *Eastside Journal* and the African American *California Eagle*, the mainstream press remained at best silent, and, as demonstrated during the June riots, at worst, they went back to repeating the rhetoric of the day, offered in ample doses by city political and law enforcement officials, that Mexican Americans were to blame for all the violence. The tide started to turn in 1944 due in no small part to Alice Greenfield's tireless efforts to turn people to the cause. One of the recommendations of the Trade Union Committee at the March 1943 Belmont conference had been a concerted effort to "change the tone of daily press." The committee suggested that a subcommittee go see the publishers of the mainstream press. Whether "daily press" meant the *Daily News* specifically is not clear from the Belmont minutes, but Greenfield had gone to work on Matt Weinstock, a writer for the *Daily News*. By early 1944, Weinstock began devoting a significant portion of his daily column to the appeal effort, and his slant had become decidedly favorable.

The process by which Weinstock came to support the SLDC's cause is not totally clear, but Alice Greenfield's persistence and contagious energy had to have played a part. But her efforts alone could never have pulled Weinstock or anyone similarly situated into the fold. In the campaign to sway the press, the young men themselves became their greatest ally. They had done as Greenfield insisted back in April 1943 by excelling in prison. When Weinstock and other members of the local media went to investigate the story that Greenfield so zealously advocated, they would have found the kind of support every newspaper person seeks: clear and convincing evidence. To find it, they would have had to look no farther than one of warden Clinton Duffy's progressive creations, San Quentin's own newspaper, the *San Quentin News*.

In a 25 November 1943 article entitled "The Neutral Corner," the prison paper described the Thirty-eighth Street boys the San Quentin community had come to know:

One day, about nine months ago, a dozen downy-cheeked youngsters stepped, as a group of newspaper-tagged Zoot-suiters, through our famous little wicket gate and at once began to make everybody in this neighborhood full of happy amazement.

First, they led off, as sturdy little individuals, to carve out shining names for themselves in local athletics. They boxed, played All-Star baseball, and scintillated in softball and handball; and, just to startle everyone, one of them sang very melodiously. Secondly, by dint of exhibiting the manners and behavior of gentlemen, they struck dead the preconceived notion of their fellow-inmates and the officials that they were twelve no-account, gang-marauding Zoot-Suiters.

But what a far cry this is from all we'd read about them!

The whole nation, at that time, was in the throes of race-riot hysteria and the zoot-suit garbed boy was catching hell for about every sin perpetrated, and twenty-two neighborhood kids, of good families, went to court and twelve of them were dispatched to Warden Duffy's safekeeping.

These kids have clearly shown that they are made of real fibre, that they would respond to kindly, decent treatment. And it would've been an easy thing to have allowed them to go sour, what with the daily press hammering away with lurid accounts of Zoot-suited unworthies and the public wishing dead every man who wore a high-waisted pair of pantalonnos. Certainly it was no fault of these youngsters if all the stores featured the so-called zoot-suit, no more than it was the fault of the kids of yester-year for wearing bell-bottom trousers and barber-pole silk shirts. Although it was their misfortune that the country was agog with race-riots and a scattering of zoot-suited characters involved in escapades when these twelve lads did whatever they did to come to San Quentin.

There is no proof that Weinstock actually read this column, but had he looked, he would have found it easily. The words would not only have forced him or anyone reading it to reevaluate the boys, but also to reconsider the role that the press played in what transpired at trial. Weinstock admitted to a sense of irony that the boys had to go to prison in order to "find democracy."

As one peruses the pages of the *Appeal News*, it is clear that there was a conscious effort on Greenfield's part to get the boys to send pictures. They obviously wanted pictures of her, but part of the reason was that she was attractive, and her image brightened an otherwise dreary cell wall. But Greenfield had a different motive in asking for their pictures. The Sleepy Lagoon trial had been about many things, but one of the most prevalent themes of the case had been image. The media had created the image of a pachuco gangster. The L.A. law enforcement community had done everything in its power to reinforce that image, trumpeting the criminal nature of the boys even over the statistical data of the time that flew directly in the face of such accusations. At trial, Judge Charles Fricke had allowed the boys to sit in front of the jury as live exhibits of the criminals the jury had been told to expect: dirty, unkempt, zoot-suited delinquents. When George Shibley and his colleagues finally challenged what was going on, the prosecution did not even attempt to deny this key aspect of its strategy. The prosecution's case relied on the boys appearing in the costumes and haircuts that characterized pachuco gangs. With them sitting together, looking like the newspapers depicted them, and the prosecution throwing out the word *gang* at every opportunity, it is easy to see how the jury convicted them on image rather than on the evidence. Of all of the documents and records that survived to become part of the Sleepy Lagoon papers, perhaps the most telling are the photos of the twelve boys taken in San Quentin. In those pictures, spread out over nineteen months, is a very different image—one that perhaps the defense team should have done a better job of bringing forth but for whatever reason did not. In the end, the jury saw one side of a complex group of young men and their lives.

When thumbing through the photographs one at a time, what one sees are kids—young, good-looking, clean-cut boys that could be anyone's sons, brothers, boyfriends, or husbands. Almost every photo depicts some of them together. What comes across is not an image of gang members, but of friends, teammates, athletes, and musicians—just regular guys. The shots of the boys as basketball and baseball players could have been of any good team of the day. The pictures of the San Quentin five in boxing trunks and gloves show five strong, wiry young men who looked every bit like true contenders. Bobby Telles could have been doing a gig at any club in the world from looking at the picture of him and his band at the Club Azteca. Forget about all the positive things that people said about them at the time and simply look at who they are: young men in their prime, looking like they could take on the world. There is no question that the judge, prosecution, and media did everything in their power to convict these boys, but when it came to their image and depicting who they really were, part of the blame has to lie at the feet of the defense team that offered nothing to contradict how their clients had been portrayed. Lost in the hundreds of pages of testimony, with counsel for both sides sparring with witnesses on whether the group was a gang or not, is the notion that some of the most powerful evidence available to a trial lawyer is the demonstrative visual evidence of pictures and images. The prosecution had created its own demonstrative evidence with the assistance of Charles Fricke: the zoot-suiters seated in a row behind their counsel. It had the boys looking exactly the way it wanted them to.

In his autobiography, prominent lawyer Melvin Belli wrote:

> Jurors learn through *all* their senses, and if you can tell them and show them, too, let them see and feel and even taste or smell the evidence, then you will reach the jury. A good trial attorney . . . is a good teacher. He doesn't overestimate the jury's knowledge, either. He has to show them.

Belli's fame lay in bringing demonstrative evidence into civil trials, most notably accident claims. However, as he points out, demonstrative evidence had been commonplace in criminal trials long before *People v. Zammora*. In the Sleepy Lagoon trial, the prosecution made generous use of it, from the board allegedly used to strike Diaz to pictures and drawings of the scene. The L.A. newspapers compounded the damage to the young men with a few inopportune photos of some of the defendants in court. It is not until one sees the images of the defendants from prison that, in retrospect, it seems clear that the members of the defense team failed to realize that part of their job lay in telling the jury who their clients really were. Perhaps the jury had already been poisoned beyond any defense lawyer's ability to bring them back and change their perception of the defendants. No one will ever know because the defense made virtually no effort to alter the perception of the boys' image.

With the boys in prison and the SLDC working to free them, the photos Alice Greenfield so persistently demanded went toward showing why the boys should be released. On 1 March 1944, the SLDC filed a formal brief with the Board of Prison Terms and Paroles at San Quentin, asking that the minimum sentences handed down to each boy be applied and that they be released at the earliest date possible. As support, the brief described the pretrial publicity and the injustices that the SLDC believed occurred during the trial; the brief then offered evidence of the boys' sterling record in prison. At the same time, supporters including Orson Welles, Charlotta Bass (editor of the Negro weekly *California Eagle*), and Gabriel Navarro (editor and publisher of *El Pueblo*) wrote letters in support of the young men's parole applications. Welles's short letter pointed out the injustice of the trial and the importance the case held for both the Mexican community and what he referred to as the "film colony" in Hollywood. Letters to the parole board have always been of some importance. How much weight is given them depends on the individual board, which in almost all cases must look to the issue of whether the convicted person deserves parole. That issue is most often resolved by looking at their record inside, which in this case was exemplary. Much of the argument being made was that the boys should never have been in prison. Although that may have been true, once convicted, the issue of guilt or innocence had been decided, and only an appellate court could overturn the conviction. Still, it did not hurt to continue to push innocence.

With the parole effort under way and the oral argument on the appeal set for 15 May, the SLDC continued its publicity and fundraising efforts. As important as Weinstock's conversion was and the added legitimacy he gave to the cause, the reaction of the remainder of the Los Angeles mainstream press only underscored the importance of the SLDC's publicity campaign. The Sleepy Lagoon trial had long ago become yesterday's news. If the case were to remain in the public view, those devoted to the cause would have to keep it there. The difficulty of maintaining support and visibility was nowhere more apparent than in the SLDC's effort to garner the support of California's highest government official, Governor Earl Warren.

In late 1943, the SLDC circulated a petition asking the recipients to sign it and send it to Governor Earl Warren. The petition asked him to exercise his power of clemency and free all seventeen boys currently serving time, whether they were in county jail, San Quentin, or Folsom. The petition followed a familiar pattern of laying out the pretrial hysteria, the inequities that characterized the trial itself, and the larger impact on national unity and international relations. It found its way to his office and then seemed to simply disappear. There is no record of Warren ever doing anything with regard to the SLDC and the young men in San Quentin. Warren's memoirs are completely silent on the issue; there is not one word about the case, the petition, or the outcome. The closest Warren gets to the Sleepy Lagoon matter is his intervention in the zoot suit riots in June 1943, but even that intervention was orchestrated by Kenny and McWilliams. Warren's final word on the matter assured Californians that "there is no reason why the good name of California should ever suffer because of a race riot."

One of Warren's biographers points out that in Warren's first year in office, most people considered him a safe conservative. As such, he was unlikely to come to the aid of the political left. Whether he knew the details of the SLDC or who was behind it is unknown. One would think that as hard as the committee worked to get the word out, it would have been difficult for Warren to not have known about the SLDC and that Carey McWilliams was its national chair. If so, McWilliams's association alone might have dissuaded Warren from getting involved. Lest one forget, Warren campaigned in the Central California Valley and promised that, if elected, his first act would be to fire Carey McWilliams from his position in the California Department of Agriculture. Whether out of spite or possibly to goad Warren into some action under the theory that bad press would be better than none, McWilliams took Warren to task in the 18 October 1943 issue of the *New Republic*. McWilliams described Warren's record on major social and economic issues to date as "almost a perfect blank." As far as McWilliams was concerned, the Hearst–Knowland–Chandler political clique of the Republican Party owned Warren. The "powers that be" had created Warren and then used their newspaper empires to keep him in favor. "The advertising boys have done a good job," McWilliams wrote, "Shirley Temple, with the same newspaper support, could make a fairly popular Governor of California."

Thirty years later, a more sanguine Carey McWilliams called Warren "a most remarkable American politician who grew to greatness." But this was 1943; McWilliams had taken on a major fight, and Warren seemed unlikely to help. In retrospect, the SLDC petitioned Warren because he was the governor and not because it believed he was a friend of the cause. Not only did McWilliams head the SLDC, but the CIO, one of its major supporters and most active voices, routinely used its own newspaper and radio organs to attack the governor. For whatever reason, Warren remained conspicuously absent from the Sleepy Lagoon fight. In a sense, his inactivity was consistent with his past. McWilliams had been correct: Warren had no record on social issues, and his first year in office hardly seemed like an appropriate time to step out of the shadows. Those whose historical perspective comes from the vantage point of the postwar baby boom have a difficult time imagining an Earl Warren who did not push a social agenda. But such was the case in World War II California.

With or without Warren, the fight continued, and, on 15 May 1944, the long-awaited battle of the postverdict period took place. The California Second District court of appeals heard oral arguments in *People v. Zammora.* The three-member panel consisted of presiding justice John M. York, Justice William C. Doran, and Justice Thomas P. White. The three men, all native Californians, had reputations as able, experienced legal scholars. Fifty-eight-year-old William Doran had served as a deputy or chief deputy district attorney for Los Angeles County for thirteen years before becoming a superior court judge in 1923. He served twelve years in that position before ascending to the appellate bench in 1935. John York, the oldest member of the panel, died on the bench in 1949 at the age of seventy-one. Unlike Doran, he left private practice in 1913 to serve as a superior court judge for Los Angeles County. In 1926, he became an associate justice for the Second Appellate District, and, eleven years later, he became presiding judge, where he served until his death. He also became an active member of the Judicial Qualifications Commission and the Judicial Council. Thomas White followed much the same career path as his colleagues. He had been in private practice until 1931, when he became a superior court judge. He moved on six years later to become an associate justice of the Second District court of appeals and assumed the duties of presiding justice when John York died in 1949. He remained an appellate judge until 1959, when Governor Edmund Brown appointed him to the California supreme court, where he served for three years before retiring. In short, the members of this panel had a lot of experience, both at the trial and appellate levels, and they seemed an ideal trio to scrutinize the Sleepy Lagoon trial.

Margolis appeared for the appellants, John Barnes argued on behalf of Los Angeles County, and Eugene Elson spoke for the California attorney general's office. Barnes and Elson went through the motions. Their arguments tracked the jury argument made during the trial in 1942 and reflected either supreme confidence in the outcome or a sense that they were defending a verdict that should never have been rendered. Margolis, on the other hand, had been waiting for over a year for this opportunity. He later recalled being more emotionally worked up about this argument than any case he had ever argued. After poring over the trial transcript, his sense of personal outrage at how these young men had been treated had reached a fever pitch, and this carried over into his argument. Margolis recalled the panel as having read the briefs well, and *Zammora* turned out to be one of the easier cases he ever argued. He remembered one or two what he deemed unfriendly questions, but, for the most part, the panel seemed very receptive. Onlookers recall the panel becoming engrossed in Margolis's argument almost from the time he began to speak.

There is no extant transcript of the oral argument. The bits and pieces that exist come from onlookers who later wrote down what they heard. However, from the written opinion rendered a little over four months later, we can glean something from the oral argument. Margolis attacked the prosecution's case at its heart, arguing a lack of any evidence as to a conspiracy. Without the conspiracy charge, some of the guilty verdicts had to be immediately overturned because they depended completely on the acts of others as part of an agreement to commit murder. Margolis contended that no such agreement ever existed. Without a conspiracy, the evidence simply did not support a finding of murder against any defendant. The remainder of the appeal focused on Judge Charles Fricke. From his improper rulings on evidentiary objections, including his admission of grand jury testimony and police statements, to his biased and disrespectful treatment of defense counsel, Margolis argued that the judge's conduct prejudiced the defense and constituted reversible error.

Perhaps the most important legal argument focused on Fricke's actions that deprived the defendants of effective representation of counsel. In the only instance where the court's opinion references the oral argument, it becomes clear that the panel must have pressed the prosecution about the seating arrangements of the defendants at trial. During the course of these inquiries, the panel established that everyone agreed that the defendants had been seated together in a group apart from their counsel. The prosecution must have also confirmed that the defendants could not confer with their attorney except by getting up and making their way to counsel table, or by having their lawyer come to them. The panel had read the entire trial transcript and fourteen hundred pages of briefs, and yet apparently made a point to confirm this particular aspect of the case. Margolis concluded his argument with a point that had become the SLDC's theme: the trial and the verdicts were the product of racial prejudice. In his summation, he told the panel that this was more than simply an indictment of the seventeen young boys; it was an indictment of the entire Mexican people.

With the oral argument done, the lawyers and the defendants could only wait for the outcome. However, the SLDC did not have the luxury of resting. A loss at the court of appeals level meant a further appeal to the California supreme court. With the verdict in limbo, the SLDC had to prepare for the worst, and that meant that they needed to continue raising money. Support from national and international sources continued to pour in, and, on 9 June 1944, the committee reported some of the best news anyone connected to the case had heard since it began with the arrest and indictment of the twenty-four boys in August 1942. The Board of Prison Terms and Paroles had granted the parole applications made on behalf of the boys by the defense committee through its attorneys, Charles Katz, Leo Gallagher, and Ben Margolis. Not everyone would get out immediately, but starting with Manuel Delgado's release on 18 August, three others would be released in September, three in December, one in January 1945, and one in May 1945. The remaining three serving life sentences—Henry Leyvas, Joe "Chepe" Ruiz, and Bobby Telles—were ineligible to appear before the parole board for seven years.

The parole applications contained a record of the work done by the defense committee, provided evidence of the public interest in the case, and contained quotes from San Quentin officials that the boys were "well-mannered" and "well-behaved," and had made the greatest contribution to San Quentin sports in years. The goal had been to refute the charges made during the trial that they were hoodlums and gangsters. The board undoubtedly had access to much more information than was contained in the application. Nevertheless, a central aspect of their parole decision had to have been the young men's prison records. Since their initial incarceration at San Quentin, some of them had done well enough to get transferred south, to Chino, a facility for minors and considered an "honor" prison. Carey McWilliams did not discount by any means the announcement of the paroles. In a written press release, he told SLDC supporters that a significant victory had been achieved by the action of the parole board, but that the legal action to reverse the case continued — not only to free the three young men who would not benefit by parole action, but to completely exonerate the other nine. "Even though they are out of prison," wrote McWilliams, "they will still suffer the disadvantages of assumption of guilt. They will have lost their citizenship rights, they will be stigmatized for life, with problems of employment, and always suspect. We have the duty to clear their names and restore their rights."

Manuel Delgado walked out of prison on 18 August. He immediately went to the SLDC's offices, where he helped stuff envelopes and talked about his ordeal. What he had to say about the SLDC's reach and the effect of some of its efforts was encouraging. As the work of the SLDC progressed, Manuel described how people's attitudes within the prison improved: "The guards and the supervisors became sympathetic and told us we had gotten a raw deal. They all read the SLEEPY LAGOON MYSTERY by Guy Endore." Manuel was paroled to the teamster's union and began driving a truck within a week of his release. Before he went to prison, he earned only day laborer's wages, even as a machinist's helper. Now he would realize the pay of any other member of the teamsters. In September, three more boys walked free on parole. By now, all of them but Leyvas, Ruiz, and Telles were at Chino. Although parole represented a huge victory for the boys and the SLDC, in a sense, it undermined the goal of freeing everyone. The four who got out first were never as connected to the appeal as they had been when they were still inside. Now free, they had jobs, families, and responsibilities. Although their hearts remained in the fight, they simply had other things to do and places to be. Fortunately for everyone concerned, the struggle continued for only a little while longer. On 4 October 1944, the Second District court of appeals handed down its decision in *People v. Zammora*. For everyone involved in the effort to free the boys, it had been worth the wait.

In a one-hundred-twenty-one-page opinion, the court of appeals reversed every conviction and remanded the entire case back to superior court for retrial. The sense Ben Margolis had during oral argument proved accurate. In an opinion as meticulous as it was definitive, Justice Thomas White, writing for the court, completely dismantled the prosecution's case starting with its lynchpin, the conspiracy claim. After six thousand pages of trial transcript and fourteen hundred pages of briefs, the court simply could not find any evidence that when Leyvas and the rest of the Thirty-eighth Street kids had embarked for the Sleepy Lagoon early in the morning of 2 August 1942, they "had murder in their hearts." More important, the agreement, if any existed, was to return to the Sleepy Lagoon and confront the gang that had beaten up Leyvas and several others a few hours earlier. When everyone arrived at Sleepy Lagoon and there was no one there, any agreement that ever existed to do anything ended. The subsequent journey to the Delgadillo house and the fight that ensued lacked any semblance of a collective intent to commit murder. As several of the defense counsel had tried to tell Judge Fricke during the hearing on the motions for new trial, when the jury found some guilty and others not, that alone served as a rejection of the prosecution's conspiracy theory.

Without a valid conspiracy case, the verdicts against each of the boys convicted of murder rested on showing that one or any of them had attacked Jose Diaz. The court pointed out what had been apparent throughout the trial: no one could even put Jose Diaz at the Delgadillo house when the defendants arrived that morning. One by one, the court examined each piece of evidence presented for each of the seventeen boys convicted, beginning with Henry Leyvas, the alleged ringleader. There was no evidence to connect Leyvas with assaulting anyone that night. The fact that someone had seen him with a knife or a club proved meaningless without some direct testimony that he had used either against any particular person. More important, the court gave much more credence to Leyvas's testimony of police abuse than Fricke had seen fit to do. The only possible incriminating evidence against Leyvas was that he lied about even being at the Delgadillo home that night. The court picked up on the fact that in its effort to refute all of the testimony, the defendants had been abused, and the prosecution had failed to provide a witness to deny that the police had beaten Leyvas. Under the circumstances, Leyvas's false denial could not be used to impute guilt.

The court addressed each defendant and separated real proof of guilt from the prosecution's efforts to establish guilt by showing that one of the defendants had a knife or carried a club. The court's most lengthy analysis came with regard to Ysmael Parra. Eleanor Delgadillo Coronado testified that Parra had pushed her and that he had knifed Joe Manfredi. However, after painstakingly going through the testimony, it became clear that Manfredi's testimony as to when he got stabbed conflicted with Delgadillo Coronado's testimony, and that her grand jury testimony was in conflict with her trial testimony. At trial, she claimed that Parra stabbed Manfredi. At the grand jury proceeding, she was just as sure that Henry Leyvas had stabbed Manfredi. The court characterized her testimony as "unsatisfactory and as well unconvincing." The court then pointed out that as to the remainder of the boys, the testimony had been sufficient to establish only that they were at the Delgadillo home that night, but nothing had been offered to tie them to any assault or murder. In his opinion, Justice White conceded that sufficient evidence existed to show that Diaz died from nonaccidental means, but nothing directly connected any of the defendants to Diaz's death or to any of the assaults.

Having resolved the issue of the insufficiency of the evidence, the court then moved to the allegations made by Margolis that Fricke favored the prosecution in his evidentiary and procedural rulings. The court concluded that over the course of the thirteen-week trial, they could not find clear proof that Fricke's rulings insofar as admitting evidence demonstrated the presence of an attitude by the judge that had prejudiced the defendants' rights to a fair trial. However, as to Fricke's attitude toward defense counsel in general, the court was not so forgiving. After reciting numerous examples in the record of Fricke's harsh and demeaning treatment of defense counsel, the court concluded, "We are satisfied that the Trial Judge injured materially the defense of the appellants by the character of rebukes he administered in the presence of the jury, when, in most instances, not even a mild rebuke was deserved." Margolis had pointed out the improper conduct to the court in his brief, but it was George Shibley who had weathered the storm and taken the lion's share of the abuse. Justice White made reference to one instance where Shibley had been held up to the jury as one who, in trying to defend his client, would resort to unethical and even "iniquitous" practices. The court conceded that a trial judge has the authority to direct the trial and control his own courtroom. However, that authority did not allow him to disparage either party. The harm in doing so lay in the effect such conduct has on the jury. Twelve laypeople cannot help but react to the guidance provided by the most powerful figure in the courtroom, the judge. By attacking Shibley and his co-counsel as he had, Fricke sent a message to the jury as to what their verdict should be, and that was simply unacceptable conduct.

Even when Fricke did not attack defense counsel, his habit of commenting on the evidence drew a rebuke from the court. By commenting on evidence or rendering his own opinion as to the nature of testimony, the judge provided an opportunity for the jurors to evaluate what he thought, as opposed to relying on their own impressions. As the American Bar Association canons stated, impartiality is crucial for a judge, and Fricke's repeated instances of commentary and open efforts to try and summarize defense evidence when he grew impatient with their attempts to make a point served to prejudice the jury against the defendants.

Although the court found no evidence of a pattern of evidentiary rulings that prejudiced Leyvas and his codefendants, it did find specific instances where Fricke allowed statements into evidence that should not have been admitted. One example came with Fricke's willingness to allow statements made by one codefendant into evidence under the theory that it was somehow an admission by that witness against his own interest, when in reality it also served to prejudice codefendants who had not made the statement. The court properly concluded that given the number of defendants and the length of the trial, there was little hope that the jurors could exclude in their own minds what part of the statements were proper and what were not. The most glaring example provided by White in his opinion related to Henry Leyvas. Joe Carpio, who was actually acquitted, had made the statement to his brother on 3 August that "we had a mean battle, and I think somebody got killed." But then Fricke allowed the rest of his statement into evidence: "he [Leyvas] uses a knife . . . when he fights with the boys. . . . Yes he has been in lots of gang fights." Although the court did not say so, with no evidence pointing to anyone's direct guilt, a jury already poisoned by negative media coverage and under community pressure to convict could only take such statements as some proof that Leyvas had acted consistently with his alleged habits that night at the Delgadillo house.

The court had already indicated that evidence of police abuse had tainted some of the testimony made by Henry Leyvas and others at the grand jury proceedings. However, Justice White directly addressed the defense's allegations that the boys' statements made to the police and transcribed were inadmissible because they had been unlawfully confined and had not been apprised of their legal rights, including their right to counsel. As important as this opinion would be for other matters, specifically the right to counsel at trial, White's analysis of the admissibility of the statements taken under custodial interrogation reveals how far America remained from a world dictated by *Miranda* and the difference in the outcome of certain issues as a result.

Citing two California cases, *People v. Rogers* and *People v. Gonzalez*, the court conceded that a statement made while in custody may be inadmissible, but custody alone does not render such a statement either involuntary or inadmissible. A *Miranda* analysis would ask, was the defendant in custody such that he was not free to leave, and, if so, was he apprised of his rights, including the right to counsel? If not, any confession is out—but that was not the law or the analysis in 1942.

First, the California penal code, §849 and §825, specifically addressed the proper procedure for bringing an arrested person before a magistrate and stated that two days between arrest and arraignment constituted "unnecessary delay." As the court broke down the period of time between arrest and arraignment for the defendants, it found that all of the boys were held too long under the penal code provisions relating to arrest and arraignment. However, the unnecessary delay alone did not render the statements involuntary. Margolis had cited several United States Supreme Court cases to support his argument that excessive periods in custody tainted the statements. Justice White addressed two of them, *McNabb v. United States* and *Anderson v. United States*. Both *McNabb* and *Anderson* involved federal statutes requiring U.S. marshals and FBI agents to immediately take defendants before the most accessible U.S. commissioner or nearest judicial officer for commitment. Any statement made while in custody under circumstances where the officer failed to comply with the statute was inadmissible. However, White distinguished both *McNabb* and *Anderson* by pointing to the United States Supreme Court's most recent decision in *United States v. Mitchell*. Handed down on 24 April 1944, six months after Margolis filed his brief, *Mitchell* involved a case where the defendant admitted guilt almost immediately after he was arrested. It took eight days to get him arraigned, but there was no showing that the confession had been coerced by violence or any other means. The majority opinion conceded that the detention had been illegal under the statute, but that illegality had no bearing on his confession, and, because the confession was clearly relevant, it could be excluded only under some other evidentiary theory. White then cited old California law, *People v. Divine*, an 1873 court of appeals case to the effect that throwing out a confession that was not otherwise tainted simply because of a delay in taking a prisoner before a magistrate finds "no countenance either in principle or authority." On the basis of his analysis of the case law, White permitted the admission of police statements not otherwise tainted by force or duress so long as they were used against the defendant who made the statement. He did not cite *Chambers v. Florida* even for the propositions that lengthy custodial interrogation alone, absent violence, still tainted a confession.

In the end, it did not matter because none of the statements had risen to the level of admissions, and, even with the statements in evidence, the court found insufficient evidence to convict any defendant. However, White's analysis of the issue provides insight into just how profound a decision *Miranda* would be, and just how far removed America was from that view of the police in 1942. But having allowed the statements into evidence, White then found fault with Fricke's refusal to allow the defendants to testify as to the facts and circumstances surrounding the statements, specifically the police conduct in eliciting the statements. Consistent with the spirit of *Mitchell*, while a custodial confession was not inadmissible simply because the period of custody exceeded the legal limits, even the Court in *Mitchell* allowed for the exclusion on some other evidentiary ground. White concluded that the jury should have been allowed to hear testimony as to how the statements were secured and to judge for themselves how much weight to give them.

Near the opinion's conclusion, the court surmised that some issues raised by the appellants had become moot. However, as if it had saved its most enduring issue for last, the court then took up the issue of right to effective counsel. After reciting the oral argument in May and the fact that everyone had agreed to the defendants' seating arrangements, the court then repeated verbatim within the opinion the exchange between Shibley and Fricke that occurred on 12 November 1942 outside the presence of the jury. Fricke took it upon himself to readmonish defense counsel about trying to speak to the defendants during recesses. Shibley took the opportunity to openly challenge the entire arrangement whereby he and the other defense counsel could not converse with their clients during the proceedings. During the trial, Fricke had listened to the objections of Shibley and others, then simply concluded, "The Motion will be denied upon the ground there are twenty-two defendants and five counsel, that the courtroom is not big enough to permit any such arrangement, nor are there any facilities here." Fricke's solution to the seating situation did not pass muster with the court. Although the trial court may have seemed oblivious to the larger issues, Justice White and his colleagues understood full well what had happened, and, in no uncertain terms, they explained to Fricke and any other trial judge in California the gravity of the issues at stake.

The right to be represented by counsel at all stages of trial proceedings was not within a trial court's discretion. It was both a federal and state constitutional guarantee. The ability to freely and instantly confer with one's attorney is more important during trial than perhaps any other stage: "A defendant in a criminal case is not required to leave his defense in the hands of his counsel, because the Constitution guarantees him the right to 'appear and defend in person with counsel.'" The federal Constitution was clear, and the state constitution explicitly said a defendant has the right to appear with counsel. The panel was emphatic that denying a defendant the ability to converse freely with his attorney at trial deprived a defendant of both life and liberty interest under the Fourteenth Amendment to the United States Constitution. The right to counsel means the unhindered and unobstructed ability to consult freely and as often as necessary. In order to be able to do so, a defendant must be able to sit with his attorney. It is the trial court's duty to provide adequate quarters and facilities. The fact that the facilities were limited was a direct result of Fricke's failure to make proper arrangements. In language that wove *Zammora* into the evolving fabric of a defendant's right to counsel, the court left no doubt where it stood:

> Under such circumstances, it is not the Constitution or the rights guaranteed by it that must yield. That a joint trial of numerous defendants speeds the wheels of justice and provides not only an expeditious but a less burdensome method for disposing of criminal cases furnishes no valid argument for depriving a defendant charged with a crime of his right to the effective and substantial aid of counsel at all stages of the proceeding. To do that, as was said in *Powell v. Alabama* . . . "is not to proceed promptly in the calm spirit of regulated justice but to go forward with the haste of the mob."

The court acknowledged the state's effort to defend Fricke's actions by distinguishing the single piece of authority cited in its brief in support of the seating arrangement, *United States v. Gilbert*. The fact that the only authority the state could find dated back to 1834 foreshadowed the strength of their position. The opinion written by Justice Joseph Storey had sustained a conviction despite allegations that the defendant had been unable to sit with his counsel. Justice White was quick to point out that in *Gilbert*, the court had allowed the defendant and his counsel virtually unfettered access to one another during trial, living up to its promise that "every delay of time for this purpose will be cheerfully given." No such freedom of exchange and consultation existed in Fricke's courtroom. The panel concluded, "To hold under the circumstances here present that the defendants were accorded their constitutional right to 'appear and defend in person with counsel' would simply be to ignore actualities."

The court declined to consider any further grounds raised by the defendants because there was simply no need. The court understood the gravity of the offenses and the need to protect society, but it felt that it was of equal or greater importance that guaranty of a fair trial be assured. In a final word, the court chose to address the assertion that the prosecution of the defendants had been racially based. The panel found the claim to be "without foundation." True, the defendants were Mexican, but so were the victims. To many people, it seemed as if the court missed the entire context in which the case played out. However, what people often forget is that the appeals court did not look at the media coverage or any of the pretrial hoopla because it was not part of the six-thousand-page trial record they reviewed. From the face of the record alone, there is no apparent effort to prosecute the defendants on the basis of race. To see the racial overtones, one had to look beyond the record. All that mattered now was that after almost two years, the law could be heard clearly again.

CHAPTER 10

Whither *Zammora*

Judge Clement Nye's Los Angeles superior courtroom stood filled to capacity on the morning of 23 October 1944 as the final act of a two-year ordeal prepared to play out. The appeals court's decision overturned every conviction and reversed the denial of every motion for new trial. However, the decision alone did not end the case; it merely sent the entire matter back to Los Angeles superior court for a possible retrial. Whether the case would continue or not depended on the Los Angeles district attorney. Shortly after Judge Nye took the bench that morning, Deputy District Attorney John Barnes stood and addressed the court. In a short motion, he formally laid the case to rest. With both George Shibley and Ben Margolis in attendance, Barnes did just as he had with the two defendants whose case had been severed from the main case. Barnes asked Judge Nye to dismiss the case on the basis of lack of evidence. Barnes tried to name each of the seventeen defendants but could not. Shibley and Margolis struggled to help him. Alice Greenfield sat in the crowd, screaming inside, "I can remember. I betcha I could do it alphabetically—backwards even!" Finally Nye handed Barnes a complete list, he read the names into the record, and, without any delay, and certainly absent the fanfare that had dominated the case when it began, Judge Nye dismissed *People v. Zammora* as to all counts and all defendants. The battle to free the boys was over.

The courtroom exploded in a spontaneous release of emotion as reporters, friends, family, and other spectators, no longer able to contain their excitement, reacted to the ruling. Judge Nye, although destined to be a mere footnote in the overall ordeal, nevertheless must have sensed its importance. In a fitting epitaph for the case that died in his courtroom, he said as he brought order to his court, "And you people in the audience whose sons these boys are not. You who struggle and struggle. For Mooney and Scottsboro, Sacco and Vanzetti. Who spend bitter years in the struggle and not too often reap the happiness of this particular moment. Please don't make a demonstration. It offends the dignity of the court."

The crowd quickly moved out of the courtroom and into the halls to wait for the release of the last four young men. Four were already out on parole, and the rest had been released from county jail. Now an anxious crowd that included Henry Leyvas's mother and sister and Bobby Telles's mother, Margaret, stood and waited for them to appear. Leyvas had been moved from Folsom back to San Quentin after the 4 October court of appeals verdict. Then the four still in prison were moved to the Los Angeles Hall of Justice for final release. The delay seemed to last forever. Margolis went to be sure the judge's order had made it to the jail for the boys' release. He had tears in his eyes, and the crowd applauded as he moved toward the elevator. Greenfield and George Shibley went upstairs to assure the boys that they would be out soon. The deputy sheriff allowed them to see only one at a time, and Greenfield chose Leyvas. Standing across from him, she saw how tired and thin he looked. She leaned over and said:

"Baby, it's all over. You'll be out of here in a few minutes."

"When do we go to court?" he asked.

"You don't have to go to court. We already had court. The case is dismissed."

"I'm free? I'm free?" Alice leaned over and kissed him and the sergeant was right there, "Here, here — We can't have any of that. Sit down and stay on your side of the table. We can't have any of this."

Greenfield and George went back downstairs. Moments after they returned to the waiting crowd, the elevator door opened, and Henry Leyvas, Bobby Telles, Gus Zamora, and Joe "Chepe" Ruiz stepped through the open door and into freedom. The celebration continued for over an hour, and then the crowd broke up. Leyvas, Ruiz, and Telles made their way to the Sleepy Lagoon Defense Committee (SLDC) offices, where they saw firsthand where so much hard work had taken place to secure their release. It seemed as if all they could say while in prison was, "If we ever get out of here, we will never be able to pay back what the people are doing for us. We wish we could thank every single person." Of course that wasn't possible, but just being at the SLDC offices let them thank a few. Amid the celebration, Alice Greenfield could not help but keep working. She took a call to the office from the CIO radio station in Los Angeles that brought a request for the boys to appear on the evening broadcast, and they were only too happy to comply.

That evening, Henry Leyvas, Bobby Telles, and Joe Ruiz appeared on *The Daily Bread*, and the elation felt by everyone was impossible to contain. While the boys still basked in the feeling of newfound freedom, the DJ and interviewer, Vern Partlow, could not help but exude a sense of pride in his own efforts and those of the CIO. The CIO had stepped to the forefront early on and remained a staunch supporter of the SLDC for the duration of the fight. Partlow explained to his listeners how labor had seen the fight for what it really was: a fight for "equal treatment before the law of our minority group . . . the preservation of our democratic practices, civil rights — the issue of the good neighbor policy." Partlow tried to describe the jubilation that morning at the Hall of Justice but could not, and, out of ways to explain the joy, he turned to his guests and let them tell their own story:

"Henry, you've been free for exactly six and one-half hours, how does it feel?"

"Like being born again, everything looks so wonderful to me. I have to keep telling myself it's true," Henry answered. Bobby and Jose both agreed. Partlow had always hoped to have them on the program, but he never believed he would have them on their first day of freedom, and he had to ask the obvious question, "What do you guys plan to do next?"

"We plan to get jobs and work right now. But I guess it won't be long before we go in the service. That's OK with me. I figure there's something to fight for now," said Bobby.

"They can make mine the Army uniform," answered Joe Ruiz.

"The merchant marine appeals to me," said Henry. "My brother is in the army and he's in the Hawaiian Islands. Maybe I could deliver some of the goods to him." Partlow pointed out that not only were they free, but all their rights of citizenship had been restored. Henry agreed; his only complaint was that he could not register to vote in San Quentin so he could not vote for FDR in November. With the program winding down Booby [*sic*] Telles spoke up.

"Before we go, Mr. Partlow, I want to tell you that we speak for all of us, not just the three of us here, when I say that we are grateful to everybody who helped us. We will never forget it for the rest of our lives." Partlow assured them they were welcomed, "Well, boys, I'm sure our audience knows how you feel. But they ask no thanks. Winning the Sleepy Lagoon Case was just a step in the fight to end discrimination not only in our courts but in every aspect of American Life. We need your energy and your enthusiasm. That will be your ways of expressing your thanks."

"We're with you," said Henry.

"You can count on us," added Jose.

As Partlow signed off, a long and rewarding day drew to an end. But many unanswered questions remained. The boys had their whole lives ahead of them, and, for people like Ben Margolis, Carey McWilliams, and Alice Greenfield, life would also go on. What would everyone do with this new opportunity?

For the immediate future, those who worked so hard took a little time to enjoy the moment. It has been said: victory has many fathers . . . defeat is a bastard child. In effect, everyone wants to be part of a win, just as no one wants to own up to a loss. Many individuals and groups could claim some aspect of fatherhood for the Sleepy Lagoon triumph. For starters, the families of the defendants had done their part, particularly Lupe Leyvas and Margaret Telles. Despite its initial hesitance, the local Mexican American community had stepped up. Lost amid much of the state and national efforts were the local dances, assemblies, and fund-raising efforts. Local leaders like attorney Manuel Ruiz had worked tirelessly to bring the various racial groups within Los Angeles together and had publicly criticized the L.A. police for their role in the riots in 1943. Bert Carona and Josefina Fierro de Bright, the wife of screenwriter John Bright, both were there in the early days of the Citizens' Committee for the Defense of Mexican American Youth (CCDMAY). Josefina Fierro de Bright worked tirelessly thereafter, using her Hollywood connections to draw publicity to the cause and help raise money. But although the local Mexican American community stepped up and did its part, it was not the driving force behind the efforts to free the young men once they were convicted.

Labor could certainly claim a large share of the prize. The CIO brought the full force of its membership and resources to bear on the fight. The International Labor Defense (ILD) and its connections helped bring the two lawyers crucial to the ultimate outcome into the fray: George Shibley and Ben Margolis. Whether she actually started the CCDMAY or not, LaRue McCormick's personal connections and her energy gave the boys a fighting chance in the early weeks of the trial when she convinced Shibley to come on board. Hollywood also made its presence felt. Orson Welles, Anthony Quinn, Joseph Cotton, and Rita Hayworth were just a few of the stars who lent their celebrity to the cause. Guy Endore played a huge part in the success. His pamphlets galvanized the movement and gave the cause a story that everyone could understand. Shortly after the case was dismissed, Endore wrote a short letter entitled "Victory for Democracy." He had clearly come to take it personally, and his vindictiveness found a target in Charles Fricke. Endore pointed out each place where Fricke had failed. But perhaps the best part of the short piece was that it reflected the breadth of the effort:

But the case soon swelled into the broadest kind of democratic movement. Unions, large and small collected dimes and dollars in their shops, Motion picture people contributed their talents and their money. Los Angeles businessmen sent in their checks. The newsboys at one of their union meetings voted to push the sales of the SLEEPY LAGOON MYSTERY. Lawyers gave generously of their time and their experience. Good wives baked cakes and made sandwiches for pay-parties to help the boys. Girls gave up their afternoons to address envelopes. From all over the country came letters of inquiry and approval. Wires of encouragement came from high officials in Latin America, and in particular from ex-President Lazaro Cardenas of Mexico.

All these people rejoice now in a victory for American democracy and for American love of justice.

However, what all of these diverse groups and individuals had in common was that they came together behind the efforts of the SLDC, and the driving force behind the SLDC was Greenfield and McWilliams. The SLDC remained alive for a short time after the boys were released. Announcements of the appellate decision in both English and Spanish flowed across the country and beyond its borders. But with little left to do, on 29 December 1944, Carey McWilliams issued a short letter announcing the end of the SLDC. It had accomplished its goal, and an audit had been performed of all of its receipts and disbursements. Not only were the boys now free, but also the SLDC's efforts had had a positive effect on relations with Mexico and Latin America, a point McWilliams spoke of with pride. He hoped that the end of the SLDC would not be the end of the struggle to fully integrate Mexican and Mexican American people into American society. He thanked the thousands of people who contributed to the fight in some form or another, and, with this short note, one of the most successful volunteer efforts in American history came to an end.

In retrospect, it is difficult to call the SLDC's efforts anything but a complete victory. One source of debate in the Chicana/o historical community is the importance of the SLDC in the struggle to free the boys. The tendency is to try and downplay its importance or to overstate the role of the local Mexican American community in its success. One historian has commented that although it was a major victory, "it was a limited victory in retrospect." Irreparable damage had been done to the boys and their families. Fricke remained on the bench, and the L.A. police continued to harass East Los Angeles communities. Although all of this is true, it is also irrelevant in judging what the SLDC had accomplished. In this respect, Judge Nye's comment bears closer examination because success for the SLDC was far from a foregone conclusion. On the basis of similar efforts in the 1920s and 1930s, it could have easily failed.

Three sensational trials between 1916 and 1932 generated organized efforts to overturn the verdicts rendered in those courts. When Alice Greenfield visited Henry Leyvas at Folsom, the warden had expressed a belief that the Sleepy Lagoon boys were no different than "them dynamiters." The warden referred to a bombing at San Francisco's Preparedness Day Parade on 22 March 1916. Ten people died and forty were injured in the explosion, which occurred during the height of anarchist activity in America. Labor leader and socialist Tom Mooney and a nineteen-year-old associate, Warren K. Billings, found themselves convicted of murder on the basis of perjured testimony. Mooney's sentence of death by hanging sparked a worldwide movement to free him spearheaded by his wife, Rena. Mooney's defense committee included supporters from across the globe and counted members from labor and government as well as Hollywood celebrities. In 1918, on his own initiative, President Woodrow Wilson contacted California governor William Stephens to request the sentences be reduced. Stephens commuted the sentences to life, but despite all of this support and the apparent lack of any evidence to convict, the effort to free Mooney and Billings took twenty-three years. Mooney was finally pardoned in 1939, and he died three years later. Billings lived until 1972, but, by the time of his release in 1939, he had spent his most productive years in jail.

While Billings and Mooney languished in prison, the volunteer effort that developed to free Nicola Sacco and Bartolomeo Vanzetti fared even worse. Convicted and sentenced to death in 1921 for murdering two employees at a shoe factory in Braintree, Massachusetts, the verdict sparked a nationwide effort to free the two men. Like both the Mooney and Sleepy Lagoon cases, contemporary observers expressed shock at the weakness of the evidence used to convict the two men. After almost seven years, numerous appeals, and stays of execution, both men eventually went to their deaths. Although today historians argue that Vanzetti may have been innocent and that Sacco was probably guilty, the fact remains that both men were convicted on very thin evidence. Yet despite a strong popular effort that brought both money and competent attorneys to the fight, they could not escape execution.

Legal historians look to *Powell v. Alabama* as the genesis of the U.S. Supreme Court's efforts to define the Sixth Amendment right to counsel. However, beneath that decision is a tragic story. After the Supreme Court ruled in 1932, the boys spent another four years in jail. Despite the efforts of the Scottsboro Defense Committee, none of the Scottsboro defendants saw freedom after the reversal of their convictions. The state of Alabama chose to retry them, and, in 1936, after numerous retrials, the ILD and its defense team managed to get four of the boys released. However, the remaining five ended up serving long sentences in Alabama prisons; the last of them did not get released until 1950. Those who did time lost not only years while in prison, but their rights of citizenship. The lesson in the Mooney, Sacco and Vanzetti, and Scottsboro cases is that just making the effort to help is not always enough; winning matters. The SLDC had not changed society overnight, but it had given seventeen boys a second chance, and, for three of them, that meant not serving life sentences. Their releases were unconditional, and, although it was not possible to make up for the time they lost, the defendants left jail and prison with their rights of citizenship intact.

In less than two years, the SLDC raised almost $30,000 – a huge sum for the time. The organization's very existence had made the fight possible. Through McWilliams's leadership and Greenfield's ability to translate what he wanted into action, the SLDC had bridged racial, political, and cultural divides, and, even if that unity did not endure, the SLDC is not to blame. The challenge is to defeat evil and injustice where one finds it and to win the war one small battle at a time. What those who helped and those who were saved chose to do with that experience and with the second chance they received was up to them. Still, even as crucial as the SLDC's role had been, the search for the father of the Sleepy Lagoon victory ends in the same place as so many other great legal cases in history: with the men who fought the fight. All the pamphlets, letters, rallies, events, and donations would have been meaningless had not two lawyers refused to be denied.

Ben Margolis's name will forever be associated with the court victory. With only a hope of payment – payment that eventually left him short about $5,000 out of his own pocket – he stepped up and agreed to pursue the appeal. Anyone who has ever waded through thousands of pages of trial transcript knows the enormity of the task that lay before him. His brief to the court was unbelievably detailed, and, by every eyewitness account, his oral argument was brilliant. The result was a complete victory, and the photograph taken of him, the young men, and Greenfield shortly after their release shows a group of well-satisfied clients. But forty years later, in an interview he gave in his law office, Margolis passed the baton of victory to only one man: George Shibley.

Shibley had not only fought the lopsided struggle at the trial level, but he did so knowing that no matter what was happening to him and his clients, there would be another day. For him, the trial became an exercise in preserving error. What is remarkable was his ability to remain focused in the face of the hostility that he received day in and day out from Fricke. Shibley not only did not wither under the fire, but as his colleagues tired, with some actually turning their clients over to him, he grew stronger. He took the fight to Fricke—a fight he waged with absolutely no likelihood at the time that he would ever get paid. He did it because that's what lawyers do. He was always polite and ever persistent, and, over time, Fricke lost control of himself. Much of the conduct the court of appeals sanctioned came at the point when Fricke had begun to personalize the struggle between himself and Shibley. In the end, with Margolis's help, Shibley won. The seventeen young men walked free because of what two men did in court. Although the question "what is next for the boys" lingered, nothing that happened afterward could taint their accomplishment.

What was next? What became of the seventeen boys? A deputy sheriff in the crowd the morning they were released had an answer: "Them guys? They'll be back here. Back here before you know it." No doubt the deputy's opinion was based on the fact that the boys' victory had been a defeat for others—not the least of which was local law enforcement. But bitter or not, his snide remark proved prophetic, at least for some. Angel Padilla, Joe Ruiz, Manuel Delgado, and Henry Leyvas all went back to prison. It is hard to say why, after their experience, they did not stay on the straight and narrow. After Leyvas's death from a heart attack in 1971, his sister, Lupe, commented that the incarceration and beating Leyvas took after his arrest in August 1942 broke him. Perhaps the qualities everyone saw in Leyvas as a leader proved his undoing. With the proper outlet, those gifted with the ability to lead can flourish, but if there is no place to focus such skills, leadership can take on aspects of defiance, particularly of authority. For whatever reason, Leyvas spent a good portion of his life in and out of prison. The same fate befell Padilla and Ruiz. Only Manny Delgado broke the cycle. The rest of the boys stayed clear of prison, with some living fulfilling lives while others struggled.

Jose Diaz's family never recovered. Diaz's killer remained at large, and, without closure, the family all but disintegrated. Eduardo Pagan offered a couple of alternative theories. Years later, Lorena Encinas confessed that her brother, Louie, told her that he had killed Diaz. But there was no way to corroborate his story, and unfortunately Louie committed suicide in 1971 in the midst of a failed bank robbery. Another theory points to the two young men who left the party with Jose Diaz around 11:00 P.M. that night. No one ever questioned them, and Diaz's father had testified that Diaz had gotten paid that day. Diaz had been found with his pockets turned out; robbery seems a likely motive for the beating that left him near death. Encinas's story can never be verified, and anything else, even based on some of the evidence at trial, is mere speculation. What should have been apparent to both law enforcement and the prosecutor was that given Diaz's disappearance from the party that evening, there was sufficient time for almost anything to have happened to him. That alone should have signaled that on a level playing field, they would never convict anyone beyond a reasonable doubt.

George Shibley and Ben Margolis went on from Sleepy Lagoon to have solid and at times spectacular legal careers. Shibley had a successful practice in California and would one day defend Robert Kennedy's assassin, Sirhan Sirhan. During the trial, the young men had quickly grown to trust him, and, for years after the case ended, he maintained connections with some of them. When he died on 4 July 1989, those of the seventeen still surviving were there at his graveside to mourn. Ben Margolis likewise went on to have a stellar career. He continued to represent people under attack by the government. Almost immediately after the Sleepy Lagoon case, Margolis defended the Hollywood Ten, a group of feature film writers, directors, and producers cited for contempt and sent to federal prison by the Congressional Committee on Un-American Affairs. In 1952, he was called before the same committee, and, before going, he told friends and supporters that "he would fry in hell" before giving up anything on any of his clients. Throughout the McCarthy era, Margolis defended high-profile clients against the government. When he died on 27 January 1999, obituaries in newspapers in America and Great Britain mourned the passing of a lawyer who built a career on defending underdogs.

Carey McWilliams quickly found new causes to occupy his efforts. In 1946, he supported close friend Robert Kenny's unsuccessful run for governor against Earl Warren. By 1949, he had written eight books in ten years. In between, he had lent his talents to a new effort to organize agricultural workers in California. The McCarthy era proved a troubling time for McWilliams; anyone on the left found himself having to prove their loyalty to America. The political climate drove him closer to *The Nation*, the country's longest continuously running newspaper, and, by 1955, he had taken the reins as its editor. He remained there for twenty years, and, by the time of his retirement in 1975, he had put his own stamp on the paper and transformed it into the leading journal of homegrown American radicalism. After his retirement, he began work on his memoir, *The Education of Carey McWilliams*. Published in 1979, it was his least favorably received work. Most critics thought that it added little to what we already knew of McWilliams. The book ended up being more about *The Nation* than him personally. A year before it came out, McWilliams fell ill, and surgery revealed he had a rare form of cancer. He fought the disease for two years, finally dying on 27 January 1980. After his death, people struggled to define McWilliams's legacy. For those who knew him and the times in which he lived, his legacy was that of dissent. He unashamedly adopted a position as a left-wing radical and never backed down. It was this very belief that drew him to Sleepy Lagoon, to the good fortune of seventeen young Mexican Americans.

Alice Greenfield McGrath was the last survivor of the Sleepy Lagoon mystery. Eventually, she moved to Seattle, Washington, continuing her lifetime avocation as a labor and social activist. In the days immediately after the end of the case, she took on less imposing tasks. She planned W. E. B. DuBois's eighty-third birthday party, and they remained friends for the rest of his life. Later she took jobs as a publisher's sales representative, a retail clerk, and a figure model, and she even taught self-defense to girls and women. In 1984, she made her first trip to Nicaragua and discovered a place and people she loved. Over the next twenty years, she made more than eighty trips, bringing friends and organizing tours to the country. After moving to Ventura, California, she discovered the local bar association had no pro bono program, an omission she set out to remedy. For two years, she worked almost full-time as a volunteer for the fledgling pro bono program. In 2003, she made two contributions to the University of Washington's Harry Bridges Center for Labor Studies and continued to be active in the community. She also remained a close friend of the Leyvas family.

The prosecutors, John Barnes and Clyde Shoemaker, slid back into the obscurity from which they had emerged in 1942 when they tried the case for the state of California. The same cannot be said for the presiding judge. Charles Fricke remained on the bench and in time became almost an icon of the California bar. He continued to publish, and, after his death in 1959, his three most popular volumes, *California Criminal Law, California Criminal Evidence,* and *California Criminal Procedure,* continued to be mainstays of California criminal law. In what has to be the greatest of ironies, Fricke told his publisher not only that he wished for his writings to continue after his death, but that he entrusted his legacy to an up-and-coming Hispanic lawyer, Arthur Lawrence Alarcon. Alarcon became a superior court judge in 1964 and eventually rose to become the senior justice on the United States Ninth District court of appeals. In deference to Fricke's written wishes, he revised the seventh edition of Fricke's *California Criminal Evidence,* published in 1966. To read the preface written by Alarcon, one would never suspect that Charles Fricke was the same man who presided over *People v. Zammora* in 1942. Alarcon's words speak about a far different jurist than the one who presided over the Sleepy Lagoon murder trial: "Throughout his lifetime he was an enthusiastic and learned student of the criminal law. Those attorneys who were privileged to have practiced before him as defenders or prosecutors came away from his court more effective trial lawyers because of the high standards of advocacy and scholarship demanded by Judge Fricke." This, not *Zammora,* became Judge Fricke's legacy.

The only other significant state official at the time played no part in the case and seemed to do his best to distance himself from it during the appeal. Earl Warren eventually served three terms as governor of California. In 1953, President Dwight D. Eisenhower looked to fill the vacancy created by the death of Fred Vinson. Ten years earlier, Warren had been described as a "safe conservative." Ike hoped he was at least a moderate conservative. To everyone's surprise, Warren emerged as a constitutional liberal; his efforts revolutionized the American social and legal landscape. Anyone watching him handle the racial turmoil of World War II Los Angeles would never have foreseen what Warren became. However, although he said nothing about Sleepy Lagoon, either at the time or in his memoirs, some of what he saw and heard in those years must have affected him. Warren's trans-formation had profound consequences for Mexican Americans.

In 1954, the same year the Supreme Court handed down the land-mark school desegregation decision in *Brown v. Board of Education*, Warren wrote the opinion in *Texas v. Hernandez*. Pete Hernandez, an agricultural worker, was accused of killing his employer, Joe Espinoza. He was indicted by an all-white grand jury. His lawyers moved to quash the indictment on the grounds that no Hispanic had served on a grand jury or trial jury in Jackson County, Texas, in twenty-five years. Hernandez's lawyers argued that no fair trial could be obtained unless the jury pool contained Mexican Americans. The trial court overruled Hernandez's motion to quash, an all-white jury convicted him, and, on appeal, the Texas court of criminal appeals echoed what Hispanics had argued during the school desegregation fight of the 1930s and 1940s: "Mexicans are . . . members of and within the classi-fication of the white race as distinguished from members of the Negro Race." The Texas court rejected the argument that Mexican Ameri-cans were a "special class" under the meaning of the Fourteenth Amendment. Further, the court pointed out that "so far as we are advised, no member of the Mexican nationality" challenged this clas-sification as white. In an opinion as short as it was profound, Earl Warren made it clear that the Fourteenth Amendment to the Consti-tution did not see the world as only black and white. Warren pointed out that the distinction between whites and people of Mexican ances-try was made clear at the Jackson County courthouse itself, where "there were two men's toilets, one unmarked, and the other marked 'Colored Men' and 'Hombres Aqui' ('Men Here')." Warren had no reservations in declaring people of Mexican ancestry a "special class" entitled to equal protection under the Fourteenth Amendment.

The Sleepy Lagoon murder case fell into obscurity for decades. In 1978, Luis Valdez resurrected the events and the case with his play *Zoot Suit*. Admittedly a combination of fact and fiction, the lead character, Henry Reyna, was based on Henry Leyvas. But as rewarding as it must have been to see their experience remembered, the play struck a nerve among the survivors. Not only did it bring the eight surviving defen-dants of the *People v. Zammora* back together, but it briefly reunited them behind a personal cause. The play emphasized violence, often to the detriment of historical accuracy. Switchblades became a prominent theme in the play, yet historically no one associated with the Thirty-eighth Street neighborhood carried a switchblade. The deviation from facts so upset the survivors that, in 1979, the eight of them sued Valdez and others after seeing the play. In an out-of-court settlement, they received a financial interest in the proceeds from the play and the movie that followed.

Valdez should have anticipated the reaction to any deviation from historical fact. Efforts to find the survivors had proven difficult, and, when he finally located some of them, he found them reluctant to talk about what happened. Alice Greenfield McGrath had actually resurrected the *Appeal News* in September 1978 to put the word out to those of her boys who were still alive. In a short piece, she was careful to emphasize that she understood how important privacy was to them all. Her goal was to make sure they all understood that not everything about the Sleepy Lagoon case was in the public domain. If names or images were used, the subjects had to give their permission. From their collective reaction to the violence portrayed in the play, it was clear that they understood Greenfield's message.

The reaction to the play reveals an important aspect of what happened. The success of the SLDC and its attorneys in freeing the boys could not undo the damage done to the young men in being arrested, tried, convicted, and imprisoned. Ysmael "Smiles" Parra was one of the eight survivors. From the moment he came home, his mother admitted he "looked so different." His daughter, who was small at the time, said her father never really trusted again. He lost any respect he had for the law, and, for most of his life, he continued to feel the devastation of the experience. His marriage did not survive, and he and Delia divorced. He remarried, moved to Arizona, and tried to make a life for himself, but the shadow of his past seemed to haunt him even though he had been cleared. Henry Ynostroza was seventeen when he and the others were sent to San Quentin: "Smiles was our oldest one and kept us out of trouble," he remembered. But the whole experience took something from Parra. Although *Zoot Suit* might have been a financial success and an important event in the Chicana/o movement, for those who lived through the real experience, the play reopened wounds that had never really healed.

Epilogue

Sleepy Lagoon is long gone, buried beneath concrete and asphalt. Almost everyone closely connected with the story is gone as well. All but eight of the twenty-two defendants were dead by 1978, and the rest have since passed on. Ysmael "Smiles" Parra died in 2001. Henry Ynostroza, who was at his graveside, died in 2006, and Manuel Reyes followed two years later in March 2008. On November 27, 2009, Alice Greenfield McGrath passed away at age ninety-two. But the event and the story that comprise the Sleepy Lagoon case are still with us. Almost without exception, the participants lauded *People v. Zammora* as a landmark case. Without question, it belongs in the evolution of the legal interpretation and development of the right to counsel of a criminally accused person. Not only does the case follow in the path of *Powell v. Alabama* in terms of one's right to an attorney, but it goes further. It defines what it means to have effective counsel and establishes a defendant's right to effectively interact with his attorney at every stage of the trial proceeding. In the process of more clearly defining the right to counsel, it virtually eliminated the possibility of a mass trial. In 1978, George Shibley was asked in an interview how *Zammora* had affected criminal law. He explained that by forcing a court to accommodate a defendant's right to sit with and communicate with one's attorney, the California court of appeals made it virtually impossible to hold mass trials. *Zammora* remains the largest mass trial in California history for a reason. The law it established forced courtrooms to conform to defendants, not the other way around.

In 2006, the *Yale Law Journal* addressed the question as to whether a criminal defendant should be assigned a seat in court. An attorney in Houston, Texas, had demanded that he and his client be given a table to the left of the judge's bench, closest to the jury box. Michael Ramsey argued that the defense should have an unimpeded, unobstructed, and uncluttered face-to-face confrontation with the witnesses against them. Ramsey's client was Kenneth Lay, ex-CEO of Enron, and, because the judge could find no law allowing the prosecution to sit closest to the jury, he allowed the prosecution to occupy that position while it presented its case, and then allowed the defense the same seats while it presented its witnesses.

In the process of evaluating Ramsey's position, the article traced what it called the "Defendant's Journey from the Dock to the Counsel Table." During the *Zammora* trial, Shibley had condemned Judge Charles Fricke's seating arrangement as the equivalent of placing the accused in the dock, an old English practice that had been abolished long ago. Fricke had responded with a bizarre treatise on how European courts treated defendants, a point that Shibley argued was irrelevant. The California court of appeals unequivocally condemned Fricke's deprivation of counsel, and the *Yale Law Journal* comment credits *Zammora* with eliminating the possibility that a defendant could be returned to the dock under the guise of judicial economy and the physical limitations of a courtroom.

Zammora was even more than a bridge from the conceptual right to counsel in the Constitution to the concrete rights defendants enjoy today. The case also served as a warning to the bench that ethical canons and codes of judicial conduct, even if informal and/or advisory, are to be strictly followed. As Justice Thomas P. White explained in his opinion, a judge simply cannot step beyond the realm of impartiality. Any perception by the jury that a judge favors one side over the other, or that he or she has formed an opinion as to the strength or weakness of a witness or piece of evidence, renders the right to a fair trial almost impossible. Perhaps this aspect of *Zammora* has lost some of its power because the notion that a judge would act with bias toward a defendant or his counsel seems so difficult to comprehend today. However, circumstances can alter what would normally take place. The Sleepy Lagoon trial took place in an environment of fear and racial tension. Fricke knew his obligations as a judge; further, in some aspects, he was the admitted expert in California. Yet when it came time to put into practice what he knew, Fricke proved as susceptible to outside pressure as everyone else in Los Angeles. The kinds of forces then at work can reappear at any time, and *Zammora* stands as a reminder that courts must remain, in Hugo Black's words, as "havens against the winds of prejudice."

People v. Zammora stands as a signpost on America's never-ending legal journey to make the aspirations of its organic law consistent with how it acts in real life. Although it may not have enjoyed the notoriety of other landmark cases, that does not diminish its importance, either at the time or today. However, judging a case by its legal aspects is a mistake when we look to the lasting effects of an event like Sleepy Lagoon. Court cases do more than reflect on our legal system; they also provide insight into who we are as a people and a nation. The decision in *Zammora* showed a judicial system that was unwilling to ignore the failure of its trial court, even under the extraordinary circumstances of World War II. However, the fact is that extraordinary circumstances did affect the criminal system, and, although *Zammora* represents a snapshot of what America once was, many of the same circumstances at work in 1942 remain with us today. Much like World War II Los Angeles, America is again at war. As we fight terrorism at home and across the globe, we struggle with the impulse to compromise our principles to protect us from a threat to our way of life. As *People v. Zammora* demonstrated, emotion has a way of overcoming rational thought. When some of the battles in our present conflict find their way into our courtrooms, will we "proceed promptly in the calm spirit of regulated justice," or "go forward with the haste of the mob"?

Abrams v. United States 250 U.S. 616 (1919)

Alvarez v. Owen Superior Court in and for the County of San Diego (1931)

Anderson v. United States 318 U.S. 350 (1943)

Betts v. Brady 316 U.S. 455 (1942)

Bridges v. California 314 U.S. 252 (1941)

Brown v. Walker 161 U.S. 591 (1896)

Cantwell v. Connecticut 310 U.S. 296 (1940)

Chambers v. Florida 309 U.S. 227 (1940)

Commonwealth v. Boyd 92 A. 702 (Pa. 1914)

Counselman v. Hitchcock 142 U.S. 547 (1892)

Craig v. Harney 331 U.S. 367 (1947)

Debs v. United States 249 U.S. 211 (1919)

Ex Parte Milligan 71 U.S. 2 (1866)

Gitlow v. New York 268 U.S. 652 (1925)

Frohwerk v. United States 249 U.S. 204 (1919)

Gideon v. Wainwright 372 U.S. 335 (1963)

Hernandez v. Texas 347 U.S. 475 (1954)

In Re Rodriguez 81 F. 337 (U.S.D.C., W.D. Tex., 1897)

Independent School District v. Salvatierra 33 S.W. 2d 792 (Tex. App. — San Antonio, 1930)

Johnson v. Zerbst 304 U.S. 458 (1938)

Maryland v. Baltimore Radio Show 338 U.S. 912 (1950)

McNabb v. United States 318 U.S. 332 (1943)

Mendez v. Westminster 64 F. Supp. 544 (U.S.D.C., C. D. Ca., 1946) aff'd, 161 F.2d 774 (9th Cir. 1947)

Miranda v. Arizona 384 U.S. 436 (1966)

People v. Devine 46 Cal. 45 (1873)

People v. Gonzalez 24 Cal. 2d 870; 151 P. 2d 251

People v. Rodgers 22 Cal. 2d 787; 141 P. 2d 722

People v. Zammora 66 Cal. App. 2d 166 (1944)

Pierce v. United States 160 U.S. 355 (1896)

Powell v. Alabama 287 U.S. 45 (1932)

Romo v. Laird Civil Action No. 21617 (Superior Court, Maricopa County, Arizona, 1925)

Schaefer v. United States 251 U.S. 466 (1920)

Schenck v. United States 249 U.S. 47 (1919)

Times Mirror Co. et al. v. Superior Court for State of California, In and for the County of Los Angeles 314 U.S. 252 (1941)

United States v. Gilbert Fed. Cas. No. 15,204, 2 Sumn. 19 (1834)

United States v. Mitchell 322 U.S. 65 (1944)
Webb v. Baird 6 Ind. 13 (1853)
Weems v. United States 217 U.S. 349 (1910)

CHRONOLOGY

7 December 1941	Attack on Pearl Harbor; United States enters World War II.
January 1942	Media campaign against Japanese Americans begins; negative press toward Mexican American youth gangs also starts.
March 1942	Japanese American relocation and internment are complete.
August 1942	Jose Diaz found dead near Sleepy Lagoon; police dragnet of six hundred Mexican Americans results in twenty-four indicted.
September 1942	Grand jury investigation into Mexican youth crime; L.A. law enforcement officials testify.
October 1942	*People v. Zammora* trial begins; Citizens' Committee for the Defense of Mexican American Youth (CCDMAY) is formed.
December 1942	Testimony in *People v. Zammora* concludes.
13 January 1943	Jury returns guilty verdicts for seventeen of the twenty-two defendants.
1 February 1943	Motions for new trial denied; all defendants sentenced. Twelve sent to San Quentin.
14 March 1943	CCDMAY, now reorganized as Sleepy Lagoon Defense Committee (SLDC), holds a conference at Belmont Studios in Los Angeles.
April 1943	Carey McWilliams becomes national chairman of the SLDC. Ben Margolis agrees to handle the appeal and moves to Los Angeles. First edition of the *Appeal News* goes out.
June 1943	Zoot suit riots break out in downtown Los Angeles. Tenney hearings on un-American activities conclude with Carey McWilliams's testimony.
July 1943	Guy Endore's first pamphlet, *The Sleepy Lagoon Case*, is released, and the first ten thousand copies sell out within a month. His second pamphlet, *The Sleepy Lagoon Mystery*, is released in early 1944.
September 1943	The CCDMAY formally adopts the name Sleepy Lagoon Defense Committee.

October 1943	Defense files its five-hundred-page appeal brief.
December 1943	First major Hollywood fund-raising event at the Mocambo raises $1,750, which almost matches the total of what had been raised to that point.
May 1944	Oral arguments held before Second District court of appeals.
June 1944	Nine of the twelve young men in prison receive notices that their parole has been granted.
August 1944	Manuel Delgado is the first of the Sleepy Lagoon defendants released from prison on parole.
October 1944	Court of appeals overturns every guilty verdict and remands case to the California superior court for retrial. The L.A. district attorney declines to retry the defendants and dismisses the case on the basis of insufficient evidence.
1 January 1945	Sleepy Lagoon Defense Committee officially disbanded.
July 1978	Luis Valdez's play, *Zoot Suit*, opens.

BIBLIOGRAPHICAL ESSAY

Note from the Series Editors: The following bibliographical essay contains the major primary and secondary sources the author consulted for this volume. We have asked all authors in the series to omit formal citations in order to make our volumes more readable, inexpensive, and appealing for students and general readers. In adopting this format, Landmark Law Cases and American Society follows the precedent of a number of highly regarded and widely consulted series.

This project would not have been possible without the help and assistance of the UCLA Charles E. Young Library Special Collections. Within this archival collection are housed the Sleepy Lagoon Defense Committee Records, 1942–1945, the Alice Greenfield McGrath Papers, 1943–1990, and the S. Guy Endore Papers, 1925–1970. Through the auspices of the On Line Archive of California, most of the material needed for this project was available in digital form online. Among the documents crucial to this project was the 6,032-page trial transcript, styled *The People of the State of California, Plaintiff and Respondent, vs. Gus Zammora [sic], et al., defendants and appellants: reporter's transcript on appeal, 1942 October 13–1943 March.* In addition to the transcript, the Sleepy Lagoon Papers provided valuable material on the Sleepy Lagoon Defense Committee (SLDC)'s publicity and fund-raising efforts, as well as pictures, voluminous correspondence, and a complete run of the SLDC publication, *The Appeal News.*

I am also indebted to the UCLA Library's Center for Oral History Research for its lengthy interviews with Carey McWilliams and Ben Margolis. McWilliams's interview was conducted in 1978 by Joel Gardner and Margolis's interview was conducted in 1984 by Michael S. Balter, both of the Center for Oral History Research, Young Research Library, University of California, Los Angeles. The interviews provided invaluable information about the formation and operation of the SLDC as well as insight into the appeal itself.

I could not have completed this project without the assistance of the University of Texas library system. The Peter Castenada Library and the Benson Collection at the LBJ Library allowed me generous access to some primary material and most of the secondary material I used in this book. At its core this is a legal history, and the Tarlton Law Library at the University of Texas allowed me to research not only the Supreme Court cases that make up a portion of this study, but some of the more obscure opinions from state courts.

For a general history, I started with Gilbert G. Gonzalez and Raul E. Fernandez, *A Century of Chicano History: Empire, Nations and Migration* (New York: Routledge, 2003). Historical background on Los Angeles and its Mexican American population came from Antonio Rios-Bustamante and Pedro Castillo, *An Illustrated History of Mexican Los Angeles, 1781–1985* (Los Angeles: UCLA Chicano Studies Research Center Publications, 1986); Douglas Monroy, *Rebirth: Mexican Los Angeles from the Great Migration to the Great Depression* (Berkeley: University of California Press, 1999); and George Sanchez, *Becoming Mexican American: Ethnicity, Culture and Identity in Chicano Los Angeles, 1900–1945* (New York: Oxford University Press, 1999). Matt Garcia, *A World of Its Own: Race Labor, and Citrus in the Making of Greater Los Angeles* (Chapel Hill: University of North Carolina Press, 2001), provided historical context and insight into the strength of the Mexican American civil rights movement in the late 1930s and early 1940s in Los Angeles. Carey McWilliams, *North from Mexico: The Spanish Speaking People of the United States* (reprint, New York: Greenwood Press, 1968), had background on Mexican Americans as well as some good information from his perspective on the Sleepy Lagoon case. Mark Wild, *Street Meeting: Multiethnic Neighborhoods in Early Twentieth Century Los Angeles* (Berkeley: University of California Press, 2005), provided invaluable insight into the efforts by Los Angeles city officials to cope with what it deemed the "Mexican problem" in the years leading up to Sleepy Lagoon. Margaret E. Montoya's "A Brief History of Chicana/o School Segregation: One Rationale for Affirmative Action," *La Raza Journal* 12 (2001): 159–172, provided an excellent concise survey and analysis of Mexican American school desegregation cases in the early twentieth century. Luis Alvarez, *The Power of the Zoot Suit: Youth Culture and Resistance during World War II* (Berkeley: University of California Press, 2008), provided background material on pachucos and the powerful image of the zoot suit in Los Angeles at the time of the Sleepy Lagoon case. The PBS series *The American Experience: Zoot Suit Riots* provided excellent background information on many of the participants, such as Alice Greenfield McGrath, George Shibley, and Charles Fricke. In addition, some of the more general information provided the basis for more in-depth research into other sources.

Five large California newspapers proved helpful: the *Los Angeles Times, Los Angeles Examiner,* and *San Francisco Examiner,* the latter a Hearst paper, as well as the *San Francisco Chronicle* and *San Diego Union-Tribune.* The *LA Examiner* helped me verify some of the secondary accounts of media hype; it also gave me a look at how the media assault in 1942 looked for both Mexican Americans and Japanese Americans. The San Francisco *Examiner* and the *Chronicle* helped provide me with some idea of how pervasive the press coverage was outside L.A. so I could see whether media coverage was in lockstep with regard to some of the issues. I also found an article in the *Times* on Ysmael "Smiles" Parra in 2001 announcing his death. The *San Diego Union-Tribune* added to my understanding of the school desegregation issue in 1931 and published an article on Henry Ynostroza shortly after his death in 2006. Lemon

Grove is a suburb of San Diego, and the paper carried a three-part series on the *Alvarez* case. In addition, *USA Today* provided contemporary articles on both immigration and the war on terror.

The trial itself has been the subject of several secondary works, in most cases studies devoted to both the Sleepy Lagoon case and the subsequent zoot suit riots. These include Maurico Mazon, *The Zoot Suit Riots: The Psychology of Symbolic Annihilation* (Austin: University of Texas Press, 1984); Eduardo Pagan, *Murder at the Sleepy Lagoon: Zoot Suits, Race, and Riot in Wartime L.A.* (Chapel Hill: University of North Carolina Press, 2006); and Edward Escobar, *Race, Police, and the Making of a Political Identity: Mexican Americans and the Los Angeles Police Department, 1900–1945*, Latinos in American Society and Culture Series (Berkeley: University of California Press, 1999). Pagan's work offers a revisionist explanation of what caused the trial and the subsequent riots. It is not the goal of this series or this book to resolve that debate. This book arrives at its own conclusions that are set out herein and adopts aspects of both arguments. Kevin Allen Leonard, *The Battle for Los Angeles: Racial Ideology and Word War II* (Albuquerque: University of New Mexico Press, 2006), provided excellent insight into the grand jury testimony and press before the trial. It also addressed the smaller ethnic papers like *The Eagle* and *El Pueblo*.

Judge Charles W. Fricke played a central role in the Sleepy Lagoon story. In addition to the primary material in the Sleepy Lagoon Papers, much can be learned from a review of some of his writings. To that end, I consulted several of Fricke's books, including Charles Fricke, *Criminal Investigation: The Investigation of Criminal Cases, the Securing of Evidence and its Proper Presentation in Court* (n.p., 1930); Charles Fricke, *Planning and Trying Cases* (St. Paul: West Publishing, 1952); Charles Fricke and Arthur L. Alarcon, *California Criminal Evidence: Including the Complete Text of the California Evidence Code*, 7th ed. (Los Angeles: Legal Book Corp., 1966); Charles Fricke, *Sentence and Probation: The Imposition of Penalties upon Convicted Criminals* (Los Angeles: Legal Book Store, 1960); and Charles Fricke, *California Criminal Law*, 9th ed. (Los Angeles: Legal Book Store, 1965).

For research into William Randolph Hearst and his role in the media assault in Los Angeles against Mexican Americans, David Nasaw, *The Chief: The Life of William Randolph Hearst* (Boston: Houghton Mifflin, 2000), proved helpful. The trial became an example of how the media can influence judicial proceedings long before the landmark case of *Estes v. Texas* (1965). *Radio, Television, and the Administration of Justice: A Documented Survey of Materials*, Special Committee on Radio and Television of the Association of the Bar of the City of New York (New York: Columbia University Press, 1935); Douglas S. Campbell, *Free Press v. Fair Trial: Supreme Court Decisions since 1807* (Westport, Conn.: Praeger, 1994); Harold W. Sullivan, *Trial by Newspaper* (Hyannis, Mass.: Patriot Press, 1961); and Howard Flesher and Michael Rosen, *The Press in the*

Jury Box (New York: Macmillan, 1966), all provided a wealth of analysis and primary documents regarding the state of the media and a fair trial in 1942.

The notions of a sensational trial and high-profile crimes found illumination from several sources. Lynn Chancer, *High Profile Crimes: When Legal Cases Become Social Causes* (Chicago: University of Chicago Press, 2005); Robert Hariman, *Popular Trials: Rhetoric, Mass Media and the Law* (Tuscaloosa: University of Alabama Press, 1990); and an older work, C. E. Bechhofer Roberts, *The New World of Crime: Famous American Trials* (London: Eyre and Spottiswoode, 1933), all provided good context for looking at Sleepy Lagoon as a sensational trial.

Insight into Carey McWilliams came from several sources. One such source was Peter Richardson's *American Prophet: The Life and Work of Carey McWilliams* (Ann Arbor: University of Michigan Press, 2005) and his short paper, "Carey McWilliams: The California Years," delivered at UCLA during a conference entitled "The Sleepy Lagoon Case: Constitutional Rights and the Struggle for Democracy: A Commemorative Symposium, May 20–21, 2005." In addition, McWilliams's own *The Education of Carey McWilliams* (New York: Simon & Schuster, 1979) and the short piece *Carey McWilliams: The Great Exception*, produced and distributed by Los Angeles radio station KPFK in 1979, provided valuable background material. The material on McWilliams also provided valuable information on Alice Greenfield McGrath. In addition to her papers, I am indebted to the *A&S Perspectives Newsletter* (University of Washington, College of Arts and Sciences, Autumn 2003) for its piece on the eighty-six-year-old Alice McGrath. I also received access to an audio recording of McGrath at the University of Texas, *From Sleepy Lagoon to Zoot Suit: The Irreverent Path of Alice McGrath* (Santa Cruz, Calif.: Giges Productions, 1996). Although most of the information also existed in other sources, this gave me the opportunity to actually hear the woman speak, although in her later years.

Frank P. Barajas, "The Defense Committees of Sleepy Lagoon: A Convergent Struggle against Fascism, 1942–1944," *Journal of Chicano Studies* 31, no. 1 (Spring 2006): 33–62, provides material into the reluctance of the local community to embrace the SLDC and some detail of the committee's activities and efforts. It also illuminated some of the contested ground among Chicana/o scholars today as to the real importance of the SLDC.

Through the Library of Congress, I accessed Guy Endore's *The Sleepy Lagoon Mystery*, and the *Dictionary of Literary Biography* provided excellent background material on Endore and his career. I am also grateful to the Library of Congress for the U.S. National Commission of Law Observance and Enforcement's *Report on Crime and the Foreign Born* (Washington, D.C.: United States Government Printing Office, 1931). This text, also known as the Wickersham report, helped me get a handle on the extent of Mexican crime from a source outside of Los Angeles. A dated but interesting study of U.S.

race relations in the 1930s came to my attention while at the Library of Congress: Bertram Johannes Otto Schricke's *Alien Americans: A Study of Race Relations* (New York: Viking Press, 1936). Schricke's observations provided food for thought on why Americans react as they do to ethnic change.

Other research contributed to small but important aspects of this book. My thanks to the online journal *Women and Social Movements in the United States, 1600–2000: Basic Edition*, edited by Kathryn Kish Sklar and Thomas Dublin (New York: Binghamton, 2009), for its material and original documents on Kate Richards O'Hare and her efforts at reform within the California penal system. This material provided insight into the conditions in which the Sleepy Lagoon boys found themselves in 1943 when their prison terms began. San Quentin during the 1940s was described in excellent detail, as were the efforts to reform it, in Alan Bisbort's *"When you read this, they will have killed me": The Life and Redemption of Caryl Chessman, Whose Execution Shook America* (New York: Carroll & Graf, 2006).

Melvin Belli's autobiography, *Melvin Belli, My Life on Trial* (New York: William Morrow, 1976), provides good historical background on the use of demonstrative evidence in court. The defense in *Zammora* clearly waged an uphill fight. However, part of the problem lay in the inability to portray the defendants in a light other than that established by the prosecution.

There are dozens of books on Earl Warren. For insight into his years as governor and his efforts, if any, with regard to the SLDC, I consulted Jack Harrison Pollack, *Earl Warren: The Judge who Changed America* (Englewood Cliffs, N.J.: Prentice-Hall, 1979), as well as Warren's own words in *The Memoirs of Earl Warren* (Garden City, N.Y.: Doubleday, 1977).

I am grateful to the Web site *California Courts: The Judicial Branch of California* (http://www.courtinfo.ca.gov/index.htm) for its excellent biographical sketches of former justices, which enabled me to research the backgrounds of the three-judge panel that heard the *People v. Zammora* appeal.

The *Los Angeles Bar Bulletin*, published by the Los Angeles Bar Association, and the *California State Bar Journal* provided material ranging from studies on juvenile delinquency in Los Angeles and California and the bar's perception of the Mexican youth problem to commentary on appropriate judicial conduct in the years before the enactment of California's canons of judicial ethics. The articles and reports published between 1941 and 1943 painted a very different picture of the crime problem in Los Angeles than had been portrayed in the popular press.

Catherine S. Ramirez's *The Zoot Suit Women: Gender, Nationalism and the Culture Politics of Memory* (Durham, N.C.: Duke University Press, 2009) told the story of some of the girls who made the ill-fated ride to Williams Ranch that night and found themselves incarcerated in juvenile facilities. Some remained even after the Sleepy Lagoon defendants were all freed.

The Sleepy Lagoon case provides an example of voluntary efforts by citizens' groups and/or defense committees to overturn a perceived injustice in the courts. However, it was not the only instance in the early twentieth century of such an effort. The SLDC's success can be measured at least in part by the other three significant efforts in the 1920s and 1930s. Ethan E. Ward, *The Gentle Dynamiter: A Biography of Tom Mooney* (Palo Alto: Ramparts Press, 1983) and Thomas Henry Hunt, *The Case of Thomas J. Mooney and Warren K. Billings* (New York: De Capo Press, 1971) provided background and information on the Mooney and Billings Defense Committee. Bruce Watson, *Sacco and Vanzetti: The Men, the Murders and the Judgment of Mankind* (New York: Viking, 2007) and Dan T. Carter, *Scottsboro: A Tragedy of the American South* (Baton Rouge: Louisiana State University Press, 1979) did likewise for Sacco and Vanzetti and the Scottsboro Boys cases.

As I tried to explain why *People v. Zammora* seemed to disappear in the years immediately after the decision, I looked to a variety of California law school journals and reviews. A comment entitled "Some Proposals for Modernizing the Law of Arrests" appeared in *California Law Review* 39 (1951): 96 and provided the first mention of the case I could locate. The *Yale Law Journal* 115 (2006): 2203 offered a valuable comment on the status of *People v. Zammora* today. It traced the evolution of a defendant's place in the courtroom and established *Zammora* as having fought back against efforts to return defendants to the dock.

Yolanda Broyles-González's *El Teatro Campesino: Theater in the Chicano Movement* (Austin: University of Texas Press, 1994) provided excellent material on Luis Valdez's play, *Zoot Suit*. The play resurrected the Sleepy Lagoon case, and its blend of fact and fiction both elated audiences and caused some consternation among the Sleepy Lagoon survivors.

In trying to come to grips with some of the similarities between World War II and today insofar as the immigration issue and how it has evolved over the last forty-five years, I consulted Wayne A. Cornelius and Jorge Bustamente, editors, *Mexican Immigration to the United States: Origins, Consequences, and Policy Options* (La Jolla, Calif.: Center for U.S.–Mexican Studies, University of California, San Diego, 1989). Victor Davis Hansen's *Mexifornia: A State Becoming* (San Francisco: Encounter Books, 2003) provided good material on how America, and California in particular, is coping with the social change brought on by Mexican immigration. I also consulted Thomas Mueller, Thomas J. Espenshade, and Donald Manson, *The Fourth Wave: California's Newest Immigrants* (Washington, D.C.: Urban Institute Press, 1985).